Turkish Drama Serials

TURKISH DRAMA SERIALS

The Importance and Influence of a Globally Popular Television Phenomenon

Miriam Berg

UNIVERSITY
of
EXETER
PRESS

First published in 2023 by
University of Exeter Press
Reed Hall, Streatham Drive
Exeter EX4 4QR, UK

www.exeterpress.co.uk

Copyright © Miriam Berg 2023

The right of Miriam Berg to be identified as author of this work has been asserted by her in accordance with the Copyright, Designs and Patents Act 1988.

A CIP catalogue record for this book is available from the British Library.

This book is published under a Creative Commons Attribution Non-Commercial No Derivatives 4.0 International licence (CC BY-NC-ND 4.0). This license requires that reusers give credit to the creator. It allows reusers to copy and distribute the material in any medium or format, for non-commercial purposes only. If others remix, adapt, or build upon the material, they may not distribute the modified material.

https://doi.org/10.47788/AGLL1722

Further details about Creative Commons licences are available at http://creativecommons.org/licenses/

Any third-party material in this book is published under the book's Creative Commons licence unless indicated otherwise in the credit line to the material. If you would like to reuse any third-party material not covered by the book's Creative Commons licence, you will need to obtain permission directly from the copyright holder.

Every effort has been made to trace copyright holders and obtain permission to reproduce the material included in this book. Please get in touch with any enquiries or information relating to an image or the rights holder.

ISBN 978-1-80413-042-1 Hardback
ISBN 978-1-80413-043-8 ePub
ISBN 978-1-80413-044-5 PDF

Cover image: iStockPhoto/NatanaelGinting

Typeset in Adobe Caslon Pro by S4Carlisle Publishing Services, Chennai, India

Contents

	Introduction	1
1	The Turkish Television Industry: From National to Transnational	11
2	Turkish Drama Serials in the Arab World	28
3	Fluctuating Turkish–Arab Relations and the Soft Power of Drama Serials	41
4	The Importance of Socio-Cultural Factors in the Appeal of Turkish Serials among Arab Viewers	72
5	Why Turkish Dramas Resonate with Arab Women: An Analysis of the Responses of Women Viewers in Qatar	95
6	Turkish Drama Serials in Chile	114
7	Turkish Drama Serials in Israel	146
	Summary and Conclusion	170
	Notes	197
	References	214
	Index	240

Introduction

In little more than a decade, Turkish serials have grown from being simply a popular television format in Türkiye, to solidifying their place within international popular culture, having won the hearts of audiences across the globe.[1] This book explores a significant development in television that started with Turkish dramas taking Arab screens by storm, and later expanding across the globe.

The sudden popularity of Turkish drama serials, particularly within the Arab world, saw Türkiye becoming the second-largest producer of scripted television serials worldwide,[2] and in 2016 the world's fifth-largest TV-programme exporter.[3] Their popularity has dramatically increased, moving from the Global South to countries in the south of the Global North, with Spain and Italy becoming the latest in a long list of nations that have been captivated by their unique allure.[4] As the international success of Turkish serials is a relatively new phenomenon, research examining the reasons for their appeal, or the nature of the viewing experience, is still an evolving area,[5] raising new questions centring on the audiences' viewing experience and the key factors contributing to the serials' wider success. At this point it is relevant to acknowledge that the popularity of Turkish television dramas is simply one example of how content produced in and for one nation has transcended national and cultural borders. The phenomenon of travelling television content is nothing new, having been scrutinized by various scholars in the past.[6] But it is the first time that drama serials from a Muslim-majority country have managed to attract audiences from across the globe. This poses a significant question: what is it about Turkish serials that enables them to resonate with audiences outside their geo-cultural and geo-linguistic region?

This book takes an audience-centric approach by examining rich audience data from Qatar, Chile, and Israel to answer this question. It attempts to find out what it is about Turkish dramas that appeals to Arab, Chilean, and Israeli audiences alike. Also, how can they at times even surpass national, regional, and Western productions in terms of popularity?

The book also analyses the role and importance of Turkish dramas as a soft-power tool by scrutinizing how they have impacted viewers' perceptions of Türkiye, its people, and its culture. I adopt a multi-theoretical perspective, including concepts such as cultural proximity, uses and gratifications, lifeworld, and soft power, to analyse this evolving phenomenon.

Throughout the book I argue that the successful penetration of Turkish drama serials into the Arab television markets, and their enthusiastic reception, represents a pivotal moment for them, as they transition from being successful nationally, and within their geo-linguistic region, to becoming popular across international markets. What started in September 2008 as an experiment by the Saudi Arabian-owned satellite network,[7] MBC (the Middle East Broadcasting Center), with the broadcasting of its first dubbed Turkish drama serial *Noor* (*Gümüs*, 2005–07, Türkiye: Kanal D) during the month of Ramadan, not only generated unforeseeable viewership figures,[8] but also quickly catapulted Turkish dramas into becoming a region-wide sensation. Their sudden and enormous success sparked international news coverage and global attention,[9] which unquestionably triggered other countries' interest in testing Turkish dramas in their own markets. The vast demand for Turkish serials over the past decade, particularly from countries across the Middle East and North Africa region (MENA), has positioned the Arab world as an important export market,[10] and contributed to the further expansion of the serial-production sector in Türkiye, transforming it into a highly profitable industry. Consequently, this book pays particular attention to the popularity and appeal of Turkish dramas to Arab audiences, which has been critical in their transition from domestically popular formats to internationally recognized serials.

In order to provide readers with a complete picture, the book is organized so as to give readers some background information and context regarding the Turkish television industry, both past and present. The book also offers a sense of the historical and current relationships between Türkiye, the Arab world, Latin America and the Caribbean (LAC), and Israel. It explores the role of Türkiye's economic enhancements and multidirectional foreign policy in paving the way for Turkish drama serials to enter foreign television markets. It also examines the essential factors in the Arab, Chilean, and Israeli television markets that make them favourable to Turkish drama serials, before providing the reader with the audience findings in each country.

In line with the core argument, the book first examines the reach and reception of Turkish dramas across the Arab world: a key moment that has allowed Turkish television dramas to become an internationally successful format. The book utilizes the diverse audience of the Gulf State of Qatar as a case study. It examines Turkish dramas' significance as a soft-power tool, audience viewing motivations, and the socio-cultural factors that facilitated the attraction and appeal of Turkish drama serials for Arab audiences.

As its second case study, the book examines Chilean audiences. Chile was the first country in the LAC region to broadcast dubbed Turkish serials. What the Chilean station Mega started in 2014 as an experiment transformed into a region-wide trend. As with the Arab world, the successful entry of Turkish dramas onto Chilean television represents a landmark that propelled them into an entirely new market, ultimately reaching millions of television viewers across the region. At present, Chile still incorporates the largest percentage of Turkish content within the LAC region into its television programming;[11] and the unexpected popularity of Turkish drama serials has also contributed to Chile becoming the distribution hub for the region, and the Spanish translation hub for Turkish serials.[12]

In the third and final case study, this book examines Israeli audiences. The rationale for selecting Israeli viewers is that Turkish dramas did not arrive on Israeli television when diplomatic and trade relations flourished (as in the MENA or LAC regions) but, in contrast, when diplomatic ties between the two former allies had reached a historic low. Through audience responses, this book provides an insight into why Turkish television serials' reach and reception transcended the diplomatic crisis that saw Türkiye and Israel transition from being long-time allies to becoming rival actors, with opposing political and security positions. One needs to recognize that, despite Israel being part of the developed world, in reality a significant proportion of Israeli Jews migrated from, or were raised by parents who were born in, countries that were either part of the Ottoman Empire, or countries from the Global South. This makes Israeli viewers highly fascinating, while offering the reader a broader understanding of an evolving and underexplored area.

This book has benefited from my ability as an author to study first-hand the socio-cultural factors behind the popularity of Turkish serials in the Arab world, initially while working for a Qatar-based media network in 2008, and later as an academic and PhD student residing in the country. I also had the opportunity to interview various industry professionals in Türkiye, as far back as 2010, in order to understand how the popularity of Turkish serials in the Arab world has been perceived from the outset, and to gain an insight into the impact this popularity has had on the television and production sectors in Türkiye over the last ten years.

This book provides a rare perspective, incorporating a mix of empirical data gathered in Qatar, Türkiye, Chile, and Israel, along with scholarly analysis spanning almost a decade. Alongside interviews with Turkish television-industry professionals, based mainly in Istanbul, it includes online surveys and focus-group discussions with Qataris and other Arab nationals residing in Qatar and other parts of the Arab world, and online surveys conducted with viewers in Chile and Israel. Additionally, there are accounts taken from numerous informal chats with industry professionals and academics, in Türkiye, Chile, and Israel, along with discussions with numerous viewers (predominantly women). In addition to the empirical data, I have examined countless articles in Arabic, English, Hebrew, Spanish, and Turkish, as well as ratings reports and public-opinion polls.

The findings provide insights into the reasons for the international appeal of Turkish drama serials—a developing area of scholarly research. The reader will be in a position to comprehend why Turkish serials are increasingly shaping the global media scene and have become an important soft-power tool for their country of origin. As the author, I recognize that the empirical findings presented in this book are not a reflection of all attitudes to Turkish serials. Nor should the reader assume that research participants are representative of particular social groups—all women, for instance—in the way they receive Turkish dramas simply because they are recognized as the predominant audience of Turkish serials.

However, the significance of this study is not based solely on the quantitative demographic distribution of the various ways that Turkish serials are received. Instead, the central question is: how do Qatari, Chilean, and Israeli audiences respond to Turkish drama serials? And what makes them so attractive to these audiences?

INTRODUCTION

One needs to be aware that people's responses to questions about their viewing experiences and preferences should not always be taken at face value. Often these occur subconsciously during everyday life, rather than as a result of rational thought.[13]

As I drafted the various chapters of this book, my hope was that this volume would provide the reader with a better understanding of the rise of Turkish drama serials as an important development in popular culture, all the while becoming the subject of intense political, academic, and journalistic interest.

The subject matter of the seven chapters is summarized below, while a more detailed introduction to the content may be found at the start of each chapter.

Chapter 1—The Turkish Television Industry: From National to Transnational

The chapter examines the growth of the Turkish television industry, which has become the world's second-largest exporter of scripted TV dramas. It explores the economic and political factors that have contributed to the expansion of the industry and the impact of changes in foreign policy and trade relationships. The chapter also looks at the ideological and technological transformation of the TV production industry and the rise of video-on-demand services that increasingly produce serials for digital and global viewers. Streaming platforms are enabling Turkish serials to reach international audiences with ready-dubbed content, bypassing geopolitics and distribution companies.

Chapter 2—Turkish Drama Serials in the Arab World

The second chapter examines the parallel development of Arab media industries and the impact of Arab-Turkish diplomatic and trade relationships on the successful entry of Turkish serials into the Arab world. It starts with a brief history of private satellite networks in the 1990s, including the rise of Saudi-owned MBC as a leading entertainment network. MBC was the first to introduce Turkish dramas to its large audience in the MENA region. The chapter also analyses the impact of technological convergence on the region's production, distribution, and consumption of content. It shows how financial interests have intersected with politics, with Turkish dramas being offered on regional digital platforms while being banned on free-to-air satellite channels. The chapter concludes by describing the shift in Turkish influence in the cultural industry, from dubbed dramas to content produced specifically for the Arab world.

Chapter 3—Fluctuating Turkish–Arab Relations and the Soft Power of Drama Serials

Chapters 1 and 2 provide an overview of the Turkish and Arab TV industries, exploring why Turkish drama serials became popular on the Arab world's largest media network, MBC. Chapter 3 examines the impact of the growth of diplomatic and economic ties between Türkiye and the Arab world on the popularity of Turkish TV dramas in the MENA region. By analysing audience data from Arab nationals in Qatar, the chapter seeks to understand whether the growing awareness and positive perception of Türkiye among Arabs is due to Turkish foreign policy or exposure to Turkish dramas. This is relevant, as Turkish political influence, economic strength, and engagement have intersected with the success of Turkish serials in the Arab world. The chapter covers the historical background of Turkish-Arab relations, Türkiye's multidirectional foreign policy, the factors that have made Türkiye a regional soft power, and the current political developments between Türkiye, KSA, and the UAE. The key findings show that Turkish drama serials have been the main reason for increased awareness and a positive perception of Türkiye and its people among Arab study participants. The serials raise awareness of Turkish culture and history, and function as a soft-power tool as they come from a Muslim-majority country and offer a relatable mix of glamour, Western-style modernity, and socio-cultural elements. The dramas have motivated many Arabs to visit Türkiye and change their perception of shared history from a period of Arab oppression to a time of Muslim glory and importance, primarily shaped by Ottoman period dramas where Turkish actors are depicted as Muslim heroes instead of villains.

Chapter 4—The Importance of Socio-Cultural Factors in the Appeal of Turkish Serials among Arab Viewers

Chapter 4 examines the impact of cultural and historical ties between Arabs and Turks on the positive reception of Turkish dramas in the MENA region.

It uses Qatar as a case study to explore the appeal of Turkish dramas, focusing on the cultural and socio-cultural factors that facilitate their popularity. It finds that cultural similarities, such as common religion, heritage, and ethnic types, enhance acceptance of dubbed Turkish dramas. Chapter 4 also reveals that the interplay between cultural proximity and distance makes Turkish dramas particularly engaging to Arab viewers, as they can portray characters and storylines that are relatable and authentic but considered taboo in the Arab world.

Chapter 5—Why Turkish Dramas Resonate with Arab Women: An Analysis of the Responses of Women Viewers in Qatar

Chapter 5 explores the viewing motivations of Arab women, who are the primary audience of Turkish drama serials, using the uses and gratifications theory. It builds on Chapter 4's findings of intertwined histories and cultural similarities as significant factors in the positive reception of Turkish dramas. The chapter starts by examining the status of women in Qatar and finds that Turkish dramas offer a level of emotional authenticity that other media have failed to provide, satisfying women's needs beyond just escapism and fantasy. The combination of multiple viewing motives creates a unique viewing experience that only Turkish dramas have been able to offer to date.

Chapter 6—Turkish Drama Serials in Chile

This chapter explores the success of Turkish dramas in Chile, despite the absence of shared language, ethnicity, history, or religion between the two countries. It examines Chilean viewers' motivations for watching Turkish dramas and their relevance to Chilean audiences' lives in an emerging economy in the Global South. The chapter also provides context on recent diplomatic and trade relations between Türkiye and Latin America, particularly Chile. Empirical data suggests that Chilean audiences relate to the same topics as Turkish and Arab audiences, and cultural similarities contribute to the success of Turkish dramas in Chile. Türkiye's dramas are also recognized as a powerful soft-power tool for Türkiye and Muslim nations among viewers with limited exposure to Türkiye or the Muslim world beyond Western stereotypes.

Chapter 7—Turkish Drama Serials in Israel

This chapter examines the appeal of Turkish drama serials to Israeli audiences. Like Chapter 6, Chapter 7 seeks to identify the factors that attract audiences from different geo-cultural and geo-linguistic regions to Turkish drama serials. To provide background context, the chapter explores the past and present diplomatic relations between Türkiye and Israel, which have transitioned from allies to opposing actors and are now gradually improving. The chapter also explores how Turkish drama serials have successfully entered the Israeli television market despite the highly strained relationship between the two nations. Unlike in the Arab world or Chile, the Israeli case illustrates how popular cultural products can rise above diplomatic tensions. The core findings of the chapter reveal that television serials can transcend conflict and opposition if they meet the needs of the audience. The empirical data also shows that Turkish dramas create a positive image of Türkiye among Israeli viewers and reveal many cultural similarities between the two countries. The portrayal of a Turkish society and culture that values conservative traditions while embracing Western-style modernity holds strong appeal for Israeli audiences. The constant interplay between tradition and modernity resonates with their everyday life, and the realization of these commonalities elevates their attraction and engagement with Turkish dramas.

A brief note on method

This book draws its analyses from qualitative and quantitative data to better understand the appeal of Turkish drama serials to Arab, Chilean, and Israeli audiences. The survey portion of the study used open-ended questions to gain in-depth insights into participants' perspectives and experiences regarding the consumption of Turkish dramas. In addition to open-ended questions, the surveys also included Likert Scale questions investigating the significance of cultural factors, dubbing, viewing motivation, and production values—all deemed important for viewers. Lastly, respondents were questioned about their perceptions of Türkiye, and whether these had changed after watching Turkish dramas. While survey data, focus-group discussions, and interviews were conducted in English in Qatar, in Chile they were administered in Spanish, and in Hebrew in Israel. Responses were later translated into English.

The data gathered in Qatar spans almost a decade. Research participants were a mix of women and men from various Arab countries and diverse socio-cultural backgrounds. All focus-group discussions were segregated by sex to avoid gender constraints. Twenty focus-group discussions were conducted between 2013 and 2014, and another twenty between 2016 and 2017, with university students aged 18–25 (with a 50:50 female to male ratio), along with two hundred online surveys targeting people aged 18–25 (with a 70:30 female to male ratio). The participation criteria required that participants should either themselves be a viewer of Turkish serials, or have a family member in the household who was a regular viewer of Turkish dramas.

In addition, fifty semi-structured interviews of predominantly female viewers of Turkish dramas in Qatar were conducted from 2016 to 2017. Participants were aged between 18 and 56 (consisting of stay-at-home mothers, students, and professionals). In 2018 an online survey was administered to Arab fan pages of Turkish serials on social media, in order to examine viewer reactions to the banning of Turkish drama serials on KSA and UAE free-to-air satellite channels. Three hundred participants responded, hailing from various Arab countries. The ages of participants were 18–60, with the majority being female respondents.

For the focus-group and face-to-face interviews, research participants were recruited first through personal contacts and later through snowball sampling.[14] Both were audio-recorded and immediately transcribed. When participants did not wish to be audio-recorded, handwritten notes were taken and later checked with individuals for accuracy. The focus-group discussions lasted between 60 and 90 minutes and included six to eight participants. The individual interviews lasted 45–60 minutes. In order to respect research participants' privacy and guarantee anonymity, all participants were assigned numbers; only gender, nationality, and occupation are clearly stated in the study. A thematic analysis was utilized.[15] A preliminary codebook was created after the transcription of focus-group discussions and interviews with viewers. After coding three samples of the transcripts, the codebook was developed, and ambiguities were clarified. In the final step, each transcript was coded. In the process of eliciting the codes and merging them into superior categories, particular focus was given to themes reflecting viewing motivation, dubbing, the importance of cultural elements, visual aesthetics (production values), and the perception of Türkiye before and after viewing Turkish dramas. The same coding process was utilized for all the survey data containing open-ended questions that required participants to answer in their own words.

In order to study Chilean audiences, two hundred surveys were conducted between 2019 and 2020 (with an 80:20 female to male ratio), with participants aged 18–63. Sixty surveys were conducted with Chilean university students aged 18–30 (with an 85:15 female to male ratio). Once more, the participation requirement for university students was either to be a viewer of, or to share a home with a regular viewer of Turkish dramas. The same sample size was repeated in Israel. Two hundred Turkish drama viewers were surveyed (with a 70:30 female to male ratio), along with sixty university students aged 18–33 (with a 90:10 female to male ratio). Along with conducting surveys and interviews with viewers, I also carried out semi-structured interviews in English with ten Turkish industry professionals (in 2010, 2015, and 2020), one US/Latin American professional (in 2020), and two Arab television executives (in 2015). These interviews offered valuable insights to supplement my empirical data.

Furthermore, I thoroughly analysed numerous articles in Arabic, English, Hebrew, Spanish, and Turkish, as well as rating reports and public-opinion polls. By incorporating a diverse range of sources, I aimed to provide a comprehensive and nuanced understanding of this evolving phenomenon.

1 The Turkish Television Industry: From National to Transnational

Introduction

Turkish television dramas have captured the hearts of viewers around the world, from the Middle East and Asia to Eastern and Southern Europe, Africa, Latin America and the Caribbean, and the United States. This chapter explores the impressive evolution of the Turkish television industry, which has transitioned from a dependence on foreign content to becoming the world's second-largest exporter of scripted television dramas, only surpassed by the United States. Türkiye has sustained this position since 2014,[1] and has even established itself as the world's fifth-largest exporter of all television programs since 2016. In just a matter of years, Turkish television exports have seen remarkable global success. By 2018, Türkiye's export revenue from TV dramas had reached $500 million and is expected to skyrocket to $1 billion by 2023.[2]

This chapter will examine the economic and political factors that have contributed to the expansion of the Turkish television industry. It will explore crucial changes in the Turkish economy, and in foreign policy and trade relationships since the early 2000s—changes that fuelled the growth and expansion of the domestic television sector, creating the unique conditions that made it favourable for Turkish drama serials to penetrate the Arab world, and later other former Ottoman territories and countries further afield. At the same time, the huge demand for Turkish drama serials over the past decade, particularly from the Arab world, has contributed to the transformation of the production sector in Türkiye into a highly profitable and competitive industry. Therefore, the successful reception of Turkish serials in Arab countries represents a pivotal moment for Turkish drama serials' transitioning from being successful nationally, within their geo-linguistic region (Turkic-speaking countries) and among Turkish diasporic audiences, to becoming internationally popular television serials.

In order to provide the reader with a complete picture, this chapter touches on the establishment of the Turkish television industry through to the present day. It then goes on to outline the sector's current economic, political, and cultural dynamics, with an overview of ownership and affiliations. The reader is introduced to the numerous challenges the Turkish television industry has faced—an unstable economy, fierce competition, changing broadcast regulations, and restrictive ratings systems. These key factors are analysed in light of the ever-changing foreign and trade relations that have played a crucial role in the current upsurge in the television sector, and the ongoing challenges within the highly competitive Turkish television market. The chapter concludes by examining the technological transformation of the Turkish television industry in recent years, which has resulted in the improvement of production values and growing investment in streaming platforms. It analyses significant developments in domestic streaming services, where television serials are being increasingly produced without prioritizing the domestic television audience, focusing instead on viewers in the digital realm and global markets. The discussion in this chapter is based on industry reports, academic papers, and journalistic articles written in both English and Turkish, along with numerous formal and informal conversations with industry professionals.

A historic overview of Turkish television

The state-owned broadcaster, the Turkish Radio and Television Corporation (TRT; Türkiye Radyo ve Televizyon Kurumu), was founded in 1964, and is the only public-service broadcaster in the country.[3] Currently, TRT has ten domestic channels: TRT1, TRT2, TRT, TRT Belgesel, TRT Çocuk, TRT Müzik, TRT Haber, TRT Spor, TRT Spor Yıldız, TRT Avaz, TRT Türk, TRT World, TRT Arabi, TRT 4K, TRT3.[4]

However, in contrast to the size of the Turkish state broadcaster as it is today, TRT had humble beginnings—starting from the basement of two apartments located at 47 and 49 Mithat Paşa Street in the capital, Ankara. The programming consisted of news, weather reports, forums, and music. As

THE TURKISH TELEVISION INDUSTRY: FROM NATIONAL TO TRANSNATIONAL

TRT did not have any tape-recording capabilities for later broadcasting, all programmes were produced live. According to Kale, Tunca Yönder, one of the first directors of TRT, was assigned the task of producing the first drama in the history of Turkish television.[5] Yönder chose a work by Ottoman playwright and journalist Ibrahim Şinasi, called *The Wedding of a Poet* (*Şair Evlenmesi*)— the first Turkish play written for the theatre. *The Wedding of a Poet* was performed live and broadcast on 6 February 1968. Following this first literary adaptation, many others followed. However, unlike today, they were not called *dizi* (dramas) but instead were referred to as *televizyon oyunu* (television plays). The first television play to be pre-recorded for broadcast was *Direklerarasi*, produced in 1971 for TRT's programming during Eid al-Fitr.[6] It is believed that from 1971, TRT started to outsource the production of its content to private local companies and began by broadcasting predominantly US dramas and movies. Kocabaşoğlu notes that because the production of original programming was an expensive business, a reliance on foreign content was seen as the only way to meet the ever-growing viewer demand.[7] However, TRT's strategy of filling its schedules with foreign movies, television series, and cartoons faced increasing criticism. According to Sümer and Taş,[8] the debate focused on the poor quality of television broadcasts and the lack of original national content.

Nonetheless, the comedy series *Mothers-in-Law* (*Kaynanalar*), which began on TRT in 1974, and later aired from 1997 to 2004 on the private television station Kanal D, was the first and longest-running Turkish television series (in the traditional sense), being screened over a period of thirty years.[9] Meanwhile, according to Kale, TRT produced its first mini-series, *Forbidden Love*, in 1975 (*Aşk-ı Memnu*, April–May 1975), which was the adaptation of a novel by an Ottoman author, poet, and playwright, Halid Ziya Uşakligil. Notably, *Forbidden Love* was not only the first series produced by TRT in collaboration with Yeşilçam (a sobriquet referring to the Turkish film industry), and the most expensive production of its time,[10] but it was also the first Turkish show to be exported internationally, sold to France in 1981.[11]

For many academics,[12] the 1970s and 1980s represent a significant turning point in Turkish television, as this period introduced the transnationalization of television content with the introduction of dubbed programmes to Turkish audiences, first from the USA, and later from Latin America. Shows such as *Charlie's Angels* (1977–81), *The Little House on the Prairie* (1974–83), *Roots*

(1977), *Dallas* (1980), *The A-Team* (1983–87), *The Cosby Show* (1984–92), *Knight Rider* (1982–86), and Latin American telenovelas such as *Cara Sucia* (1992), *Marimar* (1994), and *Maria La Del Barrio* (1995–96),[13] were just some of the globally successful shows made available to Turkish television audiences. According to Kaptan, these offerings were highly welcomed and appreciated by Turkish viewers.[14] Ilaslan notes that the initial criticism of this dependency on foreign programmes was replaced by an emphasis on the need to integrate with the international flow of broadcast content.[15]

Nonetheless, the heavy presence of foreign content did not mean that there was a complete lack of local material. TRT produced its own news and entertainment programmes, and turned to local production companies for dramas and comedy serials.[16] Scholars in the field agree that the mid-1980s saw the beginning of deregulation, and the liberalization of Türkiye's television industry based on global neoliberal imperatives.[17] As a result, private channels entered the broadcasting market in the early 1990s, despite legal frameworks still forbidding this move. Kaya & Çakmur stress that for the Turkish public and authorities alike, these developments in the media sector were somewhat unexpected, and many were sceptical about both the purpose and benefits.[18] The fact that satellite dishes were required in order to watch these private channels made many question their ability to succeed and their likelihood of survival.[19] Yet the advent of satellite technology, and the development of inexpensive satellite dishes capable of receiving direct satellite broadcasting, are believed to have aided in the successful establishment of the first private television station, Star TV, in 1990, despite it technically being a pirate station.[20] At the time, a high level of television penetration in the country, along with great public interest in new entertainment outlets, and the authorities' disinclination to enforce the law, are factors believed to have aided Star TV in establishing itself, while motivating other entrepreneurs to follow their example.[21]

It is worth noting that Star TV was co-owned by Ahmet Özal, the son of the late prime minister and president Turgut Özal who, during the 1980s, led the introduction of neoliberalism into the country.[22] Öncü highlights that the advance of neoliberalism, and the expansion of media markets that followed, was a definitive period in Turkish television history, as it marked Türkiye's integration into the global economy.[23] For scholars, this process was further accelerated in the 1990s by the economic transformation of media through convergence and concentration, with large conglomerates establishing and acquiring television stations and newspapers to create media empires.[24] Kaya and Çakmur describe how the sudden expansion of the broadcasting sector, and the non-existence of a judicial framework, resulted in an era of chaos. They note that the overall dissatisfaction with TRT's political coverage, together with the view that the creation of private media outlets was a technological development necessary to keep pace with the rest of Europe, were used to justify the rapid commercialization of the media industry.[25] Scholars agree that the next three years (1990–93), until the Turkish government's amendment of the constitution in July 1993, were distinguished by a lack of media policy, allowing entrepreneurs and investors flexibility and freedom to shape and develop the private broadcasting sector.[26] For many, this development had a significant impact on the dynamics between the government and the media.[27] The decentralization of broadcasting, and the upsurge of neoliberalism, subsequently resulted in big conglomerates (with investments in banking, finance, tourism, the automotive industry, construction, and the energy sector) dominating the Turkish media landscape and taking control of mainstream television channels including Kanal D, Star TV, Show TV, and ATV, among dozens of others. Despite significant growth in digital media, television still wields substantial influence in Türkiye due to high ratings and the low cost of advertising.[28]

In July 1993, Article 233 of the constitution was amended, and Law No. 3984, the Broadcasting Act, was passed in 1994,[29] along with the formation of the Turkish Radio and Television Supreme Council (RTÜK). Since its establishment, RTÜK has been responsible for allocating broadcasting licences,[30] monitoring broadcasting content, responding to audience complaints, and implementing sanctions (such as fines and the cancellation of programmes or licences) in cases of non-compliance.[31] In August 2018, RTÜK was also given the authority to regulate and monitor sound and visual broadcasting shared via the internet, and via streaming and video-sharing services.[32]

From a by-product of Türkiye's economic success to a global player in scripted serials

At present, owing to television's ongoing popularity, Türkiye has 196 channels, of which 19 are national, 12 regional, and 165 local stations.[33] As highlighted at the beginning of this chapter, just three decades ago Türkiye was in the position of having to purchase foreign content to fill its broadcast schedule. It has since moved on to producing films and serials, game shows, and entertainment formats in a comparatively short space of time, and now stands as a transnational player on the production stage. Considering that the broadcast sector was a state-owned monopoly until the early 1990s, with only TRT dominating the airways,[34] this transition represents remarkable progress. With the rise to power of the Justice and Development Party (Adalet ve Kalkinma Partisi, AKP) in 2002, Türkiye has transformed itself in less than a decade from a country that was paralysed by the economic crisis of the 1990s, to becoming part of the G20 of developing nations, with one of the fastest-growing economies worldwide.[35] As Szigetvári notes, starting from the early 2000s, Türkiye has become an emerging economy, successfully joining global economic production and trade flows, and has thereby experienced rapid economic growth.[36] This sudden economic growth also contributed to a significant expansion in the television sector.

As noted earlier, most leading Turkish media outlets are owned by large multi-sector conglomerates. Consequently, their wider economic success has helped fuel growth in the national media industry. It is also worth stressing that in the decade after the year 2000, Türkiye witnessed both the birth and the collapse of media conglomerates.[37] At the same time, the Turkish television industry shifted from a dependence on foreign content to becoming self-sufficient content producers, leading to the prime-time dominance of local serials and the relocation of foreign content to thematic channels or non-prime-time slots. However, this shift from international content to a preference for national content consumption is not a development unique to Türkiye, as in the 1990s various academics repeatedly argued that the global dominance of US entertainment content was more a question of market power than of demand.[38] Pool, for instance, argued as early as 1971 that audiences would prefer references to their own culture and to watch national content, when it could compete with US programmes in terms of production quality.[39]

Reflecting on the factors that contributed to the growth of the Turkish television sector, scholars have argued that it was not only the economic upsurge, but also the availability of trained creative professionals that contributed to the rise of local productions in the Turkish television industry.[40] Before the privatization of television in the 1990s, Türkiye's film industry had experienced significant growth throughout the twentieth century. This allowed for an experienced workforce simply to shift industries when the rapid expansion of the television sector took hold. Yesil and others note that the migration of film and theatre talent to television, and the subsequent utilization of their professional expertise, played a significant role in the development of the production sector.[41] At the same time, university degrees in media, communication, film, and drama became popular choices for young people, with many state and private universities offering courses in these subjects, contributing to the readiness of a highly trained workforce. Additionally, social acceptance of professions in the creative fields for both women and men, in what is a Muslim-majority country, equally aided in the availability of skilled cultural-industry professionals. One could argue that this aspect has been one of the Turkish television industry's most significant advantages when compared to other Muslim-majority countries, where professions in the film and television industries are still often perceived as culturally unacceptable—even more so for women.

The rising demand for television content contributed to the establishment of numerous production companies, some of which are presently among the leading production houses in the country.[42] In addition, to obtain a share of the growing television production market and meet the increasing demand from national broadcasters, film production companies also entered the television sector. At present, Turkish television channels are broadcasting almost entirely local content, with an average of 200 television serials being produced a year, in comparison to only fourteen being shot less than three decades ago.[43]

This expansion of the television market has been predominantly driven by a demand for and dependence on dramas, with over 60 per cent of television broadcasting time allocated to drama serials across the most-watched television channels.[44] As Cetin quite rightly argues, Turkish drama serials have become the *sine qua non* of Turkish television, similarly to telenovelas for Latin American television.[45]

To demonstrate effectively the degree of growth that the television industry experienced, it is useful to look back at the level of advertising revenue being generated at the start of the economic upturn in 2002, which was a reported $953 million.[46] Increases in advertising and media investment in the country over the past twenty years have been significant, and according to an industry report published by Deloitte in 2020, the total investment in advertising and media had grown to $2.48 billion.[47] Thus, advertising revenue has become a key factor in the production of both television and internet shows, with television still being the most important medium for advertisers to promote their products and services in Türkiye.

Moreover, advertising revenue has also had a direct impact on the runtime of Turkish serials. Unlike global norms where an episode of a drama is thirty-seven minutes to an hour long, depending on the country and medium on which it is shown, a single episode of a Turkish serial broadcast on domestic television is typically 120 to 140 minutes long (excluding advertisements). Each week's episode also includes lengthy summaries of the previous episode. The result is that Turkish serials end up being closer in duration to an average feature film than a weekly serial. Long episodes on television offer considerable advantages to advertisers, as they pay per episode and not for the number of times the commercial is run during its allotted time.[48] Therefore, with each episode running for more than two hours, advertisers get significantly more airtime for their commercials. Furthermore, in contrast to US or Western European serials, with an average of thirteen episodes a season, Turkish shows can have thirty-five to forty episodes a season,[49] which are filmed weekly. A successful Turkish serial can run for an average of two to three seasons, with very few exceptions.

Many researchers in the field argue that with the growing demand for serials, and persistently growing domestic competition, production companies are under constant pressure to meet the needs of audiences, channel executives, and government regulators, with serials having become an important commercial platform.[50] The production sector has faced additional rivalry with the entry of international players such as the Endemol Shine Group and MBC-affiliated O3 Productions in 2014. In 2017, Los Angeles-based Karga Seven Pictures, owned by Red Arrow, also opened an Istanbul office, as did Fox, to name just one more—each wishing to profit from the increasing demand for Turkish content.[51]

Current conditions in the Turkish television sector

The Turkish television market can presently be described as highly ruthless and ratings-driven. Television channels are investing enormous amounts of money into productions in the hope of attracting high ratings and profitable advertising revenue. Production companies, in an attempt to meet broadcasters' demands, increasingly utilize high production budgets, and cast star actors to draw in large numbers of viewers. A prime example of this was the high-budget and high-quality production value applied to the period drama *Magnificent Century*, which reached more than 500 million viewers worldwide. The drama first aired in Türkiye in January 2011 and ran for four seasons, spanning a total of 139 episodes. According to Turkish media reports, the programme employed 50,000 supporting actors and required 5,000 costumes. In addition, five Ottoman palaces were recreated as production sets, and 100,000 metres of material were used for the decor. The entire cost of the serial is estimated to have reached a total of 130 million TL (approx. 84 million USD).[52] Timur Savci, founder and owner of TIMS & B Productions, and creator of *Magnificent Century* (*Muhteşem Yüzyil*, 2011–14, Türkiye: Show TV, Star TV), stressed during an open question-and-answer session following the screening of a behind-the-scenes documentary on the series in Doha, Qatar, in October 2015, that the serial was a huge undertaking for his company. He emphasized that due to the high production costs and the potential risk of the serial not reaching desirable ratings, his production company was under enormous financial pressure. The production cost of *Magnificent Century* was much greater than any budget the industry was accustomed to at the time. However, following its domestic and international success, high production budgets started to become more common. The national broadcaster also adopted this approach, and according to Turkish media reports, TRT spent 1.1 million TL (approx. 711,000 USD) per episode during the production of *Resurrection: Ertugrul*, 1 million TL (approx. 646,000 USD) per episode for its mini-series *Seddülbahir*, and 850,000 TL (approx. 549,000 USD) per episode for its Ottoman detective series *Filinta*, to name but a few.[53]

The more recently concluded drama *Bitter Lands* (*Bir Zamanlar Cukurova*, 2018–22, Türkiye:ATV), from TIMS & B Productions, is another example of high production values playing a significant role in the appeal of the programme. The drama serial is set in 1970 Çukurova, southern Türkiye, a municipality in Adana known for its wide, fertile plains. It took the TIMS & B Productions team eight months to recreate the Çukurova of that time. According to Turkish media reports, 450 people worked on creating a family farm, which is at the centre of the story and home to the lead protagonists of the show, the Yaman family. The production team was reported to have studied hundreds of documents and photographs from the period to ensure that the set was as accurate and realistic as possible. At the same time, the costume department searched for and found original vintage clothing and accessories for the actors, in order to further enhance the serial's authentic depiction of the period.[54] The fact that *Bitter Lands* often topped the ratings demonstrates that Turkish audiences expect and appreciate serials with high production values.[55] The constant pressure to produce content to satisfy audience expectations in a country of more than 84 million appears to have converted the rating race in Türkiye from a run into a sprint, where shows compete fiercely against each other across their weekly broadcasting schedules.

One of the negative impacts of the ratings fight is that Turkish audiences will often find that they have been watching a new series for only a couple of weeks, when suddenly, and without explanation, the show is cancelled.[56] The reason for this lies within the production contract—television stations and production companies sign an agreement that stipulates the viewership numbers required for a serial to be maintained. If the serial fails to meet the required viewership numbers it will be swiftly taken off air, as the television station only pays the production company per episode, rather than per season.[57] A serial's success is also dependent on which day of the week the show is broadcast, and which other serials are aired simultaneously on competing channels. Occasionally, Turkish audiences will see shows suddenly and unexpectedly change their broadcast day and/or time. By amending the broadcast schedule, television stations try to ascertain whether a specific programme will do better when competing against shows on a different day, hoping that the competition will be less fierce.

Many industry professionals spoken to over the years stressed their discomfort with the current Turkish ratings system, introduced in 2012, which focuses only on high-television-consuming households while disregarding other audience groups. Alankus and Yanardagoglu note that prior to 2012, the education level of the 'head of the household' determined how social and economic status was allocated, whereas in the current system, the primary determinant is mass public income-level instead of education, which is seen as impacting audience preference.[58] This practice is perceived by many to limit creativity, and push the industry to use repetitive storylines in a bid to win viewers. Ratings have also been criticized as the reason why most Turkish drama serials contain love stories and romantic elements. According to industry reports, serials with romantic storylines are highly popular among female audiences, who represent an important audience base for prime-time serials in Türkiye. As a result, even action and crime serials are given a romantic subplot, with the aim of evoking a range of emotions and attracting a broader audience. This contributes to Turkish serials each trying to span multiple genres.[59] At this point, it is important to stress that the success of Turkish serials among domestic audiences is essential for both their longevity on national television and their ability to be marketed abroad. Only Turkish serials that are successful in the local market typically attract foreign buyers, because a drama serial's favourable reception among Turkish viewers is seen as an indication that it also has the potential to be successful in other television markets.[60]

Consequently, the current ratings system in Türkiye can be seen as a double-edged sword; on the one hand, productions with repetitive themes might be more likely to gain preferable ratings, while on the other hand, repetitiveness might lose the interest of international buyers, as foreign customers are equally eager to introduce fresh content to their viewers. The fact that in 2017, only ten out of the seventy serials produced that year were sold abroad, with only half of these becoming international hits, gives an indication of this dilemma.[61] One could argue that Turkish production companies appear to be left with the heaviest burden—that of coming up with creative ways of making an old formula work every time. That said, according to scholars and journalists, Turkish serials' textual strategies have become ideological, representing at their core a more conservative worldview in line with the ideology of the ruling Turkish government. This conservative ideology, however, is often challenged in situations where commercial and ideological imperatives collide, pushing the Turkish television industry to find new ways of balancing commercial success and government expectations to promote Turkish family values.[62] But to attract greater audiences, Turkish drama serials appear liberal on the surface; they contain many contradictions that are essentially opposed to the interests of the prevalent ideology. However, the liberal themes in conventional Turkish dramas are never truly liberal, as they are restricted by patriarchal perimeters and storylines that are consolidated in a normative conservative framework.

Nonetheless, despite the various challenges faced by the television industry, the fierce competition in the sector has also generated positive outcomes. This includes contributing to Turkish serials achieving higher overall production quality, and thus allowing them to compete effectively in the international television market. According to data published by French audience ratings and measurement company Glance (Global Audience & Content Evolution), in 2016, Türkiye was at the top of the foreign content-provider list, with a 25 per cent television market share (for scripted dramas). The USA, as a source of worldwide content, was positioned in fourth place, with a 7 per cent share, followed closely by Brazil and Mexico, with 6 per cent each. By comparison, 2017 data for Latin America revealed that the USA was the leading off-region content provider, with a 31 per cent share, followed by Türkiye with 23 per cent.[63] Moreover, according to Turkish media reports in 2019, 150 serials had been exported to 146 countries worldwide,[64] from the Middle East to the Balkans, Africa to Central Asia, and the Far East to South America, reaching some 700 million viewers. With a growing demand for Turkish serials, and increasing production costs, the price per episode of a Turkish programme rose steeply from $4,000 to $400,000 in only a decade.[65] These growth figures demonstrate that Türkiye has become a world-class player in the global television ecosystem, while drama serials have become the nation's most important cultural commodity. The international success of Turkish drama serials is a significant example of the ongoing trend of multiple-centre geo-flows in the media industry.[66] This trend reflects a departure from traditional Western-centric media flows and a shift towards a more diverse and decentralized landscape. The popularity of Turkish serials among global audiences is a manifestation of this trend and highlights the growing demand for alternative and diverse media content.

Digital media and streaming platforms

The following section examines the rise of streaming platforms and the implications for the production industry in Türkiye. Over-the-top (OTT) or set-top box media services have become an essential part of content consumption for domestic audiences in the last decade.[67] Before the arrival of streaming platforms in Türkiye, Turkish television stations had been offering catch-up content

THE TURKISH TELEVISION INDUSTRY: FROM NATIONAL TO TRANSNATIONAL

via their streaming services as a way for viewers to watch programmes after an episode had first screened on television. The establishment of domestic streaming platforms such as BluTV in 2015, and Puhu in 2016, and the entry of international giant Netflix in 2016, represented a gradual but essential shift in the way Turkish audiences consumed content. Turkish television viewers now generally supplement their traditional terrestrial and satellite content consumption with streaming services.

According to the Berlin-based website *JustWatch* (which allows searches for and watching of TV series and films), the largest market share of digital platforms available in Türkiye is held by BluTV with 43 per cent, followed by Netflix and Amazon Prime with 26 per cent and 18 per cent market shares, respectively.[68] These top three digital platforms now claim 87 per cent of the total market. In 2020, it was reported that BluTV had 4.2 million subscribers and Netflix 3.5 million, which might appear insignificant in a country of 84 million—yet streaming has become a serious business.[69] Realizing that there is profit to be made from online content, streaming companies are increasingly trying to attract viewers with original shows. According to a report published by Deloitte in 2020, digital media in Türkiye have taken the lion's share of investment with 54 per cent, while television broadcasters have been pushed to second place with 36 per cent. As the most successful subscription video-on-demand (SVOD) platform in Türkiye, BluTV has created a number of original shows that have moved away from the classical drama and romance recipe, in an effort to produce bolder and riskier content. This move appears to have paid off, making it the current platform market leader in the country.

During an interview with an Istanbul-based media executive at a sales and production company, the interviewee noted that the production of serials for digital platforms had several advantages. Firstly, it permits companies like his to create content outside the competitive television market by making serials that differ from the traditional drama genre. At the same time, the digital platforms allow their serials to reach 'millennials', who are one of the primary consumers of digital content in Türkiye. According to a 2019 report by Eurostat, 92 per cent of Turkish viewers between 16 and 24 have been found to consume content via video-on-demand platforms or streaming services, compared to 54 per cent among the 55–74 age group.[70] Moreover, for the Istanbul-based media executive, digital platforms allow Turkish productions to find new audiences. 'We're aiming to penetrate some new markets that we have never been successful in penetrating before, like West European countries.'[71]

Due to growing demand, in late 2020 two additional domestic streaming platforms were established, GAİN and Exxen. GAİN offers a more innovative alternative to previously established streaming platforms and network television in Türkiye. GAİN's most innovative aspect is the length of its content. Everything, from original series to documentaries, is around fifteen minutes long. The platform aims to reach younger consumers who enjoy watching shorter programmes on their smartphones. Serials produced for digital platforms try to offer more diverse storylines and edgier content, hoping that this will attract domestic audiences who do not feel catered to by network television, while also looking for greater success internationally.

Another significant factor to note is that serials produced for streaming platforms are sold in six–ten episode packages, offering international customers another alternative for 'testing' Turkish content on their audiences.[72] In contrast, Turkish serials for television have typically been sold to international broadcasters in packages of 100 commercial hours per show. In another noteworthy development, TRT has been offering its original productions free of charge for international viewers, either dubbed or subtitled, on their YouTube platforms. At the same time, Demirören Media (owner of several legacy media outlets) launched its digital platform, Dramax, a subscription system for users worldwide. The platform aims to present popular Turkish television series globally on a single platform, with more than 5,000 hours of content. All productions can be streamed with Spanish and Arabic dubbing, while also offering other language options such as Russian, Urdu, and English.[73] This move by one of Türkiye's largest conglomerates demonstrates that the Turkish television industry is striving to reach international audiences away from the traditional export routes, instead targeting them directly. In other words, by cutting out the middleman, the television production industry aims to find new revenue streams, bypassing geopolitical constraints such as those that caused the cancellation of Turkish serials on the Arab world's largest media network, the MBC Group, in 2018.[74] Turkish serials were banned from MBC's airways until 2022 (see Chapter 3 for more).

According to the majority of Turkish media executives interviewed in 2020, owing to Türkiye's economic downturn in recent years, television productions are increasingly turning to international audiences for financial gain. Whether it's establishing streaming platforms that aim to attract international subscribers, or the production of bolder and edgier content for streaming services nationally or internationally, the end goal is to attract diverse audiences and, most importantly, to extend their global reach. This rapid growth of digital media, with increased investment, illustrates a significant development in the Turkish television industry.

Driven by the demand for Turkish content and the space for further growth, the race to produce Turkish serials has now been joined by another international giant, Disney+, who entered the market in June 2022 and is offering Turkish originals. Likewise, HBO Max was expected to arrive in the Turkish market by the end of 2022, again planning to offer a selection of Turkish originals.[75] While the rising demand for Turkish serials creates growing job opportunities for people in the field and increases the production value of serials, it seems to have also ignited a domestic struggle for qualified professionals. Renowned actors have recently chosen to favour digital platforms because they find them more prestigious, resulting in domestic television networks struggling to find suitable talent.[76]

Nonetheless, the intersection between television and streaming platforms still presents a blend of the two platforms, rather than the replacement of one medium by another. Yet the ability to reach broader audiences nationally and internationally, along with the ability to move away from restrictive ratings systems, and from the limitation of only focusing on one particular genre, makes investment in the move away from traditional television increasingly lucrative for production companies. This development has the potential to shape the industry further, and to permit Turkish television serials to grow and expand into other genres and regions.

Turkish serials entering the Arab television market

In this last section of the chapter, I examine the factors and circumstances that contributed to Turkish drama serials finding their way onto the Arab world's largest television network, MBC. I also discuss changes in trade and foreign policy in the 2000s that made this development possible.

It should be acknowledged that the entry in 2008 of the first Turkish drama, *Noor* (*Gümüş*, 2005–07, Türkiye: Kanal D), on MBC, represented a pivotal

TURKISH DRAMA SERIALS

moment where Turkish drama serials transitioned from being successful domestically and within their geo-linguistic market, to becoming popular internationally. But perhaps more crucially, this development exemplifies the success of foreign-policy efforts and the broadening of trade relationships by the Turkish state. Under the AKP government that took office in 2002, a multidirectional foreign policy has been adopted, moving away from predominantly Western-orientated relations, in order to improve Türkiye's political and economic interests in multiple regions.[77] Türkiye's new political direction of improved diplomatic relations with the Arab world paved the way for important business deals, the formation of free-trade zones, and the removal or easing of visa restrictions with Arab countries.[78] This also made it possible for Turkish products and companies, including drama serials, to flood the Arab world, while also enabling Arab tourists to visit Türkiye in greater numbers.[79] According to Professor of International Relations Mustafa Kutlay and others, foreign-policy initiatives under the AKP government have been following the functionalist framework, which comprises exploiting economic opportunities and interdependence to further institutionalize its relations with neighbouring countries.[80]

When MBC executive Fadi Ismail discovered the series *Noor* at a trade show in Türkiye, the Arab world's largest television network suddenly considering the acquisition of Turkish drama serials might have appeared to come out of the blue. *Noor* was purchased in 2007, and finally aired in 2008 on Saudi-owned and Dubai-based MBC Television during Ramadan, the most popular time for television viewing in the region. At that time, diplomatic and trade relations between Türkiye and countries in the Gulf were in full swing, having reached a historic high. Trade relations between Türkiye and Saudi Arabia had gained significant momentum, proved when we compare the trade volume in 1996–97, at only $8.3 billion, with that of 2002–08, reaching $20.3 billion.[81] Moreover, along with state partnerships, private-sector trade deals also began to flourish, with Turkish businesses in energy, finance, banking, tourism, construction, communication, and the food industry securing trade deals with Saudi Arabia.[82] To further illustrate the dramatic improvement in Turkish and Saudi relations, in November 2007, Saudi King Abdullah received the Medal of Honour during his visit to the Turkish capital, Ankara, for his role in developing partnerships between the two countries. The Saudi monarch was presented with the medal at a state dinner hosted by the then

THE TURKISH TELEVISION INDUSTRY: FROM NATIONAL TO TRANSNATIONAL

Turkish president, Abdullah Gül. The medal had previously been given to only seven other world leaders.[83] King Abdullah's previous visit to Türkiye just a year before, in 2006, was the first visit by a Saudi king since King Faisal visited Istanbul in 1966.[84] Therefore, the period leading up to the purchase of the first Turkish serial by the Saudi-owned MBC network was characterized by a number of historical political, economic, security, and bilateral cultural agreements,[85] providing the necessary framework for Turkish cultural products to enter the Saudi Arabian market. Thus, the penetration of Turkish drama serials into the Arab television market represents an important interplay between economic and political integration.

The following chapter will provide a brief overview of Arab television history, starting from the 1990s, and will explore core factors that made it conducive for Turkish serials to establish themselves successfully on the Arab world's largest television network, MBC—and ultimately be shown on television screens across the MENA region.

2 Turkish Drama Serials in the Arab World

As mentioned in the previous chapter, it should be acknowledged that the successful entry and reception of Turkish serials in the Arab world was kickstarted by the Middle East Broadcasting Center's (MBC) airing of *Noor* (*Gümüs*, 2005–07, Türkiye: Kanal D), which in 2008 was dubbed into the Syrian colloquial dialect of Arabic. The airing of *Noor* resulted in unprecedented viewership figures across the Middle East and North Africa (MENA) region, attracting 80 million Arab viewers, of whom 50 million are believed to have been women above the age of 15.[1] The popularity of *Noor* and other serials that followed on MBC, such as *Mirna and Khalil* (*Menekşe ile Halil*, 2007–08, Türkiye: Kanal D) and *Asi* (2007–09, also on Kanal D), to name but two, encouraged other Arab channels to follow MBC's example of including a significant number of Turkish dramas in their daily scheduling. This resulted in Turkish dramas constituting 60 per cent of the foreign content on Arab broadcast schedules.[2]

The penetration of Turkish drama serials into the MENA region represents an important shift for these serials, which were until then only popular within the geo-linguistic market of Turkic-speaking countries and the Turkish diaspora (mainly Turks living in Western Europe). As argued in Chapter 1, the successful entry and positive reception of Turkish drama serials in the Arab world can be described as a key stage in their transition to becoming successful globally. Their popularity in the Arab world contributed to greater revenue in the sector, fuelling further growth, and created a burgeoning interest among international media, who all reported on the Arab viewer's passion for Turkish serials. This, in turn, helped to create increasing attention on Turkish drama serials in other parts of the world.[3]

Thus, this chapter first explores the various factors that made the Arab television market conducive to the arrival of Turkish drama serials by providing a brief overview of the Arab television market, from the establishment of private satellite-television stations in the early 1990s to the media environment as it currently stands. This chapter also outlines the sector's socio-political, economic, and cultural dynamics by describing the media structure, ownership, and affiliations across the MENA region. The reader is then introduced to the numerous challenges faced by the television industry, including an unstable economy, political turmoil, and the industry's dependence on income from the Arab world's largest economy, Saudi Arabia.

This chapter, therefore, pays particular attention to the Saudi-owned MBC Group. MBC is of particular interest, not only as one of the most influential media organizations in the MENA region, but also because it remains responsible for first igniting the fever for Turkish serials on Arab television and, a decade later, for banning these serials from its free-to-air satellite channels. Below we will explore the developments that led to the banning of Turkish drama serials, implemented in March 2018 by Kingdom of Saudi Arabia (KSA) and United Arab Emirates (UAE) free-to-air satellite TV stations, and their subsequent return. The chapter also analyses how over-the-top (OTT) set-top boxes, pay-TV, and streaming services have become significant factors in the region, in line with global trends. These services permit Arab audiences to select content beyond the network television schedules, allowing greater audience autonomy, and enabled audiences to bypass the MBC ban on Turkish programmes. In addition, this chapter discusses efforts by MBC to adapt to the Turkish format for drama production in the creation of local serials. The analysis here is based upon empirical data, industry reports, academic papers, and journalistic articles in Arabic, English, and Turkish. Some key findings reveal that Turkish drama serials have become an integral part of the content offering in the region, where financial interests transcend political differences via regional pay-TV and streaming services, which have continued to profit from the popularity of Turkish dramas despite diplomatic tension.

Television in the Arab world: past and present

In the Arab world, which has an estimated population of over 450 million,[4] television has traditionally been the most watched, most lucrative, and most politically influential medium.[5] However, a more recent study published by

Northwestern University Qatar, 'Media Use in the Middle East Survey', found that, compared with 2013, in 2019, significantly greater numbers of Arab nationals were using the internet and fewer were consuming traditional media across all Arab countries surveyed.[6] The study also revealed that women were more likely than men to watch television and spent more time doing so on average (watching television offline: 90 per cent women vs 83 per cent men; hours watching television offline each week: 20 hours women vs 17 hours men). The study also found that older individuals (45 and over) were more likely to watch television than the youngest group (18–24).

The shift from traditional to online media in the Arab world has seen growth for OTT services; pay-TV services also expanded their business, with increased subscription video-on-demand (SVOD) offerings benefiting from the growing market. As media scholars such as Joe Khalil note, cheaper access to the internet and improved mobile connectivity, in line with global trends, has contributed to the shift towards streaming options in the Arab television landscape.[7] Global giant Netflix launched their platform in the MENA region in 2016,[8] while the range of regional and international streaming services available to Arab viewers has grown significantly since, with numerous options now available to regional viewers.[9] Recent data from Digital TV Research estimates that by 2025, SVOD revenue in the MENA region will have reached $2.97 billion, up from $897 million in 2019.[10] Nonetheless, whether considering television or digital media, a few key media organizations continue to dominate the wider region.[11] The economic dependency of the Arab television industries on the oil-exporting countries is at the core of this imbalance. According to scholars in the field, the reliance on financial backing for production, and on the population of the Arab states of the Persian Gulf (henceforth referred to as the Gulf countries) and their high per capita spending for distribution, has provided these countries with the power to control what is commissioned or produced in the MENA region.[12] It is important to note that Arab television is not a single industry but consists of multiple sectors.[13] Therefore, to understand the Arab media landscape, the existing ecosystem, and the factors that later paved the way for Turkish dramas to enter the Arab television market, a brief historical overview of the establishment of private satellite-television stations in the 1990s is required. Academics in the field agree that this development in the 1990s has contributed to the dominance of Arab television networks, such as MBC, in the MENA region.[14]

As in Türkiye, the early to mid-1990s saw the emergence of many private satellite-television stations in the MENA region. Three decades on, these media outlets retain important positions in the Arab media landscape. In contrast to Türkiye, where liberal market dynamics have motivated Turkish media entrepreneurs to establish private satellite stations,[15] in the Arab world, the motivation for developing satellite channels (for example, in KSA) was, according to scholars in the field, driven by a fear of losing control over the 'monopoly on information'.[16] The 1991 news coverage of the Gulf War represented a significant moment when Arab viewers increasingly started watching Western media in order to access an alternative perspective on the ongoing conflict.[17] According to Pintak, this occurred despite the fact that satellite dishes were illegal in most Arab countries, and there were no Arab satellite channels available at the time. Yet dishes managed to appear on rooftops across the region.[18] As a result, the early to mid-1990s saw the emergence of private satellite-television stations. Scholars such as Rubin and Ayish note that the popularity of Western satellite television in the 1990s was driven by the increasing number of highly-educated Arab professionals who had lived in the West for several years—studying, working, or both. According to Rubin, this group, being familiar with news and entertainment networks available in the West, was one of the key audiences for satellite channels in the region. Sakr argued that the increasing anxiety over the fact that Arabs, both in the region and overseas, were opting for foreign channels, and thus potentially being influenced politically, was seen as a crucial factor driving the establishment of Arab satellite channels.[19]

As Khalil stresses, the popularity of foreign programmes also generated religious and moral panic, even prompting KSA clerics to call fatwas against specific shows.[20] The consequent establishment of Arab satellite channels, led by Saudi investment, significantly impacted television's overall development and the content produced in the MENA region—an impact which is still significant three decades later.

Several of the newly established channels in the 1990s were launched as offshore operations, broadcasting from the United Kingdom and Italy. These included MBC (1991, London, Saudi-owned), Orbit (1994, Rome, Saudi-owned), ART (1993, Rome, Saudi-owned), and Showtime Arabia (1996, London, Kuwait/USA-owned), to name but a few.[21] Not all overseas satellite channels were solely Saudi-owned: there were also Kuwaiti/US, Lebanese/

Saudi, and Syrian satellite channels, all headquartering their operations in London. According to Khalil and Kraidy, the British capital, while being a global city and international hub, was of particular interest to Arab media investors for two other important reasons. Firstly, the UK had undergone economic liberation, resulting in significant changes to its media and telecommunications sector; and secondly, the Gulf States had a historical relationship and affinity with the UK. Additionally, beside the economic, political, and geographic benefits that London afforded, the European location also provided the newly established broadcasters with a sense of editorial and creative autonomy that was not achievable anywhere in the Arab world.[22]

Nevertheless, after almost a decade in Europe, the Arab satellite channels chose to relocate, a reaction to falling oil prices from 1998 onwards, managerial problems, high operational costs, and the political and ideological clashes between KSA politics and British journalistic practices.[23] The decision was made to expedite MBC's relocation to Dubai Media City, which allowed the satellite channel to make a 30 per cent cut in its overall spending.[24] While most of the decisions to relocate were taken in early 2001, the events of September 11th of that year significantly accelerated the process.[25] Following MBC's relocation, the remainder of the Arab satellite channels also relocated their operations to the Arab world in the early to mid-2000s.

That said, MBC, which later evolved into the MBC Group, managed to establish itself as the largest broadcaster in the MENA region, serving as the barometer for the industry,[26] and attracting the largest audiences with its offering of entertainment, music, sports, and news channels.[27] MBC's multichannel service offers eighteen free-to-air satellite channels and a video-on-demand service, Shahid.[28]

It is worth noting that after a two-decade residency in Dubai, MBC and other Saudi-owned TV channels have since started to relocate to the KSA capital, Riyadh, as part of government plans to remould the kingdom as a regional business hub.[29]

Arab television audiences and markets

It needs to be recognized that, among the twenty-two Arab countries across the MENA region, in addition to significant economic disparities there are distinct social, cultural, demographic, and creative differences that impact the shaping of Arab television production and markets.[30] One of the most obvious differences between the Arab countries is that the Gulf States are more socially conservative than other parts of the Arab world. According to scholars in the field, the many differences that exist between Arab countries and their television markets make it difficult to describe Arab viewers as one audience.[31] Therefore, when discussing Arab television, it is important to take a broader perspective in order to view the industry as an interconnected set of cultural industries, where production and exchange have predominantly defined the market through the common language they share.[32] At the same time, it must be recognized that there are marked differences even within the Arabic language. There are many Arabic dialects, each of which is presented on the various Arab channels, ranging from the common Egyptian and Lebanese dialects, to the Gulf (Khaliji) and Syrian. While the majority of the Arab world is of the Muslim faith, there are also 'other religious and ethnic minorities that make up its ethnoreligious social mosaic'.[33] Moreover, there is a three-hour time difference between the Gulf and the most distant North African countries, as well as differing days of the week on which the weekend is observed. These factors make scheduling for Arab audiences particularly challenging.

However, irrespective of these challenges, networks such as MBC have been targeting a broader and more general audience across the MENA region.[34] Perhaps the most significant difference between the various markets is the economic variance (as noted earlier), with the most telling factor being the disparity existing between the wealthy Gulf monarchies and the other poorer countries. The economic differences between Arab countries have resulted in a strong interdependence between Arab television industries, with a particular dependence on Gulf countries such as KSA and the UAE.[35] It must be re-emphasized that KSA remains the most significant media market in the region, with a population of over 34 million (although immigrants do make up 38.3 per cent of the population). Even though Egypt is the most populous Arab country, with over 104 million inhabitants, KSA has a higher income per head,[36] making it the dominant market in the region. As a result, the priority for the Arab television industries has been to appeal to the preferences of the KSA audience. This is particularly true during the Muslim holy month of Ramadan, when viewership is believed to reach an all-year regional high.[37]

Ramadan TV: Turkish serials meeting Arab audiences

Although there are differences across the MENA region, and a steady shift from traditional to digital media, the Muslim holy month of Ramadan remains the most popular period for watching network television.[38] Arab television dramas, known as *musalsalāt* ('drama serials' in Arabic), have been a popular genre across the Arab world since the 1960s, and during Ramadan in particular they bring large audiences to the small screen. The Muslim holy month, known for its family *iftars* (the evening meal by which Muslims end their daily fast), has become a synonym for heavy television-viewing and drama consumption in the family setting. Ramadan has consequently been seen as shaping production, programming, and acquisition trends in Arab television for the entire year ahead.[39] The high volume of content produced for Ramadan is broadcast throughout the remainder of the year, as the shows are typically re-run across various channels.[40] Therefore, the introduction of the first dubbed Turkish drama during Ramadan in 2008 was a bold but decisive move by MBC, allowing the network to test Turkish content with potentially the largest television audience across the MENA region.

Following the enormous success of *Noor* in 2008, most Arab channels allocated some of their prime-time slots to Turkish dramas.[41] According to media reports, *Noor* had reached nearly 30 million daily viewers across the region, and the last episode was reported by media to have been watched by 92 million.[42] Consequently, purchasing Turkish serials has been seen as a win–win for Arab networks, firstly because Turkish dramas have been perceived as having the potential to attract valuable advertising revenue, and secondly because they have been particularly appealing to Arab television networks as programmes that have already been tested on Turkish audiences. Unlike, for instance, the traditional Ramadan series, where channels are buying a concept, idea, or script, Turkish dramas are offered as a finished product, making it far easier for television stations to foresee their success. The fact that many Turkish serials often consist of over 100 episodes has also been seen as favourable for generating desirable advertising revenue.[43] Turkish drama serials are typically purchased by Arab media organizations on an exclusive basis to guarantee advertisers that they will feature exclusively on their platform.

My fieldwork with audiences in Qatar, Chile, and Israel has shown that viewers enjoy the fact that Turkish dramas are longer-running programmes, allowing audiences to grow closer to the characters and storylines. Media executives and advertisers also appreciate the longer duration of Turkish shows because they create an attachment, and increase viewer loyalty to the channel. At the same time, dependent on the contract agreed, Turkish dramas can also generate income for the Arab television channel even after being broadcast, as the drama can be subsequently re-released on other platforms. And, if the network has acquired the serial's copyright, it can also sell the show to other channels, making Turkish content a highly profitable commodity.

Some scholars have suggested that the ever-growing demand for new content, and the inability of traditional Arab film and television production centres such as Cairo, Beirut, and Damascus to retain their previous influence, made it favourable for Turkish serials to enter the Arab television market.[44] The years 2010 and 2011 brought the Arab Uprisings in Tunisia, Egypt, and Libya, and a continuing civil war in Syria; a decade on, most parts of the Arab world, except for the Gulf countries, are still faced with an ongoing political and economic downturn as a result.[45]

Kraidy and Al Ghazzi's argument that the 'parallel restructuring of the Turkish and Arab media industries, by creating "push" (on the Turkish side) and "pull" (on the Arab end)', established the foundation for Turkish serials to enter the Arab media space does not explain this phenomenon sufficiently.[46] On the contrary, as will be revealed in Chapters 3, 4, and 5, Turkish drama serials do not simply fill a space on Arab television by substituting for the shortcomings in regional content production. Instead, Turkish dramas are filling a void on Arab screens by providing dramas of high production quality that are able to satisfy the audience's need for entertainment, cultural proximity, and emotional realism, while at the same time exploring themes and storylines that are familiar but generally not covered in Arab serials, owing to cultural taboos.

Banned on network TV but expanding on digital media

This section will explore why Turkish dramas were suddenly banned on Saudi Arabian and UAE free-to-air satellite channels, with a particular focus on MBC. It also examines further the robust growth in digital media within the

MENA region, and how digital platforms have become a game-changing alternative route for Turkish dramas to reach Arab audiences.

The cancellation of Turkish serials on KSA and UAE free-to-air satellite channels, in March 2018, curtailed the presence of Turkish serials on Arab satellite television—which had become the most significant international market for Turkish content. Without prior notice, on 2 March 2018, MBC took all Turkish dramas off the air. Six serials were pulled from the schedule at a cost to MBC of $25 million.[47] MBC Group's move to cancel Turkish dramas was particularly impactful because it is not only the largest free-to-air Arab TV network, with a 50 per cent market share in Saudi Arabia, but it also attracts 140 million viewers daily across the region—and beyond—that Turkish serials could no longer reach.[48]

This decision to remove Turkish content has been seen as a political response to Türkiye having remained an ally of the State of Qatar despite a blockade of the country led by Saudi Arabia, Bahrain, Egypt, and the UAE.[49] According to observers, the cultural influence and soft power of Turkish serials were seen as concerning to KSA and the UAE, for whom Türkiye had now become more a threat than a friendly nation, and where significant political and ideological differences had manifested themselves, especially since the Arab Uprisings.[50]

Four months after the ban of Turkish dramas on KSA and UAE free-to-air satellite television, an online survey was administered in the summer of 2018 to several Arabic sites for fans of Turkish serials on social media. The survey sought to gauge audience reaction and examine whether the cancellation of Turkish drama serials had prevented viewers from watching Turkish dramas. The survey was completed by more than 300 respondents, of whom the overwhelming majority were women between the ages of 18 and 50 from various Arab backgrounds. The survey responses revealed that Arab audiences were opting to watch Turkish serials either online with English or Arabic subtitles, such as via YouTube or on illegal websites, or they were visiting the official websites of Turkish television networks to watch the content in the Turkish language. Watching Turkish dramas on Turkish channels, or on online catch-up TV, is certainly not a new occurrence. Many Turkish-serial viewers I encountered as part of my fieldwork over the years were accustomed to watching a new season of their favourite television drama via Turkish channels prior to its broadcast on Arab television. Many even noted that they had managed to learn Turkish simply by watching Turkish dramas in their original language. However, these findings reveal that visiting Turkish channel websites also became a popular and viable alternative to accessing Turkish content following their cancellation on regional networks. Moreover, one-third of 18- to 25-year-old respondents noted that they started watching Turkish serials on Netflix. The survey has further shown that viewers over the age of 50 had either stopped watching Turkish dramas altogether, or were trying to watch them on other free-to-air satellite channels that were still broadcasting them, as they preferred to watch dubbed rather than subtitled content. These findings demonstrate that viewers who perhaps did not have the financial means to watch Turkish content via pay-TV or streaming services found alternative ways to watch. The survey also showed that Arab audiences had been actively seeking content that best served their needs, irrespective of restrictions and censorship. Despite television still being an important medium in the MENA region, these findings clearly show that the new media landscape permits Arab audiences to more freely seek and select media content they would like to engage with, rather than limiting their consumption to only what the state or media corporations believe they should be watching.

Moreover, recent growth in streaming services has enabled Turkish dramas to expand further their presence in the Arab market without a reliance on broadcast networks, as pay-TV and SVOD services never cancelled Turkish content for fee-paying viewers. Khalil and Zayani stress that with the advent of the digital era, KSA has intensified its pro-business approach in order to exert control over the media. They argue that, for instance, major productions have been channelled towards Shahid, a regional streaming platform belonging to the MBC Group.[51] Despite the four-year ban of Turkish drama serials on MBC's satellite channels, which came to an end in 2022, Turkish dramas were available on Shahid: this is an interesting example of a pro-business approach prevailing over politics.

Furthermore, similarly to Türkiye's media market (see Chapter 1), digital media in the MENA region are predicted to grow significantly. According to a 2020 study published by British-based Digital TV Research, the market for SVOD is predicted to almost triple across the region in the next five years, growing to some $2.1 billion. The study also suggested that SVOD revenues would grow in the region from less than $1 billion in 2020 to $2.97 billion by 2025, as Netflix and other SVOD platforms are expected to increase their investment in the fast-growing region. Market leader Netflix is predicted to benefit most from the projected growth, forecast to more than double its existing subscriber base from 4 million to 10.17 million, thus accounting for 38 per cent of all SVOD subscriptions in the MENA region. At the same time, StarzPlay Arabia, a subscriber service owned by Lionsgate, is forecast to more than double its SVOD customers to some 3 million by 2025, accounting for 23 per cent of the market.[52] While Turkish drama serials have been available on Netflix since its launch in Türkiye and the MENA region in 2016,[53] the streaming platform has also produced a number of Turkish originals since 2018. Additionally, StarzPlay Arabia launched an add-on partnership with BluTV in June 2021, which will allow Türkiye's first and largest local SVOD service, BluTV, to showcase its Turkish catalogue, dubbed into Arabic and accessible to subscribers in the MENA region. StarzPlay also increased its Turkish content offering just before Ramadan 2021, through partnerships with MISTCO, an international brand-management and content-distribution agency, and Calinos, an Istanbul-headquartered Turkish distributing company.[54]

The fact that SVOD services in the MENA region have been offering Turkish drama serials despite diplomatic tensions demonstrates that there is an apparent demand for Turkish content that cannot be stifled by censorship or banning. It appears that the advent of digital media has contributed to audiences in the Arab world being able to select the content that best serves their needs. However, one needs to acknowledge that the audience autonomy that SVOD services offer is limited to paying viewers, mainly in the Gulf, as they form the largest share of the total MENA revenue for these platforms. KSA alone is estimated to account for over half of the Netflix subscribers in the entire MENA region (2.11 of 4.13 million total subscribers). Capturing audiences in the Arab world's wealthiest region is, from a business perspective, a win for all parties involved. It demonstrates that while financial interests intersect with politics, digital platforms have offered media organizations an alternative way of bringing Turkish dramas to Arab audiences. As was also explored in Chapter 1, the growth in digital media enables the Turkish television market to sell serials to digital platforms in the Arab world, while avoiding the geopolitics. This allows them to reach younger audiences who, until now, have not been the typical viewers of Turkish serials on network television.

Therefore, whether it is StarzPlay Arabia having signed a partnership with BluTV, or MBC's streaming platform Shahid having accumulated a sizeable catalogue of Turkish content, it is clear that Turkish dramas cannot be removed from screens across the Arab world, even during government-imposed bans. Moreover, the facts that Turkish streaming platforms are offering serials dubbed into Arabic in order to attract Arab subscribers, that Arab media are providing exclusive Turkish content on their own platforms, and that US giants such as Netflix, Disney+, and soon HBO Max are all racing to produce Turkish originals,[55] demonstrate that Turkish serials have established a significant audience base that neither Turkish, Arab, nor international media outlets can overlook. That said, after an almost four-year absence, and with Turkish, KSA, and UAE relations back on the mend (see Chapter 3), Turkish serials have also returned and taken back their place on Saudi and Emirate free-to-air satellite channels.

Arab adaption of Turkish serials

Finally, another significant development lies in the attempt by Arab production companies and broadcasters to adopt the Turkish style of serial production, in an effort to win over Arab viewers who have become accustomed to Turkish dramas. Since entering the Turkish market in 2014, MBC-affiliated and Istanbul-based company O3 Productions has managed to produce a string of Turkish serials for domestic television, along with a number of Turkish originals for Netflix. In 2019, O3 produced an Arabic adaptation of its internationally successful serial *Bride of Istanbul* (*Istanbullu Gelin*, 2017–19, Türkiye: Star TV), renaming it *The Bride of Beirut* (2019–20, MBC). What is unique about this production is that rather than dubbing Turkish content, or filming the adaptation of *Bride of Istanbul* in the Arab world, O3 Production decided to use its expertise in producing Turkish dramas by shooting the serial, using Arab actors and locations, primarily in Türkiye.[56] Furthermore, in October 2022 the MBC Group signed a five-year agreement with Turkish production companies Medyapim and Ay Yapim. The partnership will see a host of Turkish content shared exclusively with MBC Group via 'first look' and volume deal agreements, along with original Arabic-language content produced specifically for the MENA market.

One could argue that the adaptation of Turkish serials and Turkish expertise in drama production has the potential to be the next step in a more mature approach to content production in the Arab world, where Turkish influence in the cultural sphere changes the way stories are told.

The next chapter will discuss the reasons behind the ever-changing nature of Turkish–Arab relations. It examines whether Turkish foreign policy, or exposure to Turkish drama serials, instigated a more positive perception of Türkiye among Arab nationals.

3

Fluctuating Turkish–Arab Relations and the Soft Power of Drama Serials

In the last decade, Turkish political influence, its growing economic strength, and the success of Turkish dramas in the Middle East and North Africa (MENA) region have intersected, all set against the backdrop of what has become a constantly changing political climate between Türkiye and the Arab world. As explored in Chapters 1 and 2, the crossing of paths between the Turkish television industry and the Arab world's largest media network, MBC, was initially driven as much by demand for content as by improved diplomatic ties and a flourishing trade relationship between Türkiye and the Arab world's most influential nation, the Kingdom of Saudi Arabia (KSA). This chapter attempts to reveal the answer to a central question: has the changing Arab perception of Türkiye in more recent years, from the previous negative image (that of the Arab oppressor dating back to Ottoman rule, and later from Türkiye being perceived as a defender of Western interests),[1] to a more positive one, been due to Turkish initiatives in foreign policy, or exposure to Turkish drama serials? Or are the two interconnected?

The analysis in this chapter is drawn from fieldwork conducted in Qatar between 2013 and 2018, consisting of focus-group discussions and interviews with university students from various Arab backgrounds and female Arab serial viewers of various nationalities, and drawing on academic papers, opinion polls, and journalistic articles in English, Turkish, and Arabic.[2] The main findings in this chapter reveal that Turkish drama serials have been the prime facilitator for the increased Arab awareness and positive perception of Türkiye. Turkish drama serials were found to be an essential soft-power tool and to play a pivotal role in creating a positive image of the country. Period dramas in particular were instrumental in presenting Türkiye's imperial past as an era of Muslim glory instead of Arab dependence and oppression.

To provide the reader with important context and background information, the chapter first explores the various factors that have contributed to Türkiye's increasing prestige and confidence as a nation, which in turn has contributed to the country being increasingly seen as a significant soft-power nation in the MENA region.[3] The chapter then provides a brief historical account of Turkish–Arab relations. Commencing with the establishment of the Turkish Republic in 1923, it examines the paradigm shift under the ruling Justice and Development Party (Adalet ve Kalkinma Partisi, AKP), which moved from alignment with the West to rapprochement with the Arab world and other parts of the Global South. The chapter provides critical insights into the so-called neo-Ottomanist foreign policy that has seen Türkiye reconnect with the Arab world. For many observers, Türkiye's neo-Ottomanist foreign policy is believed to have enabled the country to expand its diplomatic and cultural influence dramatically in the MENA region—which is seen as a core element contributing to Turkish soft power.[4] The chapter also explores the reasons behind the fluctuations in Turkish–Arab relations. It examines more recent geopolitical constraints such as the Qatar diplomatic crisis of 2017, which represents a significant turning point in the positive relations between Türkiye and its most important trading partner in the Arab world, Saudi Arabia. The final section of the chapter then discusses empirical findings.

2000 to 2013: the golden period

The uninterrupted rule of Recep Tayyip Erdoğan's AKP since the 2002 general election represents the beginning not only of historical changes in Türkiye's foreign policy, but also a drastic shift in the country's economic development. The years 2002–13 can be described as a golden period firstly because they represent an era during which Türkiye managed to transform itself, experiencing a wave of economic, cultural, and international sporting success. Secondly, this was a period during which Turkish–Arab relations flourished and the rise of Turkish soft power was widely discussed. According to scholars in the field, these success stories represented essential factors contributing to Türkiye's growing soft power across the MENA region.[5] This can be clearly illustrated if we look at Türkiye's impressive economic development in the 2000s, where in less than a decade the country was able to transform itself from a nation paralysed by the financial crisis of the 1990s, to becoming part of the G20 group of developing countries with one of the fastest-growing economies worldwide.[6] Türkiye started to become more attractive to its Arab neighbours for economic reasons, being increasingly perceived not only as an important financial partner but also as a gateway to the wider world.[7]

The success stories of the 2000s were pivotal in Türkiye's position as a regional soft power, but they also helped the country to gain confidence in other areas—as seen, for example, in Türkiye's accomplishments on the football field, the home of the nation's most popular sport. The Turkish national team enjoyed their greatest success in the 2000s, most notably finishing in third place at both the 2002 FIFA World Cup and the 2003 FIFA Confederations Cup, while also reaching the semi-finals of UEFA Euro 2008. Another example of Türkiye's increasing global presence and prestige was Miss Türkiye winning the 2002 Miss World beauty pageant. The pageant was shrouded in controversy after bloody riots forced it to relocate to London from Nigeria's capital, Abuja, where the event was branded immoral. More than 220 people were killed and 30,000 driven from their homes in sectarian rioting in Nigeria's north. The unrest was allegedly sparked by a newspaper article suggesting that the Prophet Mohammed might have taken one of the contestants as his bride.[8] One could argue that a woman from a Muslim-majority country winning a competition that created sectarian violence in another country has crucial soft-power potential—with Türkiye consequently being perceived as a Muslim yet progressive nation where women can participate in an event such as a beauty pageant without being judged as having committed an immoral act.

Then, after years of fruitless efforts, Türkiye won the Eurovision Song Contest for the first time in 2003 with Sertab Erener's 'Everyway That I Can'. Despite Türkiye having competed at the contest since 1975, it had always had difficulties reaching a respectable position, consistently returning home with low scores until the win in 2003. The following year Türkiye hosted the 2004 Eurovision Song Contest, with thirty-six countries coming together in Istanbul.[9] As with its football and Miss World successes, Türkiye once again featured prominently on the global stage. The Eurovision Song Contest, until

Türkiye's exit from the competition in 2012, was seen as a national priority, and a significant opportunity to show the European Union (EU) how progressive the country was.

On the diplomatic front, in 2005, after a wait of almost two decades, Türkiye finally began negotiations with the EU as it sought to become a full member. The Arab media celebrated the start of these discussions not only as an achievement for Türkiye, but also as something that would be beneficial for the rest of the Muslim and Arab world. It was claimed that around 200 Arab media outlets were present at the European summit in Brussels in December 2004 when the decision was made to start the accession negotiations with Türkiye.[10] One could argue that the scale of Arab media interest demonstrated Türkiye's changing position in the MENA region. International Relations Professor Meliha Benli Altunişik proposed that the increased interest in Türkiye was due to some in the Arab world realizing the potential for a positive spill-over effect from Türkiye's developing relations with the EU and presumed eventual membership. She went on to argue that liberal reformists saw this as a chance to promote democratization in the region, while Türkiye's engagement with the EU was seen as an opportunity to foster regional stability and peace. But most importantly, many Arab countries perceived Türkiye's march towards the EU as an opportunity to gain access to economic prospects that would be highly beneficial to the wider Arab region.[11]

In 2005 another significant development intensified Türkiye's relationship with the Arab and Muslim world, and in so doing increased its prestige. The first democratic vote took place to elect the Secretary General of the Organization of Islamic Cooperation (OIC), established in 1969; and for the first time a Turkish candidate, Ekmeleddin İhsanoğlu, was elected. Türkiye had tried unsuccessfully in the past to take over the OIC presidency, but for the first time the Gulf Cooperation Council (GCC) countries had strongly supported Türkiye's candidacy. The election of a Turkish diplomat as the ninth secretary general of the OIC, the second-largest intergovernmental organization after the United Nations, can be seen as a significant indication of Türkiye's increasing status and soft power in the Muslim and Arab world. Moreover, 2008 was another critical year for demonstrating Türkiye's economic resilience on the global stage, when the country emerged relatively unscathed from the global financial crisis.[12] For Çevik, Türkiye's 'relative' economic prosperity occurred while the EU and the USA were undergoing financial turbulence, aiding Türkiye to invest in its foreign policy and develop its softer approach to power.[13]

In the same year, the first Turkish drama serial *Noor* (*Gümüs*, 2005–07, Türkiye: Kanal D) made its impressive entry onto the Arab world's most-watched satellite-television station, MBC. The serial is believed to have attracted over 80 million viewers across the region, becoming an instant sensation.[14] Turkish drama's enormous appeal to female viewers,[15] and also the question of its harmful influence on Arab society, was instantly highlighted by both media and scholars alike—as was the impact of Turkish drama serials on Turkish soft power.[16]

However, it is crucial to recognize that all these examples of Türkiye's success are linked back to its hard power, which appears to have created the soft power to which its Arab neighbours have been particularly receptive. Türkiye's economic achievements were not only seen as beneficial to the Arab world, but they also began to be perceived as a tangible model to emulate. At the same time, the Arab Uprisings created an environment conducive to the idealization of Türkiye's model of governance in the MENA region. Türkiye's potential role in and contribution to the democratization process of the Arab countries that had already experienced these popular revolutions was greatly debated by Western think tanks and media alike.[17] Türkiye was increasingly presented as an inspirational example of a Muslim-majority country with a secular state, democratic system, and a flourishing and striving economy, which many argued was the key formula for Turkish soft power. As Yilmaz notes, Türkiye was portrayed as an ideal model to emulate, offering a counterweight to pro-Islamic and fundamentalist movements.[18] In addition, the evolution of political Islam in Türkiye under the rule of the AKP added another important component to the appeal of Türkiye's soft power. The AKP government was seen as a successful example of the reconciliation between democracy and Islam.[19] It should also be acknowledged that the EU and the Obama administration were pivotal external dynamics that helped promote Türkiye as a role model for the Arab world, as they believed that Türkiye, historically an ally of the West but with connections to the Middle East, would have the demonstrable ability to reshape the region and lead by example.[20]

TURKISH DRAMA SERIALS

Turkish–Arab relations: a historical overview

Many scholars in the field have argued that the foreign-policy changes that facilitated the reconciliation with the Arab world under the AKP government represent a significant paradigm shift.[21] The AKP government's foreign-policy direction has been a stark contrast to the previous Kemalist and Western-orientated governments that succeeded the Ottoman Empire. Since the establishment of the Turkish Republic in 1923, a unidirectional foreign-policy goal had been maintained, with the focus on strengthening Türkiye's Western credentials. Cooperating militarily and working closely with the USA and Israel was at the core of the country's foreign-policy agenda.[22] The rest of the Middle East was largely ignored and regarded as a 'backward zone of conflict' in which Islam brought an element of irrationality to international and domestic politics.[23] As scholars such as Dal note, the Kemalist elite often conceptualized the Middle East 'with the Western Orientalism stereotype of inefficiency, superstition and dubious morals'.[24] Or as Middle East Studies Professor Dietrich Jung argues, the region was perceived as an 'uneasy and unattractive neighbourhood', only to be dealt with if essential for Turkish security needs.[25]

For most of the twentieth century, Turkish–Arab relations were marked by mutual distrust, the roots of which go back to the dissolution of the Ottoman Empire and the First World War. The Great Arab Revolt of 1916, led by Hussain bin Ali, Sharif of Mecca, against the Ottoman Empire, with the encouragement of Britain, signifies a crucial moment in history that contributed to constructing mutually hostile Turkish–Arab narratives. For Turks, Arab collaboration with the British was seen as a betrayal, being stabbed in the back during the collapse of the Ottoman Empire. This experience left Turks with a sense of resentment and distrust towards Arabs which is still present as conventional wisdom in Turkish society. In contrast, many Arabs felt that the Turks had turned their backs on Islam, particularly during the interwar period. Following Arab independence from British and French rule, the period of Ottoman rule was often held responsible for Arab ills. These mutual hostilities resulted in a Turkish policy of 'non-involvement' in Middle Eastern affairs, and a lack of political support for Turkish causes from the Arab world.[26] Despite many experts in the field agreeing that Türkiye's Kemalist elites never

FLUCTUATING TURKISH–ARAB RELATIONS

established a specific foreign policy for the Middle East, relationships with the region were seen as an extension of Türkiye's pro-Western policies.[27]

One essential characteristic of overall Turkish foreign policy was the country's approach to detente without engagement, by remaining neutral but without being isolated.[28] However, Türkiye's attempt to remain neutral changed during the Cold War, pulling the country back into the centre of international politics. With the manifestation of a bipolar international system, neutrality could no longer guarantee the security and integrity of the Turkish state. The permanent threat wielded by Russia pressured Türkiye into allying with Western powers. Subsequently, the Turkish Republic inherited the Ottoman role of counterbalancing Russia's influence in the eastern Mediterranean by taking on a crucial role in the USA's containment policy against the USSR.[29] For Turkish politics professor William Hale, Türkiye's geostrategic position at the intersection of several great powers' interests helped Türkiye to turn foreign policy into an economic resource.[30] International relations scholars largely agree that because of these constraints, Türkiye's elite combined domestic Westernization with a foreign policy of Western integration. But as time went on, Türkiye began to be perceived as an image of the West in the East, and of the East in the West, because of its contradictory status as an Islamic state in Europe and a secularist role model in the Middle East.[31] One could argue that while integration into Western institutions might have best served Türkiye's security interests during the twentieth century, it contributed significantly to distancing the country further from its Middle Eastern neighbours over time. This led to geostrategic constraints and stereotypical images reinforcing each other; the Arab narrative of the 'terrible Turk',[32] and the notion of Ottoman Turkish oppression, slowly shifted to one in which Türkiye was seen as an instrument of imperialistic Western interests.[33] Türkiye was characterized as being party to the 'axis of evil' with the USA and Israel.[34]

For scholars such as Nachmani, the Arab world's hatred of Türkiye for its alliance with the West was made visible in caricatures created in the region. An Egyptian newspaper in 1951 published an offensive caricature that portrayed Türkiye 'as a small dog sniffing at the rear quarters of a larger hound (the United States, and the United Kingdom), or a lapdog being dragged by its Western master'.[35] And for many observers, the reality that Türkiye was the first Muslim-majority country to recognize the State of Israel profoundly

47

impacted upon the country's negative perception in the Arab world.[36] Thus, in contrast to previous regimes, the AKP government's efforts at reconciliation with the Arab world, and its engagement with the Arab public, have since been a critical mission and a core factor in its soft-power-based policy, conceived as neo-Ottomanism.

At this point, it should be noted that neo-Ottomanism originated as a mid-nineteenth-century movement, with the main aim of bringing about reforms in the Ottoman Empire through internal dynamics. The movement loosely gathered intellectuals from various fields, such as literature, journalism, art, and politics, and criticized the imitative nature of the modernization reforms of the Tanzimat era (1839), as compared with the idea of advocating for greater restrictions on the monarchy and the establishment of a parliament, and synthesizing ideas of Islam and democracy.[37] Moreover, it was not the AKP government that first revived the neo-Ottoman vision. In the aftermath of the Cold War, former prime minister and president Turgut Özal had also attempted to initiate a rediscovery of Türkiye's imperial heritage. During his period as president from 1989 to 1993, Özal and his Motherland Party (Anavatan Partisi) tried, with some success, to reach a new consensus in the country between Türkiye's multiple identities (Western, Muslim, secular, Kurdish, and Turkish).[38]

The introduction of soft power in Turkish foreign policy

Once the AKP government came to power, Türkiye's relationship with the West was no longer solely ideational but far more pragmatic,[39] resulting in a change of political direction that has been described by some scholars and observers as re-Islamization, or even Middle Easternization.[40] Ahmet Davutoğlu, who had been an academic prior to serving as foreign-policy advisor, foreign minister, and prime minister of Türkiye, is widely acknowledged as the author of the AKP's neo-Ottomanist policies. His book, *Strategic Depth* (*Stratejik Derinlik*), published in Türkiye in 2001, is regarded as the seminal application of Türkiye's new foreign-policy direction. Davutoğlu rejects the 'neo-Ottoman' label,[41] but emphasizes the importance of the move away from strict Eurocentrism in Turkish foreign policy, and the adoption instead of a broader approach combining pan-Islamist, postcolonial, and pragmatic geostrategic rationales, enabling the country to play a more constructive role in world politics. According to Davutoğlu, this in turn creates the potential for Türkiye to develop an enhanced relationship with the USA and Europe, as well as serving as a bridge between the West and former Ottoman territories such as the Balkans, Caucasus, and the Middle East.[42] It is significant that Davutoğlu's de facto neo-Ottomanist foreign policy outlined five steps necessary for establishing Türkiye as a regional and global player:

(1) Democratization should go hand in hand with security and stability;
(2) Türkiye should have 'zero problems' with neighbouring countries;
(3) Türkiye should not forget that it is heir to a nation that combines European, Middle Eastern, and Asian identities;
(4) Soft power should seek to incorporate economic, cultural, and demographic elements, alongside security and political goals; and
(5) Foreign policy should adopt multidirectional foreign relations and move away from predominantly Western-orientated relations and policies.[43]

However, as scholars such as Oguzlu argued, Türkiye's realization of its Islamic character and the legacy of the Ottoman Empire should not be understood as the country facing away from the West and towards the East, but rather as a deliberate strategy to improve Türkiye's political and economic interests in both regions.[44] Türkiye's policy of 'zero problem with neighbours' was seen as partly established to serve its economic interests in a stable and open region.[45] For international relations scholars such as Faruk Yalvac, Türkiye's implementation of fundamental changes in its foreign policy and geopolitical vision can best be understood as an attempt to redefine state–society and economic relations in the country along neoliberal lines, within the context of changing international capitalism.[46] According to Yalvac, these new policies represented 'an articulation between neoliberalism and Turkish Islamism and due to its Islamic ideology … [were] viewed as more cosmopolitan in outlook than the realist–nationalist Kemalist foreign policy adopted by the traditional civil–military bureaucracy'. Yalvac also argues that the previous Kemalist style of foreign policy was seen as 'timid, defensive and too passive for a globalized world'. Therefore, under the AKP's new geopolitical direction, Türkiye had responded to the urgent need to take a more proactive role as a soft power in the region.[47]

Consequently, the reinforcement of positive relations with the Arab world became an essential political reality, and an ongoing strategy in Türkiye's pursuit and exercise of soft power, facilitating the country's aspirations to move from being a middle-sized regional power to becoming a dominant regional actor.[48]

An important part of this ambition has been to replace its previous negative image as an instrument of Western interests with that of the role of a natural regional leader, historical big brother, and protector of Muslim interests.[49] Thus, in line with its new vision of being a big brother to weaker Muslim nations, Türkiye has increased its aid efforts in the Muslim countries of North and sub-Saharan Africa, as well as in the Turkic countries of Central Asia.[50] Moreover, along with providing physical aid, the strategic use of rhetoric has become an essential tool in generating positive perceptions. Türkiye came to the realization that how the country and its policies were perceived, the language used to analyse those policies, and the framework in which the policies were placed could be more significant than objective reality.[51]

One significant example of rhetoric becoming an influential soft-power tool is Erdoğan's clash and so-called 'one minute' incident with Israeli president Shimon Peres at the 2009 World Economic Forum in Davos. During a panel discussion titled 'Gaza: The Case for Middle East Peace', Erdoğan refused to be silenced by the moderator, *Washington Post* columnist David Ignatius, when attempting to respond to Peres's justification of the Gaza War (2008–09). The Turkish prime minister's clash with the Israeli president transformed him overnight into the champion of the Arab world and defender of Muslim interests.[52] Türkiye's criticism of Israel on a global stage may be seen as demonstrating the country's ambition to establish itself as a leading Muslim country, with the power to react to international issues and conflicts in ways that might not align with Western interests—part of Türkiye's strategic attempt to correct its negative image in the Arab world and grow its soft power across the region.

At this point, it is vital to provide a brief overview of the notion of soft power, which has become, in recent years, a popular theory in world politics. The concept has found wider audiences within the foreign-policy discourse of mid-range regional powers, such as Türkiye.[53] The soft-power theory was first introduced by Joseph Nye in the 1990s as a critique of the ongoing decline of American power, and it has been continuously revised since its inception.[54] Soft power is rooted in the idea that alternative power structures exist in international relations alongside economic and military power (hard power), and that these need to be utilized in order to succeed within international political diplomacy. In contrast to hard power, soft power operates through attraction and seduction. It is comparable to a relationship or marriage, in which power is not always in the hands of the overtly dominant partner, but in the 'mysterious chemistry of attraction'.[55] For Nye, similar principles can be applied in the world of business and international politics. Soft power is a 'value-based' definition of power that depends on how attractive a country appears to be, and how capable it is of functioning as an exemplar for others. Nye outlines three key resources of soft power: 'its culture (in places where it is attractive to others), its political values (when it lives up to them at home and abroad), and its foreign policies (when they are seen as legitimate and having moral authority)'.[56]

In light of this definition, a country's culture, values, and policies, as well as its overall behaviour over time, all enable it to influence the interests and preferences of other nations, and to define its soft-power capacity. However, all power depends on 'who relates to whom under what circumstances', since 'soft power depends more than hard power on willing interpreters', and the 'preferred outcome' is more likely 'in set-ups where the culture is fairly similar rather than greatly dissimilar'.[57] Thus, it is possible to argue that the AKP government realized that they had entered an era where the traditional metrics of power were no longer the sole and ultimate determiners of a country's influence. Instead, historical connections and cultural similarities could represent an equally important framework for Türkiye's soft-power capacity in its former Ottoman territories.

Observers have highlighted the following key factors as having contributed to the early rise of Turkish soft power:[58] Türkiye's modernization process, its social and cultural achievements, its economic accomplishments, its political and economic stability, and its democratization and good governance.[59] Türkiye's soft power has been described as different from that of other nations because of the way that it draws on cultural proximity within a diverse region, ranging from the Balkans and the Middle East to the inner parts of Central Asia, with which it shares significant historical ties.[60] In line with Türkiye's new approach, in January 2010, the Office of Public Diplomacy was launched within the Turkish Prime Ministry.[61]

Nonetheless, some have questioned Türkiye's soft power and its credentials as a role model for other countries, particularly given its ongoing economic and democratic deficiencies. Turkish democratization, which started in the nineteenth century, is a long and ongoing transitional process. Its greatest challenge, in the view of some commentators, is to get Turkish society to a point where it truly embraces freedom and human rights.[62] Others have argued that the 'Turkish moment', which was celebrated with the idealization of the Turkish model of governance following the Arab Uprisings, has disappeared and never rematerialized, being replaced instead by the realization of the harsh realities that come with building a democracy.[63] But perhaps the most significant shortcoming of Turkish soft power has been defined by scholars as the lack of a clearly outlined mission advancing both diplomacy and foreign-policy goals.[64] According to Bryant and Hatay, what has made American soft power effective is Americans' collectively shared belief in their ideology of freedom, regardless of their political orientation. They argue that the weakness of Turkish policy is that it has still not settled on a unifying ideal or goal. Bryant and Hatay stress that the neo-Ottoman label of its recent political direction may indicate a revival of Türkiye's 'greatness' and help to turn the myth into a mission; however, selling this idea to Türkiye's neighbours would be problematic, as many do not have fond memories of their former Ottoman rulers.[65]

Furthermore, for several academics in the field, Türkiye's newly gained prestige and soft power under the AKP started to decline in 2013 with the Gezi Park protests.[66] At the same time, a combination of geopolitical stress, domestic political issues, and a deterioration of economic fundamentals after 2018 caused the Turkish lira to become one of the worst-performing currencies in the emerging markets, resulting in Türkiye being perceived by observers as losing soft power.[67] According to international studies scholar Senem Çevik, until 2013 Türkiye was recognized as a major stakeholder both in the region and on the soft-power stage, while also being a key democratic leader, providing stability in what is widely considered to be an unstable region.[68]

Ever-changing Turkish–Saudi relations and the cancellation and reintroduction of Turkish drama serials

At this point, it is useful to examine Turkish relations with the KSA, the Arab world's most influential nation, which shifted from a historic peak before the

Arab Uprisings, back to a progressively declining state. Since the summer of 2022, the relationship appears to be on the mend again.

One could argue that Türkiye's soft power is fluctuating, much in the same way as its relations with some Arab regimes are. One example of Türkiye's soft power having inconsistent effects on different groups within the Arab world is its constantly changing relationship with KSA's ruling elite. As one Turkish political analyst notes, Turkish–Saudi relations can best be 'described with a metaphor of a roller-coaster', having had numerous ups and downs over the past five decades.[69] However, as stressed earlier in the chapter, the 2000s represented a historical peak for Turkish–Saudi relations, characterized as they were by numerous political, economic, security, and cultural agreements between the two nations. Along with state partnerships, private-sector trade deals flourished, and Turkish businesses in the energy, finance, banking, tourism, construction, communication, and food industries secured trade deals with the KSA.[70]

Türkiye was also visited by Saudi monarch King Abdullah in 2006, the first visit of a Saudi monarch to the country since 1966.[71] Some observers have argued that the Turkish–Saudi honeymoon during the 2000s came to an unpleasant end with the Arab Uprisings that began towards the end of 2010. The fact that the two states have held opposing views on the outcomes of the Arab Uprisings, and have both wielded their influence in the MENA region through various means, has been described as the beginning of the end of this rapprochement.[72] Furthermore, the Qatar diplomatic crisis, which began in June 2017 between Qatar and a Saudi-led quartet (including Bahrain, the UAE, and Egypt), again demonstrated critical policy differences between Türkiye and KSA.[73] When KSA led a blockade of the country, banning Qatari planes and ships from using airspace and sea routes, and closing Qatar's only land border with KSA, Türkiye provided Qatar with food aid, along with diplomatic and military support.[74]

A telling example of the drastic shift in relations from that point on occurred when the Turkish prime minister, Recep Tayyip Erdoğan, was named by Crown Prince Mohammed bin Salman in 2018 as a member of 'the devil's triangle', a term coined by him to describe the relationship between Qatar, Türkiye, and Iran—the latter two countries having both supported Qatar during the blockade. In the same interview with the Egyptian press, the crown prince also accused Türkiye of supporting the Muslim Brotherhood and trying to turn the Middle East back into an Ottoman Caliphate.[75]

TURKISH DRAMA SERIALS

Before the downturn of Turkish relations with KSA and the UAE, the two Gulf Cooperation Council states were Türkiye's most important trading partners in the MENA region. The scale of bilateral trade between Türkiye and the Gulf countries had tripled between 2005 and 2015. It increased from a trade volume of $5.2 billion in 2005 to $15.8 billion in 2015;[76] and by 2016 the annual commercial exchange between KSA and Türkiye stood at some $8 billion, with 800 Saudi companies operating in Türkiye. At the same time, some 200 Turkish companies were operating in KSA, generating an estimated business volume of $17 billion per year.[77]

Saudi–Turkish opposition is rooted far deeper in history, going back to the time of the Ottoman Empire. Yet the chronology illustrated above is of particular interest, as it demonstrates key diplomatic shifts that led to the sudden ban of Turkish drama serials on KSA and UAE free-to-air satellite channels. The decision in March 2018 by the Arab world's largest private broadcaster, the MBC Group, to pull the plug on Turkish drama serials and movies on eleven of its channels, without prior notice,[78] highlights the significant role that Turkish drama serials seem to have played as an instrument of Turkish soft power in the MENA region.[79] The move was widely considered to have been politically motivated, the result of rising tensions between Türkiye and KSA after the eruption of the Qatar diplomatic crisis. According to Saudi media, the decision was intended to end Türkiye's use of soft power in promoting a positive image of the country in Arab homes via Turkish dramas.[80] It could be conjectured that this critical shift in Arab public perception of Türkiye and the region's Ottoman past was what motivated MBC to launch a historical television serial in November 2019—one that is supposed to present a counter-narrative, and to illustrate Arab oppression under Ottoman rule. The period drama *Kingdom of Fire*,[81] produced with a budget of $40 million and financed and supported by KSA and UAE governments, can be understood, as author and journalist Fatima Bhutto wrote, as 'an expensive salvo against Turkey's cultural neo-Ottomanism', while the selection of a British director could be interpreted as 'added cachet'.[82] One could argue that *Kingdom of Fire* has been an attempt to eliminate Türkiye's soft power and bring back the age-old perception of the 'terrible Turk',[83] one that is a violent suppressor of Arab nationalism by Ottoman rule. Türkiye's increased cultural presence, in the form of drama serials that managed to acquire prime-time spots in broadcasting schedules across the region,[84] appears to have been increasingly perceived as a threat affecting the Gulf monarchies' position towards Türkiye and its growing influence in the region. The ban not only revealed that the ruling elites were apprehensive about Turkish soft power, but also demonstrated that the serials had become the latest casualties in the power struggle between the two most influential nations in the Muslim world, with both governments realizing that Turkish drama had helped to create a significant cultural impact in the region.

While the blockade on Qatar came to an end in late 2020, relationships between Türkiye and the Saudi-led quartet did not meaningfully improve until 2022. In 2020, Saudi businessmen and retailers called for an informal boycott of Turkish imports such as meat, eggs, and other products, over the political tensions between the two regional rivals. As a result, in March 2021, the value of Saudi Arabian imports from Türkiye reached a record low.[85] However, February 2022 saw President Erdoğan visit the UAE, and in April 2022 he also travelled to KSA, following nearly ten years of tension. This apparent thaw in relations between Ankara, Abu Dhabi, and Riyadh signals the beginning of a new era, cemented in the UAE by the signing of numerous bilateral agreements spanning different sectors, including defence, trade, technology, agriculture, and commitments to invest in Türkiye. In June 2022, following Saudi Crown Prince Mohammed bin Salman's visit to Ankara, President Erdoğan and the crown prince announced in a joint statement that the two countries were determined to normalize ties fully and were starting a new period of even stronger bilateral relations.[86] Once more, along with significant bilateral agreements, Turkish dramas were allowed back on UAE and KSA free-to-air satellite stations, illustrating, yet again, the intertwined nature of diplomacy and cultural products.

The recent developments serve to affirm the argument that the relationship between Türkiye and Gulf monarchies remains in a state of continuous flux. That said, one thing has remained constant: the unique appeal of Turkish dramas among Arab viewers.[87]

Soft power and Turkish drama serials

At this point, it is crucial to conceptualize the notion of soft power in the context of cultural products, in order to better understand the role of Turkish drama serials as an important source of soft power, and to scrutinize the shift from Turkish dramas being an accidental success, to becoming a more strategic and deliberate tool.

It is important to re-emphasize that the success of Turkish drama serials in the Arab world was not a planned soft-power initiative by the Turkish government but was rather a by-product of Türkiye's economic success (hard power), which the government later utilized to promote Türkiye in its former Ottoman territories. Although unplanned, the international success of Turkish dramas fitted perfectly into the soft-power strategy of the Turkish government, who started to use these serials strategically, focusing on improving the country's persona and seeking to generate soft power, particularly in the Arab world. The Turkish government realized that drama serials were a highly effective platform by which to promote the country's cultural image and the Turkish way of life, as well as having a positive impact on other industries, such as tourism.[88]

Since the entry of Turkish drama serials onto MBC in 2008, and later other channels across the MENA region, the number of Arab visitors to Türkiye has risen dramatically.[89] At the same time, the number of Arab nationals purchasing property in the country has also witnessed a significant increase.[90] With Turkish drama serials being recognized as a key export product, Turkish TV producers were offered a seat on the Council of Exporters in 2010, joining representatives of other export-orientated industries in Türkiye.[91] One important example of the Turkish government utilizing Turkish drama serials more strategically is the Culture and Tourism Ministry's announcement in 2012 of multiple distribution deals to provide Turkish serials internationally, free of charge. During a speech, former Vice Culture and Tourism Minister Abdurrahman Arici acknowledged that Turkish television serials had enabled Türkiye to spread its cultural influence by entering homes across the Arab world. This in turn had attracted tourists eager to visit the locations they had seen on television.[92] With Turkish television stars' growing popularity, they have also been increasingly utilized as cultural envoys to instrumentalize their fan memberships as a soft-power source.[93]

However, it should be acknowledged that the Turkish government's strategic use of television serials is not unusual or unique to Türkiye. Other nations such as the USA, Japan, and Korea have utilized their popular culture to similar effect. Nye highlighted that the global success of American popular culture 'has made the U.S. seem to others exciting, exotic, rich, powerful, trend-setting—the cutting edge of modernity and innovation', so much so 'that people want to partake of the good life American-style'.[94] Furthermore, according to scholars such as Kunczik, products of popular culture can hold critical importance, as media foster the construction and shaping of a nation's image.[95] In a similar vein, Anholt also argues that 'cinema, music, art, and literature' can contribute 'colour, detail and richness to people's perception of a country', and aid in viewers' getting to know a nation and a place 'almost as well as if they'd been there; better, in fact, because the picture that's painted is often a little idealized, and all the more magical for being intangible and incomplete'.[96]

Moreover, extensive academic research in the field has explored popular culture and its effects, particularly those in the realm of critical theory. It has established that popular culture attains a cultivation effect among the intended audience by exposing them to values and messages emerging from the source country. Scholars such as Nissim Otmazgin have also argued that culture can be utilized as a tool of public relations, and a method to strengthen a country's influence. For Otmazgin, Hollywood is the most evident example, and therefore the most important American tool in perpetuating soft power, which he suggests is converted into accessible consumable products marketed globally.[97]

On the other hand, Press-Barnathan suggests that attractive popular culture is not capable of influencing foreign policy, as attraction does not necessarily equate to power. According to Press-Barnathan, citizens will not necessarily make the connection between an attractive TV show and politics—a connection which, it is hoped, would translate into a more positive approach towards the other state's policies and political behaviour. Press-Barnathan argues that trying to influence a leader's perception by using popular culture fails to work. For example, both Kim Jong-il and Saddam Hussein are believed to have been followers of Hollywood movies, yet their preferences did not translate into pro-American policies. Instead, Press-Barnathan suggests that popular culture might have a significant political influence in a less direct way. The consumption of a specific country's cultural products might result in the adoption of their culture, which in turn could ultimately shape a country's cultural market and regional discourse, along with its vision of modernity, the world, the international system, etc. While Press-Barnathan acknowledges that the idea of the 'American dream' is the best example of American soft power, which people across the world have learned about through popular culture, she argues that there are significant limitations to governmental use of popular culture as soft power. The main issue is that governments cannot use soft-power resources without diminishing their value or abusing them to a degree. In addition, cultural commodities are predominantly produced and disseminated by private societal actors who may not necessarily deliver the message that the government wants to convey, and may fail to deliver a universal message. The growth of the popular-culture industry is driven 'from below by economic incentives and not from above, as part of a governmental cultural diplomacy'.[98]

Conversely, for Otmazgin and Ben-Yari, culture can be transformed into an element of policy that is seen as manageable through technology and political channels, and utilized to contribute to economic and political goals. Culture can be treated similarly to other national assets, even though it is more challenging to manage. They suggest that 'popular culture can potentially serve as a tool to convey a state's core values and ideology, and as its front window, selling its attractive culture abroad'.[99]

Nonetheless, it is important to recognize that trade and investment between Türkiye and the Arab world has done more than enhance Türkiye's economic image in the region. The findings in this chapter reveal that Turkish drama serials have been among the most influential exports to the MENA region; and my fieldwork has established them to be the key catalyst for the increased awareness and positive perceptions of Türkiye.

Findings

The following section reveals the findings of my fieldwork, which attempted to answer a core question: has the changing Arab perception of Türkiye, becoming more positive in recent years, been due to Turkish initiatives in foreign policy, or to exposure to Turkish drama serials? Or are the two interconnected? The key findings are organized by themes that became obvious during the analysis of the empirical data.

Turkish drama serials: the most significant catalysts for increased awareness and positive perception of Türkiye

Throughout my fieldwork in Qatar, I asked research participants what they thought of Türkiye, and what image and/or reputation Türkiye had among

Arabs, while also probing whether their perceptions of the country had changed, as far as they could recall. As an academic living in Qatar for many years, I predicted that Türkiye's image had changed among Arabs. Still, I did not anticipate that so many different Arab nationalities from different walks of life would perceive the country so positively.

The fieldwork for this research ran from September 2013 until April 2018. During this period Türkiye was faced with major internal and external challenges, which one might have assumed would significantly impact upon the opinions and perceptions of the study participants. Yet, surprisingly, none of the study participants mentioned any of the events that had affected Türkiye during the time frame of this study, which included the Gezi Park protests, various corruption scandals, conflicts with Kurdish minorities, the imprisonment of a large number of Turkish journalists, social-media bans, multiple terrorist attacks, coup attempts, forced closures of media outlets, an economic downturn, a declining relationship with the EU, Türkiye's military intervention in Syria and Libya, and worsening relationships with Egypt, Saudi Arabia, and the UAE.

Most notably, the Gezi Park protests during the summer and autumn of 2013 were seen by some media observers as the beginning of the Turkish Spring,[100] while others saw them as a critical event that highlighted Türkiye's democratic deficiencies, the end of its model role in the MENA region,[101] and ultimately the declining of its soft power.[102] On the contrary, my empirical findings revealed that the perception of Türkiye had been transformed in a matter of only a few years, and remained positive despite the domestic, economic, and diplomatic challenges. One telling example of Türkiye's growing soft power and more positive perception is given in this excerpt from a focus-group transcript. A Saudi university student described the changing narrative on Arab media, and her previous preconceptions about Türkiye:

> I remember when I was really young, my dad went to Türkiye for a business trip and when I would call him on the phone and he would say I'm in Türkiye, I'd imagine Türkiye as this desolate, uncivilized place as a seven-year-old. I never really bothered when I was a young teenager to see if that imagination was correct, but then when I was in seventh grade, that's when television started including Türkiye, so I said, oh, my God, it's such a beautiful place, and it made me feel like I wanted to go. But at the same time, not only shows that are on television, but there is this other show that is Saudi, and

it promotes social reform in a sense, and the host does that by comparing other countries and the good they have done. One of the countries that is featured is Türkiye. He showed, for instance, how Türkiye produced their own computer, I believe. And also, from the humanitarian side, recently, they had one of the best—taking care of Syrian refugees from Syrian refugee camps. It showed the country in a light that made it seem more beautiful, humanitarian, and more progressive in an economic sense. (Female Saudi, 2013)[103]

Or as this female Bahraini focus-group participant vividly describes:

My mum is originally from Iran but some of her family was living in Türkiye,[104] and when I was in primary school they used to go to Istanbul to meet up. They used to always complain about being conned by the taxi driver, or the hotel having bad service and people being rude, or their flights being late and no one speaking English. The only nice thing I remember were the Turkish delights they would bring back. And now everyone is watching their shows. Türkiye is on TV and in the papers. Arabs admire their economy and their help with Syrian refugees. People love travelling to Türkiye to see what they see in the shows. When my parents travel now, I join them and we no longer feel sorry for our relatives living in Türkiye, at times we even envy them. (October 2013)

Over the years, as a researcher I witnessed how, rather than talking about Türkiye's shortcomings, study participants spoke of their admiration for Turkish history and culture. The country's natural beauty was often mentioned as having a strong appeal, with most study participants mentioning this as their first response. Participants often repeatedly expressed the view that drama serials communicated a picture of the Turkish way of life that generated a positive impression, elevating the reputation of the country. Even study participants who regarded themselves as passive audiences, because in their households female relatives were watching Turkish dramas, were greatly influenced by serials when it came to their perceptions of Türkiye.[105] Therefore, as exemplified by the response of this male Syrian focus-group participant, Turkish serials have the ability to influence people's perceptions and ideas about Türkiye positively:

I've never been to Türkiye. What I know about it is from what I've heard and what I've seen on TV. I've heard great things about Türkiye. I hear it's a very beautiful country. I think they try to portray it as this convergence of the East and the West. In terms of culture and an addition to modernization, secularism, and that kind of thing. Every time I walk into the living room and my family is watching soaps, I see how beautiful Türkiye really is. I'd love to visit. (Focus group, 2013)

The fact that study participants chose to disregard Türkiye's troubles supports the argument that Türkiye's imperfections have become its greatest soft power. In a region that has been crippled by poverty, war, and conflict, Türkiye's flaws appear to be acceptable, and perhaps, to a degree, are seen as being normal. Like Kirişci's argument, my research established that Türkiye's greatest soft power appears to be its 'demonstrative effect', which positions the country as a 'work in progress'.[106] This enables Arab countries to see themselves in Türkiye's imperfections, turning Türkiye's shortcomings into its strengths.

Yet it is necessary to recognize that despite Türkiye having used multiple strategies to win the hearts and minds of the Arab public, my extensive in-depth interviews and focus-group discussions revealed overwhelmingly that Turkish serials had been the main catalyst for the increasing awareness of Türkiye in general. For many Arab study participants, their awareness of and interest in Türkiye was first triggered by their exposure to Turkish dramas, ultimately prompting both them and their families to visit the country. Older female family members in the household were found to make up the primary audience of Turkish serials—mothers, older sisters, aunts, or grandmothers—as well as being the driving force behind decisions to travel to Türkiye for family holidays. Turkish television serials seem to have helped to transform the Turkish identity into a consumable commodity. As one female Qatari serial viewer explains:

Turkish soap operas really changed people's thoughts about Türkiye. Of course, Türkiye and Qatar have been even closer after the blockade, but people never thought of Türkiye as a place to travel for shopping or relaxation. First, it was like you wanted to see what you saw on television for yourself and now it's like the most common thing to do for a short city trip. (Interview, 2017)

As the findings here reveal, Türkiye has become one of the most popular holiday destinations for Arab nationals, and in this Turkish dramas play a decisive role. One could argue that audiences with only a mediated perception of the country, or who have never visited regions of Türkiye beyond its touristic or urban areas, would find themselves in another world from that of the

Turkish serial. Unlike the often glamorous on-screen lives embedded in Western-style modernity and somewhat progressive sensibilities, life outside its urban centres could not be more different. However, despite Turkish dramas portraying an idealistic mediated projection of life in Türkiye, the positive perception of the study participants appears not to have changed even after visiting the country. Once again, this might be because tourists visit only the most popular areas, and do not experience the full reality, but another explanation could be that Türkiye's shortcomings make the country more relatable. As Nye argues, it all depends on 'who relates to whom under what circumstances'.[107] Furthermore, many study participants, when talking about Türkiye, often compared it to other countries in the Arab and Muslim world, perceiving Türkiye as more 'advanced', 'organized', 'Westernized', and 'progressive'. As this female Jordanian research participant describes it:

> When we travelled to Türkiye for the first time in 2010, we were so impressed by how modern and organized everything seemed compared to many Arab countries. It very much exceeded our expectations. Maybe it was my own prejudice, but I was expecting Türkiye to be different to what was shown on Turkish soap operas. (Interview, 2017)

These findings clearly show that drama serials are pivotal in creating an interest in, and desirable perception of, Türkiye and the Turkish way of life among the Arab public. As Anholt argued, popular culture products can hold critical importance in facilitating the construction and shaping of a nation's image.[108]

> I have to be honest, the Bosporus and mansions around it are even more beautiful in real life than what you get to see in the shows. (Interview, February 2017)

But most strikingly, as the transcript of this female Qatari viewer demonstrates, the perception of Türkiye on-screen, compared with the experience of Türkiye in reality, is often seen as an accurate and generally authentic depiction of the country.

The changing perception of Ottoman history

For most research participants that I encountered, Türkiye's imperial past was no longer seen as a period of Arab oppression. Instead, study participants emphasized their admiration for Ottoman history, which they perceived as a period when not Ottomans or Turks, but *Muslims* collectively mattered. As this research participant states:

> When you see the reputation there, what the people think of them. It is like we are bitter about Ottoman times but at least as a Muslim power we mattered then. Look at us now. (Focus group, male, Syrian/Moroccan/Spanish participant, 2013)

Similarly, this female Palestinian serial viewer equally suggests that the Arab world's Ottoman past is no longer solely perceived as a time of Arab oppression:

> Traditionally Turks have been seen as responsible for the issues of the Arab world, but Western colonizers have been not treated the same way. But again, this is changing; once people travel to Türkiye and watch shows like *Harem El Sultan*, people kind of stopped seeing Türkiye as the former oppressor. (Interview, female, 2017)

As these two transcripts illustrate, most focus-group discussions and interviews over the years revealed that Arab nationals had begun to hold a more positive perception of Ottoman history. The majority claimed to have been fascinated by Türkiye's rich culture, Ottoman heritage, and the impressiveness of its museums, mosques, and old palaces, often visited during their family vacation. This phenomenon appears to be due to a combination of two factors: first the viewing of, or exposure to, Turkish dramas played a pivotal role in how Türkiye, its culture, and people were perceived. Then travelling to Türkiye appears to have further affirmed their pre-existing positive impressions. Perhaps most importantly, the initial desire to travel to Türkiye was driven by the exposure to Turkish dramas, which created interest in Türkiye and a desire to experience the history and beauty of the country.

Television dramas dealing with Türkiye's Ottoman past, in particular, seem to create a desirable perception of Ottoman history, as these research participant responses underline:

> *Ertugrul* has been very popular among Qatari males, and I believe it is also airing on local television. Speaking for myself, it put Turkey and the Ottoman times in a more desirable position. What I appreciated about the show is that, as a Muslim man, I felt projected as the hero rather than being portrayed as a bad Muslim terrorist. (Focus group, male student, 2016)

> Most of the guys I know have watched *Ertugrul*, which is like a halal version of *Game of Thrones* but with Muslim characters. Personally, that show changed my perception a lot. I started respecting Turkish dramas more and stopped seeing them as cheesy romance meant only for women, but as something that men can also watch that is of high quality, I mean in regards to production. (Focus group, male Qatari student 2016).

> My son or husband never watch Turkish serials with me, they avoid coming to the living room when I am watching, but *Ertugrul* was something they both watched. I think it is how Turkish musalsalāt show Muslim men. It becomes more relevant to them. It is more about battles and history than just drama. People enjoy to see Muslim people as leaders and civilized rather than being always projected as backward. (Interview, Tunisian professional woman, 2017)

Throughout my fieldwork, I repeatedly found that period dramas such as *Magnificent Century* (*Muhteşem Yüzyil*, 2011–14, Türkiye: Show TV, Star TV) and *Resurrection: Ertugrul* (*Diriliş: Ertuğrul*, 2014–19, Türkiye: TRT1), which might be said to glorify Ottoman history, are perceived as depicting a period where the Muslim world had influence, a time when the East was important and stood for glory and significance. One could argue that the Ottoman period dramas' soft power is unique. The viewers are attracted to the reality that a Muslim empire was powerful. At the same time, the fact that the serials are depicted by actors who look like people of the Middle East, and are the heroes instead of the villains (as is often the case in Western productions), holds a strong appeal. The realization that a Muslim-majority country such as Türkiye can produce high-quality content also generates further admiration for many research participants.

Turkish drama serials are perceived as a window onto a model society

Over the last decade, my findings have repeatedly revealed that Turkish dramas are perceived as being a realistic window into Turkish society,[109] allowing viewers to access a relatable model of societal modernity. Simultaneously, Turkish serials appear to enable Arab audiences to satisfy their curiosity about living a secular and more Western lifestyle against the backdrop of a Muslim society. Thus, Turkish drama serials are seen as projecting an image of Türkiye that bridges East and West, successfully combining Islam with democracy and secularism, while at the same time preserving its culture and heritage. As one male Algerian-Tunisian focus-group participant put it:

> Türkiye shows other Muslim countries that you can be Muslim but democratic. That you can have a successful economy without petrodollars. (Focus group, male, 2013)

The following response by a research participant further highlights the intricate relationship between Islamic culture and modernity, particularly in the coexistence of Western-style modernity and Islam, as represented by the choice of the hijab by women. The consistent mention of Türkiye's ability to balance these two forces reflects their importance in shaping the country's unique identity and promoting a positive and attractive perception of it. This emphasizes the crucial role of finding such a balance in fostering an affinity with the country:

> Türkiye is the only Muslim country that has a democracy, and where you feel that the country is functioning and prospering and not falling into deeper conflict like some countries in the Arab world. Maybe that is just my impression, but I feel like that no matter how modern Türkiye appears that they care a lot about their culture. We have been now three times to Türkiye, and my sister and I like that women are working in the hotel or on the streets wearing a hijab and some without. (Interview, female, 2016)

Furthermore, for most study participants, the understanding of Western-style modernity and the attractiveness of what Turkish dramas were projecting were also rooted in the programmes' ability to show themes and topics that were seen as authentic but taboo in Arab media, as this next transcript illustrates:

> I sometimes feel that some stories may be a bit too much, but generally they don't shy away from showing things that would never be shown on local shows but actually happen. They show corrupt police, doctors, business people, and politicians. I think that makes them more believable, but they don't glorify it and don't make you feel like they are preaching. (Focus group, female, 2016)

> What surprised me is that they show stories about corrupt police and politicians, but also about social issues such as rape and domestic abuse. Arab producers might be hesitant to cover such topics, as we are more used to glossing over the bad rather than addressing it. (Female Qatari student, 2016)

Turkish drama serials are seen as offering an authentic depiction of a Muslim nation where people have a choice between a liberal or conservative lifestyle, but where traditional values still matter. Therefore, Turkish dramas' ability to balance modernity and tradition is pivotal in their overall attractiveness to audiences, and in their role as an essential soft-power source.

Türkiye's hard power is generating soft power

At this point, I should acknowledge that even though my empirical work has found that Turkish serials are the most significant catalyst for creating a positive perception, interest in, and awareness of Türkiye among study participants, the findings have also shown that Türkiye's economic and military achievements are an equally important source of soft power that has resonated particularly with Arab males. As this male Qatari participant notes:

> There is no other Muslim country that is as economically successful without having petrol-dollars behind them. And they are also the only Muslim member of NATO. (Focus group, 2017)

Türkiye's hosting of more Syrian refugees than the Arab nations, and its vocal support of the Palestinian cause, seem to have aided the country, elevating its status in the minds of research participants, who increasingly perceive it to be a defender of Muslim interests. As one Lebanese man puts it:

> What I have seen of Türkiye is that they have become proactive in the region. They are helping refugees and speaking up for Palestinians, which you would never see from any Arab country. They are fighting for the Arab cause and aren't even Arab. Of course, we also need to acknowledge that they are a big country with a large army. (Focus group, 2017)

Male research participants, in particular, were also highly vocal in their admiration of President Recep Tayyip Erdoğan and his role in strengthening political Islam, and the country's economy and military, as the following statements demonstrate:

> People love the fact that the current government is trying to have more Islamic rules and apply Islam to the government and the country's legislation. Erdoğan, many people really admire him and during the Gaza crisis, he stepped up and with other crises as well. The Turkish government stepped up as the representative of the Muslim people and he was really admired. They are strong economically and as a military force, which is very rare for Muslim and especially Arab countries. (Focus group, March 2014)

The Turkish president is perceived as an inspirational Muslim leader who has the power and authority to stand up to the West. One could argue that the Turkish president himself has become a source of soft power for many in the Arab world.

> The West loves to disrespect Erdoğan and Türkiye, but they are the only country in the region who stands for something. As was said before, they don't suck up to the West like some other countries. They help where they can, which cannot be said for many other Muslim countries. (Focus group, 2017)

Intriguingly, male study participants, when expressing their admiration for President Erdoğan as a regional leader, often linked Türkiye's new-found prestige directly to his leadership. Similarly to my own empirical findings, a survey administered in 2019 to 25,407 participants across ten Arab countries by the Arab Barometer for BBC Arabic found that President Erdoğan was the most popular world leader among Arab youth.[110]

One could argue that President Erdoğan's popularity among young Arabs is also aided in part by the lack of Arab nations who seem able to win the hearts and minds of the Arab and Muslim world, along with the Arab world's growing distrust of the West. At the same time, war and the political and economic turmoil affecting most parts of the Arab and Muslim world seem to have strengthened Türkiye's position as a powerhouse and defender of Muslim interests. Most significantly, in the minds of the research participants, Türkiye's achievements are admirable because the country's accomplishments are seen as being for the greater good of the Muslim world—as illustrated in the words of a male Egyptian student:

> Our generation is very different; we see the West for what it is. Türkiye is where all Muslims feel welcome, and you can walk the streets without being treated like a terrorist. You feel it is a home away from home. You look at the Ottomans' impressive accomplishments and look at their accomplishments now, and you feel that as a Muslim you can feel proud because they put a Muslim country on the map. (Focus group, 2014)

Once again, this participant's words summarize the findings of this research, underlining how Türkiye's achievements are increasingly seen as a collective Muslim achievement, rather than as simply a Turkish one. In this context, scholars such as Philip Seib have argued that the Middle East is a value-driven region where the Islamic religion has an important position in the sociopolitical sphere.[111] This argument offers another perspective on why the economic, military, diplomatic, and cultural achievements of Türkiye as a Muslim-majority county have resonated exceptionally with Arab nationals.

Conclusion

As the analysis presented in this chapter has revealed, Turkish drama series have significantly contributed to the rise of Türkiye's soft power, even though the drama sector's initial expansion, growth, and penetration into the MENA region was linked to Türkiye's hard power. Thus, the drama industries' finances have been far from soft, representing a major economic/trade interest, with important benefits for tourism. Although unplanned, the international success of Turkish dramas has fallen neatly into the soft-power strategy of the Turkish government. The fieldwork presented in this chapter demonstrates that Turkish drama serials have a significant soft power among Arab audiences, partly owing to their portrayal of Türkiye as a nation where people can choose between a liberal or conservative lifestyle, and where modernity and tradition, democracy and Islam coexist harmoniously. This projection of Türkiye as an ideal fusion of different values and lifestyles offers an attractive and relatable narrative for Arab viewers seeking cultural models reflecting their own aspirations.

Türkiye's culture, political theories, and policies have come to be seen as attractive, which is the essence of soft power. At the same time, Türkiye's unstable relations with the EU, and with the Arab world's most influential nation, KSA, along with its domestic political issues and economic deficits, are perceived as acceptable rather than damaging to Türkiye's new-found image as a model nation, peace broker, and defender of Muslim interests. Türkiye's unique soft-power resource is its 'demonstrative effect', which has led to Türkiye being perceived as a 'work in progress', enabling Arab countries to see themselves in Türkiye's imperfections, in addition to experiencing a different societal model. Meanwhile, the fact that Türkiye is a Muslim-majority country resonates with Arab nationals in an exceptional way, where religion plays a pivotal role in the socio-political and cultural sphere across the region.[112]

Turkish drama serials, as well as having helped create a more desirable image of Türkiye among Arab viewers in Qatar, have also contributed to an Arab admiration of the Ottoman Empire. Instead of viewers seeing the Ottoman Arab history, spanning a period of 400 years,[113] as a time of Arab oppression, their shared history is perceived as an era where not Turks, but Muslims, were influential on the global stage.

The 2018 ban of Turkish drama serials from KSA and UAE free-to-air satellite channels validates my findings that Turkish serials are a powerful instrument in creating not only a positive perception of the country among Arab audiences, but also an affinity and familiarity with Türkiye, its culture, and its history, that no other public diplomacy incentive could possibly achieve. Ironically, the network that first ignited the fever for Turkish serials extinguished their existence on Arab screens for four years, replacing them with regional productions—albeit owing to political influences rather than commercial motivations—and then in 2022, decided to reintroduce them on their free-to-air satellite channels. However, with international, Arabic, and Turkish streaming platforms offering Turkish content ready-dubbed for Arab audiences to consume, the banning of Turkish serials on MBC, the Arab world's most-watched free-to-air satellite network, appears to have had a smaller impact than was anticipated or intended. On the contrary, with the growth of digital media in Türkiye and the MENA region, rather than being extinguished on Arab screens, drama serials seem to have gained a broader audience. The fact that paying audiences in the MENA region were permitted to watch exclusive Turkish content reveals that where commercial interests and politics collide, economic interests appear to prevail over the political agenda (see Chapters 1 and 2).

It does, however, need to be acknowledged that while Turkish serials have entered households across the MENA region, this has not ensured a uniform soft-power appeal to all. Turkish cultural products seem to result in contradictory reactions from different groups within the Arab world. The unstable relationships with Gulf monarchies such as those of KSA and the UAE demonstrate that the ruling elites are wary of Turkish cultural influence in the region. Strangely enough, it is still only the regional elite who can afford to watch streaming services and pay-TV platforms in order to consume Turkish content. The recent thawing of relations between Ankara, Abu Dhabi, and Riyadh, including the signing of various bilateral agreements spanning different sectors and commitments for investment in Türkiye, is an important indicator that diplomatic and trade relations are back on the mend—which has also resulted in Turkish dramas reappearing on Emirate and Saudi free-to-air stations. These developments, once again, highlight the intertwined nature of Turkish foreign policy and the reach of Turkish drama serials. 'Attractive popular culture' does not automatically equate to influence on foreign policy, because attraction may not translate into power;[114] still, Turkish drama serials have been found to be a powerful tool in creating an affinity and familiarity with Türkiye and its culture among Arab audiences.

The findings in this chapter reveal that possibly one of the most significant appeals of Turkish serials, and their greatest soft power, is their ability to project Türkiye successfully as a perfect combination in one attractive package of many hitherto separate (and seemingly opposed) political, economic, and socio-cultural elements. Recent arguments regarding soft power, or the power of attraction, have stressed the significance of creating emotional investment and connection as a core element in how soft power functions.[115] While the attraction of Turkish cultural products may not directly translate into policy goals, they appear to have created a level of emotional investment with a genuine sense of admiration, warmth, and closeness towards Türkiye and its culture. At the same time, with Turkish dramas expanding on streaming and pay-TV platforms, the continued consumption of Turkish cultural products has the serious potential to influence the Arab world's understanding of modernity, as well as to shape Arab audience taste and the cultural market at large where Turkish visual aesthetics become the regional standard.

FLUCTUATING TURKISH–ARAB RELATIONS

As explored throughout this book, the enormous success of Turkish dramas in the Arab world has not only further fuelled the growth of the serial-production sector and aided in increasing Turkish soft power in the region, but, most importantly, it has helped Turkish serials to transition from being only successful nationally to becoming internationally popular television programmes.

Thus, it is even more pressing to scrutinize what it is about Turkish dramas specifically that appeals to Arab audiences. In the next chapter, I will examine the significance of socio-cultural factors in this successful reception.

The Importance of Socio-Cultural Factors in the Appeal of Turkish Serials among Arab Viewers

The rapid expansion of Turkish drama serials since 2008, most notably throughout the Arab world, has been described by scholars as the 'Noormania and Muhannad effect',[1] as a 'fever that hit Arab satellite television',[2] and as 'Neo-Ottoman cool'.[3] These descriptions, in many ways, illustrate the enormous popularity and impact these serials have had in the Middle East and North Africa (MENA) region, which not only aided Turkish soft power as revealed in Chapter 3, but also transformed them into a transnational format and the Arab world into its most important export market, accounting for the largest international consumption of Turkish drama serials.[4] Nonetheless, the unprecedented entry and acceptance of Turkish cultural products in former Ottoman territories has not always been celebrated as a welcome addition in terms of media offerings on Arab television. On the contrary, Türkiye's strong cultural presence has at times been negatively viewed by news media and certain segments of Arab society.[5] Rather than being welcomed, it has been seen by some as a Turkish cultural invasion and as cultural imperialism.[6]

As discussed in earlier chapters, the reach of Turkish dramas was curtailed in the MENA region in recent years, partly due to actions taken by the Saudi-owned MBC network and the UAE's Abu Dhabi and Dubai TV. These included removing all Turkish dramas from MBC's free-to-air satellite channels and from Abu Dhabi and Dubai TV, respectively. However, despite Turkish dramas having only returned to UAE satellite channels in 2021,[7] and MBC in 2022,[8] the ban on free-to-air channels did not manage to stop Turkish drama serials' continued expansion, spurred on by a greater intensity and wider geographic dispersion, now reaching an audience of 700 million in over 150 countries.[9] The introduction of cheaper and faster internet (particularly in the

Arab world), combined with a more technologically educated audience, and the rise of streaming services,[10] appear to have helped expedite the broader reach of Turkish drama serials (see Chapters 1 and 2).

In order to explain the pulling power of Turkish dramas in the Arab world, and why linguistic elements have become secondary in their selection and reception by Arab audiences, the notion of cultural proximity is used as an analytical tool throughout this chapter. By utilizing the diverse audience of the Gulf State of Qatar as a departure point, the chapter examines the socio-cultural factors that facilitate the attraction and appeal of Turkish television dramas. The discussions are drawn from qualitative and quantitative fieldwork carried out in Qatar between 2013 and 2018,[11] with women and men originating from various Arab countries and with diverse socio-cultural backgrounds. At the same time, I have also drawn on ongoing informal conversations with Arab nationals over the past decade to understand the reasons behind the popularity of Turkish drama serials among Arab audiences. The central findings in this chapter demonstrate that the close cultural and historical relationship between Arabs and Turks is a critical factor in explaining audience choices and reception in the region. This relationship spans more than half a century and, despite rivalries and political differences (see Chapter 3), is based on a shared culture, heritage, and religion which have been found to be decisive factors attracting and motivating Arab audiences to engage with Turkish dramas. Furthermore, the findings also illustrate the significance of the dubbing of Turkish programmes into a colloquial Syrian dialect, which offers access to a more diverse audience, including those who might have encountered difficulties with subtitling. The popularity of dubbed Turkish dramas has made dubbing as a means of translation more widely utilized in order to localize foreign content, in a region that has been traditionally accustomed to subtitling. More crucially, the dubbing of Turkish dramas has aided in bringing an entire country and its people closer—a country and people that many in the Arab world were unaware was so proximate.

Brief overview of the notion of cultural proximity

This section provides a brief overview of the cultural proximity theory utilized as an analytical framework, before revealing the findings of the fieldwork conducted in Qatar. Cultural proximity ties together the ongoing changes in media industries and technologies, with audiences' cultural, linguistic, and historical identities. Joseph Straubhaar introduced the concept to frame the ongoing success of national and regional media products, vis-à-vis global products, particularly those produced in Hollywood. Straubhaar defines cultural proximity as 'nationally or locally produced material that is closer to and more reinforcing of traditional identities, based in regional, ethnic, dialect/language, religious, and other elements'.[12] Audience preferences are also perceived as dynamic and relational. They often respond to the limitations characterizing national production, and social and historical subnational and supranational differences that impact different groups' media choices.[13] At the same time, La Pastina and Straubhaar argue that shared histories and migration can also trigger an interest in programmes from geographically distant countries.[14]

Findings

The following section presents the results of my fieldwork, which aimed to investigate the socio-cultural factors that contribute to the popularity of Turkish television dramas among Arab audiences and to understand why linguistic elements are no longer the primary factor influencing their selection and reception. To facilitate clarity, the findings have been categorized by themes that emerged during the data analysis.

Turkish serials are discredited as 'just' a women's genre

Before exploring the importance of cultural similarities in the appeal and selection of Turkish dramas, it is necessary to briefly discuss those for whom Turkish serials appear to resonate less: younger audiences (both expatriate and national).[15] The empirical findings from my research focusing on university-level students has shown that the younger generation claims not to be the primary audience of Turkish television dramas. Most students involved in the study declared that they had watched at least one Turkish serial, and female students stated that they had watched up to three serials, either fully or partially. For the most part, however, university students underlined that they were only occasional viewers or passive audiences. Audiences have been identified as passive when they are not viewers of Turkish serials by personal choice, but

THE IMPORTANCE OF SOCIO-CULTURAL FACTORS

have been exposed by female relatives (mothers, sisters, aunts, grandmothers, or sisters-in-law) who are regular viewers of Turkish dramas in their households. Passive viewers end up watching portions of a show owing to the programme being screened in the living room or other communal areas of the house.

For the majority of university students, Turkish drama serials were perceived as a women's genre, something that 'housewives' find enjoyable to watch. Female students also noted that watching Turkish television dramas was (largely) perceived as something embarrassing and shameful, given that they are considered to be programmes for the older generation:

Female Lebanese student: I admit, I watched several Turkish shows but only because my mum and sister-in-law are obsessed with them. (Focus-group discussion, 2014)

Male students described the viewing of Turkish television dramas as a weakness of the female gender because they were used as a means of fulfilling the female need for romance, while compensating for a monotonous lifestyle:

Male French Algerian student: I seriously can't think of any Arab men that watch Turkish shows. I am sorry to say it, but they cater more for desperate housewives who have nothing better to do. OK ... sorry, I am taking away the desperate, but housewives.

Moderator: Why do you think they are only watched by housewives?

Male French Algerian student: They are so cheesy; everyone is always in love with someone or just crying. Can't see that being something men in general find interesting.

(Focus-group discussion, 2014)

The use of expressions such as 'I admit' and 'They are so cheesy' reflects the perception that Turkish dramas are seen as only appealing to older women or, as they described it, to 'housewives'. For many, Turkish drama serials were also seen as too dramatic and overly emotional, while the episodes were too long to maintain viewer focus. Yet an overwhelming majority of female and male students acknowledged that Turkish serials appear to have surpassed local and regional television content in terms of production values, and were comparable with content from the USA. These findings were most intriguing, as Turkish dramas are prime-time serials in Türkiye and thus are aimed at reaching a broader audience. However, after the students had been asked why other people liked watching Turkish dramas, they started to discuss their female relatives' viewing patterns/motives in such detail that at times one suspected that, owing to the presence of their peers, they were not being honest with their claim that they themselves were not also viewers. As the focus-group discussions went on, most were able to demonstrate an in-depth knowledge of the characters and plotlines from various programmes, as well as to discuss numerous aspects of their appeal in a comprehensive manner. Yet it should be acknowledged that the perception of Turkish serials as a women's genre has been further deepened by Arab broadcasters, such as MBC. Prior to their cancellation by the network, MBC4 (in particular), whose target demographic is predominantly women viewers, offered multiple re-runs of Turkish serials throughout the day.

The importance of cultural proximity and the success of dubbing

The empirical evidence has consistently demonstrated the crucial role of cultural proximity in the selection and reception of dubbed Turkish dramas. The analysis of both qualitative and quantitative data has shown that dubbing has been instrumental in facilitating audiences' ability to imagine and accept the idea that Turkish actors were speaking Arabic instead of their native language of Turkish.

> I wouldn't have tried to watch a Turkish show if they wouldn't have [*sic*] introduced it with subtitles, to be quite honest. The dubbing was what made me watch Turkish dramas. You can enjoy the series without concentrating on the reading. Seriously, even if I would have known more about Türkiye before watching *Noor*, I would have still not tried it with subtitling. I find it too exhausting. Watching TV should be relaxing. (Interview, female Qatari, 2016)

Similarly to this female serial viewer, an overwhelming majority of research participants over the years expressed the view that the dubbing of Turkish shows into a Syrian colloquial Arabic dialect greatly contributed to their broader reach and positive reception. This played a pivotal role in allowing

Turkish dramas to enter a foreign geo-linguistic market—a region where cultural proximity between Turks and Arabs remains a core factor. Cultural proximity is defined by similarities in history, ethnicity, religion, language, and geography,[16] with similar language often highlighted as an important determinant of audience preferences.[17] According to Sinclair, language can be seen as a vehicle of culture;[18] however, it is not only similarities of language that provide access to foreign markets, but culture more broadly. Besides language, there are other cultural elements at play, such as 'dress, ethnic types, gestures, body language, definition of humour, ideas about story pacing, music tradition, religious elements'.[19] Additional factors can include gender images, lifestyle, personal experiences, education, family, and organizational affiliation, often shared across national borders.[20] Straubhaar argued that audiences are more inclined to select content from their own culture, or, when this is not available, from cultures similar to their own but not necessarily sharing the same language.[21] This is why, for instance, telenovelas appeal across Latin America;[22] why Japanese and Korean cultural products gained popularity across other parts of Asia;[23] and, as this chapter argues, why Turkish dramas appeal in the Arab world. Straubhaar has also formulated other proximities, such as genre, value, and thematic.[24] 'Genre proximity' refers to a familiarity with specific genres and their style of storytelling, for instance *musalsalāt* (Arabic: 'drama serials'), a popular television genre in Arab countries; 'value proximity' refers to shared values, ethics, or moral codes; and 'thematic proximity' refers to topics—for example, gender inequality, upward mobility, and other issues relevant to the country or region in question.

Straubhaar has tied the notion of cultural proximity to the broader concept of cultural capital, which focuses on a person's education, and more specifically, their knowledge and intellectual skills.[25] Building on Bourdieu's concept, Straubhaar suggests that the preference for local cultural products is not always a given, because cultural proximity is limited by social-class stratification. This means that groups that might be united by language and/or national culture can at the same time be fragmented by both economic and cultural capital. Therefore, cultural proximity can exist on multiple levels, and can be thought of as a complex interaction between cultural text and audiences, where individuals do not have a single identity but rather multidimensional and complex identities—geographic, cultural, or linguistic.[26]

My research over the years has identified that cultural proximity between Turks and Arabs remains a central factor contributing to the acceptance of the dubbing of Turkish dramas into a Syrian colloquial dialect. This in turn has contributed to the dramas' accessibility for a broader audience that would typically not consume foreign content, owing to a lack of cultural proximity, or unease with subtitling, or both. It is also significant that the use of a conversational form of Arabic has allowed people from all walks of life to understand the dubbing. As one Qatari woman noted, the dubbing of Turkish shows allowed Turkish serials to reach audiences who would not usually consider such content:

> No one likes to read subtitles. It was clever that they dubbed Turkish soap operas. I might have tried it with subtitling, but I know my mother or grandmother wouldn't have. (Focus-group discussion, 2016)

The dubbing of Turkish serials not only enabled audiences to gain access to content they would otherwise have found difficult to consume, but also aided in launching a successful new industry. In fact, Turkish dramas were the first television serials to be dubbed into a colloquial Syrian dialect, whereas Arab media translations had typically been provided through subtitling. The Syrian dialect was chosen following negative feedback received during earlier attempts at dubbing Latin American telenovelas into Modern Standard Arabic—a form of Arabic that is considered throughout the Arab world to be a 'high variety', typically used only in the written language (i.e. in academic material, news, research, and government transactions). The 'low variety' consists of the local colloquial dialects of Arabic that are used in everyday conversation. Unlike in Türkiye, or in most parts of Europe and Latin America, where dubbed rather than subtitled US television serials and movies were commonplace following the advent of television in the 1970s, in the Arab world the dubbing of serials and feature films has been slow to catch on,[27] despite there being a large market and a high level of illiteracy (with female illiteracy being higher than male).[28]

Fadi Ismail is widely recognized in the Arab world as being the media executive who introduced the enormously successful Turkish series *Noor* (*Gümüş*, 2005–07, Türkiye: Kanal D) to MBC, and is therefore credited with the rise of Turkish television content on Arab networks.[29] He brought the series to the attention of Adib Khair following its purchase at an Istanbul trade show.[30] Adib Khair is the late owner of the Damascus-based production company Sama Art International. Fadi Ismail and Adib Khair decided to test the colloquial Syrian dialect for dubbing,[31] not imagining that this experiment would ultimately become a regional trend. Dubbing opened up a whole new sector, where the Syrian colloquial dialect became the preferred choice.[32] Other channels quickly followed suit, with requests for the dubbing of Indian, Iranian, and Korean serials into the same colloquial Syrian dialect. The dubbing of Turkish serials not only helped them to gain access to the Arab television market, but also helped make dubbing widely accepted by Arab viewers, who were previously accustomed to the subtitling of foreign content.

Perhaps most importantly, the dubbing of Turkish content not only translated a language and localized a television format, but it also brought an entire culture and its people much closer—a culture that many in the Arab world were unaware was so proximate. As this female Palestinian serial viewer notes:

> Until Turkish soap operas aired on MBC, people didn't know much about Türkiye or what a Turkish person or culture is about. People started watching these shows, maybe at first not even realizing that they are Turkish or dubbed because it was not common at the time and the dubbing was done quite well. Once people started watching, everything felt very similar, even though on the surface things look less conservative. (Interview, 2016)

Many research participants encountered over the years, whether committed Turkish-serial viewers or passive viewers, stated that they felt that the dubbing was well received by Arab audiences, not only owing to a conversational form of Arabic being used, but also because Turkish actors were seen as Middle Eastern in appearance. This helped to ease Arab audiences into this relatively new way of localizing foreign content. The dubbing also helped audiences imagine and believe that the Turkish actors were actually speaking Arabic rather than Turkish. The possibility of Turkish actors conversing in Arabic prevented the serials from encountering cultural discount.[33] The dubbing seems to have contributed positively to Turkish serials being experienced as more real and relatable to Arab audiences:

> When people look similar and have similar lifestyles, it is becoming more realistic that they speak Arabic. I think that was one of the things that drew a lot of women to Turkish soaps, who would normally watch Arabic shows. (Interview, 2017)

Dubbing appears to have made everything Turkish more accessible to Arab audiences, helping viewers discover and appreciate the many similarities they share with the Turkish culture and Turkish people. However, it would be wrong to say that Turkish serials became Arabized simply through dubbing. Instead, the serials have contributed to the wider rediscovery of ethnic and cultural similarities that exist between Türkiye and the Arab world.

The role of cultural and ethnic similarities, and intertwined or overlapping histories

Although audiences in this study all originate from various Arab nationalities, it is necessary to re-emphasize that they possess diverse, complex cultural identities owing to these varied nationalities and different socio-cultural backgrounds. One way to think about cultural text and audiences is to imagine that cultural proximity has multiple levels.[34] Therefore, in the broader sense of the term, ethnicity is something that unites Arab audiences and makes them proximate to Turks. One cannot overstate the importance of Ottoman–Arab history, during which many aspects of culture have intertwined and overlapped, whether in ethnicity (resulting in similar physical appearance), body language, customs and traditions, commonalities in the type of food consumed, or music that one finds familiar[35]—all of which have been identified as important factors in the appeal of Turkish serials. The ability of audiences to recognize themselves or identify with 'a familiar or desired ethnic type on screen'[36] appears to have contributed to the increase in the cultural proximity of Turkish programmes and their relatability among Arab viewers. Similarly, Iwabuchi found that viewers in Hong Kong favoured Japanese dramas over Chinese productions, perceiving them as more believable because the characters had a similar appearance (e.g. hair colour), fashion sense, and way of life. According to Iwabuchi, this allowed viewers to relate to them in a more realistic way, rather than as fantasy.[37] As this female Lebanese viewer also described it:

> Irrespective of the fact that they look like people from the Levant, the themes are very Arabic. The emotions are very Arabic. The clothes and fashion they show appeals to Arab taste. I never feel that an American show would make me cry because I can't relate to it on that level, but with Turkish

shows they cover issues and characters that you can connect with and that touches you. (Interview, 2017)

But maybe more significantly, and as articulated here by a male Egyptian student, the drama serials appear to have contributed to Turks being rediscovered by Arab viewers as people of the Middle East with a similar ethnic and cultural background:

> Before all these shows started airing, I didn't know much about Türkiye. To be honest, I only watched *Valley of the Wolves* before and was actually surprised that you didn't see many differences between Turks and Arabs. I am not just talking about their looks but the entire lifestyle they show ... Now thinking about it, other than Muhannad [the actor Kivanç Tatlituğ] that all women were crazy about, most actors look just like people in the Arab world. (Focus-group discussion, 2014)

At this point, a question may arise as to why Türkiye, which shares a lengthy history with the Arab world, was for so long not recognized as culturally similar or interesting to the MENA region, and has only recently been rediscovered and understood as a comparable country. As explored in Chapter 3, despite being geographically close to the region, with the fall of the Ottoman Empire and the establishment of the Turkish Republic in 1923, Türkiye's foreign policy and security interactions during the twentieth century were alliant with the West, and contributed to the country distancing itself from its Middle Eastern neighbours.[38] For Turks, Arab collaboration with the British during the collapse of the Ottoman Empire was also seen as a betrayal. This experience left Turks with a sense of resentment and distrust towards the Arab world. However, with the rise to power of the Justice and Development Party (Adalet ve Kalkınma Partisi, AKP) in 2002 as a political force, Türkiye started to reconcile with the MENA region.[39] My fieldwork over the years has established that, along with reintroducing and aiding audiences to discover the many cultural proximities between Turks and Arabs, Turkish dramas have also impacted the way in which Arab audiences experience their mutual history. Turkish period dramas, and productions such as *Magnificent Century* (*Muhteşem Yüzyıl*, 2011–14, Türkiye: Show TV, Star TV), believed to have reached more than 500 million viewers worldwide,[40] or later, *Resurrection: Ertugrul* (*Diriliş: Ertuğrul*, 2014–19, Türkiye: TRT1), which are both based on Ottoman history, seem to be particularly appealing owing to their ability to connect with and remind viewers of their shared past. By turning history into fiction, the dramas draw viewers into a glamorous and romanticized version of their shared Ottoman story:

> My mum and I loved watching *Harim Al-Sultan* [the Arabic title of *Magnificent Century*]. It was entertaining and educational, and gave one a feeling for how things were in the old days. I liked this Ottomanness without all these national divisions and borders. It made me read more about Ottoman history. (Interview, female Qatari serial viewer, 2017)

Period dramas appear to attract audiences while helping them comprehend their commonalities rather than their differences. The negative image of the 'terrible Turk' dating back to Ottoman rule,[41] and until recently perceived as conventional wisdom in the Arab world,[42] seems to have faded away. Instead, the rediscovery of similarities has come to be an important factor. A similar opinion was voiced by Timur Savci, founder and owner of TIMS & B Productions and maker of *Magnificent Century*, during an open question-and-answer session following the screening of a behind-the-scenes documentary on *Magnificent Century* in Doha, Qatar, in October 2015. In response to my question as to why he thought Turkish serials are particularly successful in the Middle East, Savci answered that they are successful because of their ethnic and cultural similarities, and that these similarities (which people might not otherwise have realized were there) shine through in the shows. The same question was also answered by Halit Ergenç, the Turkish actor who portrays Sultan Süleyman in the series. Ergenç claimed that the serials' success was due to Turks and Arabs having a shared history, and that Turkish shows represent both the East and the West, as well as a feeling of being cosmopolitan, which, according to him, resonates with Arab audiences.

One could argue that perhaps the most significant appeal of Turkish period dramas relates to the fact that many Arab and Muslim viewers have grown tired of how Hollywood movies and TV series often portray Muslims as 'bad guys', terrorists, and anti-Westerners. Throughout my fieldwork, I found that many research participants felt that Arabs and Muslims were more often than not portrayed as villains. The only time they were 'good guys' was when they worked as informants or spies for the West. On the other hand, Turkish period dramas, which some could argue glorify and romanticize Ottoman history, are instead experienced as depicting a period where Muslims attained glory. They are perceived as projecting Muslim people as heroes instead of villains. The ability of dramas to influence audience perception of an Arab–Ottoman shared past, and to generate a feeling of 'us', rather than 'them', not only appears to increase viewer engagement and identification with stories and characters, but also, as outlined in Chapter 3, increases the soft power of Turkish television.

The importance of the Islamic religion

Religion is not only a primary source of cultural capital that has the unique ability to intersect with social class, but it also possesses the ability to determine or mediate viewers' media choices.[43] The fact that Turkish serials originate in a Muslim-majority country, and that important religious elements are portrayed within them, have been seen as important factors in contributing to their appeal. As this female Qatari serial viewer explained:

> You can see the series is based in a Muslim country because sometimes you can see things that can be only found in a Muslim society. (Interview, 2017)

Even though Turkish serials do not display religion overtly but rather provide a more subtle projection of Islamic norms and customs, including brief views of mosques, Islamic funeral proceedings, or the wearing of the hijab (more often by the older female members of a Turkish family), these religious aspects appear to contribute to the perception of Turkish serials as culturally proximate, which in turn contributes to their successful appeal and reception. As this female viewer notes:

> It's nice to see very modern surroundings and then the grandmother of the family praying. It satisfies your need for something different but also something very familiar. (Interview, 2017)

The existence of Islamic elements in Turkish dramas provides audiences with a degree of distinctiveness when compared to other foreign content, which in turn offers the viewer a level of affinity. As Straubhaar suggests, 'cultural affinities create forms of cultural capital that inform cultural proximity',[44] which one could argue legitimizes the projection of a more liberal and Western lifestyle, as well as the breaking of boundaries that would otherwise be seen as culturally unacceptable. As expressed by one Palestinian-Jordanian woman, the fact that Turkish shows are from a Muslim country is an important factor impacting audience choice:

> I think for many families it is more comfortable to watch Turkish programmes as a family in your living room than an American programme because they are from a Muslim country. I feel like they still have boundaries about what they show. (Focus-group discussion, 2016)

As this transcript demonstrates, even though Turkish serials are projecting a more liberal lifestyle to most parts of the Arab world, and often deal with themes and storylines that are deemed taboo or even *haram* ('forbidden') in Islam, viewers still perceive Turkish serials as mostly *halal* ('permissible') entertainment. One could argue that this is mainly due to a lack of nudity or lurid scenes; but also, despite clashes between conservative norms and modernity, all are eventually consolidated within a traditional normative framework. It was remarked upon by most research participants that traditional values are often played down in Western productions, and instead values contradictory to Islam and people of faith are promoted. At the other end of the spectrum, local and regional productions have been criticized for inaccurately projecting societal realities, and for lacking overall production values, as noted by this male Qatari student:

> As a young man I feel disconnected to most content produced in the region. Themes are not honest enough and production quality is quite low. The projection of social life is neither realistic, nor does it offer entertainment or escapism. (Focus-group discussions, 2017)

Viewer attitudes like these reveal that audience preferences are dynamic and relational; they can be responses to the limitations characterizing national production, or to social and historical subnational and supranational differences, each of which can influence media choices.[45] As Qureshi argues, 'relations and perceptions of distance and proximity are not given but created in processes involving the national state, the media, local authorities and people themselves'.[46] It appears that Turkish serials have managed to fill a gap that national, regional, and international serials were unable to address, while creating a cultural closeness that is not achievable by Western productions. At the same time, it should be emphasized that the media and the state have a significant bearing on the way people form a sense of belonging or feeling of proximity.[47] One could suggest that cultural proximity has occurred on both sides: Türkiye has become more conservative/religious since the ruling AKP government came to power in 2002, which has increasingly impacted upon the cultural industry, pressing it to project more conservative values in productions. However, the empirical findings of my fieldwork have consistently shown that Turkish serials' projection of traditional values against the backdrop of a modern society resonates profoundly not only with Arab viewers but also, as I will reveal in Chapters 6 and 7, with Chilean and Israeli audiences.

The significance of family values

The family is regarded as the primary foundation of Muslim society and culture: the Islamic religion influences the family structure and the nature of relationships between family members. The importance of maintaining these structures, irrespective of liberal storylines or of how Western female characters are dressed, is an important element. The projection of a traditional family structure in Turkish serials, set against the backdrop of a modern but Muslim society where family ties and respect for the older generation are considered important, has been perceived as another key factor contributing to their appeal. The fact that Turkish serials place an emphasis on conservative family values, a concept that appears to be neglected or even contested in Western productions, increases their cultural proximity to, and makes them resonate deeply with, Arab audiences. As this male student highlights, respect for parents and grandparents, in the context of enjoyable family dinners, holds a strong attraction for viewers:

> They always have these lavish breakfasts and dinners altogether. Where everyone is well dressed, and quite often, the grandmother is the matriarch. I like that about these shows a lot because for us grandparents are as important as parents. Not visiting them or dumping them in a care home is not something we do. (Focus-group discussion, 2014)

Another way to understand this appeal is to consider that Turkish drama serials might ease Arab audiences' fear of modernity by portraying a society that, despite being comparatively modern and Westernized, pays attention to values that are core within Muslim societies—such as the family.

Some residents of Qatar, whether citizens or expatriates, have been anxious about the rapid development and urbanization within the country in recent years. Qatar has experienced not only radical changes to its infrastructure, but also a rapid expansion of its population, which at times has worried many owing to the potential deterioration of the country's traditional Islamic values and identity. For some, modernity and advances in technology are associated with Westernization and a subsequent loss of core beliefs. Therefore, Turkish dramas not only possess cultural proximity on multiple levels—historical, religious, and ethnic—but they also portray a society that is different but similar enough to associate with and relate to, but equally is able to relieve audiences' fears about transitioning into Western-style modernity. Many of the storylines in Turkish serials deal with struggles between generations, and various conflicts between the norms of modernity and tradition. These conflicts are typically contained within a traditional and somewhat established structure that resonates with audiences. As this female Qatari serial viewer noted:

> Most of the shows have a focus on love stories but family is very important. They might break taboos or show things that are not acceptable in Muslim culture, but they never project it as if it is a good thing. (Interview, 2017)

Turkish serials offer a cultural blend

As noted earlier, despite Turkish drama serials' breaking of Arab gender roles, and dealing with taboo subjects such as alcohol consumption, premarital sex, adultery, and abortion (and despite Western productions being rejected for the same reasons), Turkish dramas are still perceived as culturally proximate and relatable. As this female Iraqi student noted:

> Turkish shows are allowed to get away with things that Arab shows wouldn't be allowed to. I think if an Arab show would show the things Turkish serials do, people would be boycotting the channel and its actors … my mum and

sister-in-law would refuse to watch them, but because they are Turkish they don't mind. (Focus-group discussion, 2013)

As reflected by this transcript, there is a clear paradox at play, whereby Turkish shows are afforded a certain level of tolerance when it comes to displaying taboo topics such as sex, the consumption of alcohol, and immodest attire, topics that otherwise would be considered un-Islamic. One could argue that Turkish serials enable Arab audiences to satisfy their curiosity about living a more modern and Western lifestyle. The fact that this more modern lifestyle is displayed by Turks, who are not Arab but who are close enough ethnically and culturally, removes the viewers' anxiety about transitioning into a too-open society. Cultural proximity between Arabs and Turks makes this possible, whereas Western productions fail to have the same impact, mainly because of the lack of cultural closeness. Yet the sensation of experiencing difference, or experiencing the 'aesthetics of the exotic', also seems to be a strong motivating factor for Arab viewing habits.[48] Therefore, it is possible to argue that there are two contradictory aspects at play contributing to the appeal of Turkish dramas: cultural proximity and cultural remoteness.

Turkish drama serials appear to successfully combine local elements, such as cultural and ethnic similarities, social relations, and family ties, with a modern, more Western-style way of life that is still in a recognizably Arab and Muslim cultural context. Whether one defines this as a cultural blend or a cultural mixture, both describe levels of hybridity, which cultural studies scholar Kraidy has defined as 'the fusion of two hitherto relatively distinct forms, styles, or identities ... which often occurs across national borders as well as across cultural boundaries'.[49] As this female Qatari student encapsulates it, Turkish serials have succeeded in combining separate and seemingly contradictory socio-cultural elements into one captivating package:

> They have everything in them, things that are more Arabic Middle Eastern to things that you would more associate with the West. Basically, there is something for everyone. (Focus group, October 2013)

The blend of both Eastern and Western elements appears to make Turkish television dramas an ideal mixture, enabling them to attract and be proximate to Arab audiences, yet to represent the unfamiliar: an alternative modernity that is new and exciting for Arab viewers to discover and explore. As one female Qatari viewer summarizes it, the combination of cultural proximity and cultural distance—the known and the unknown—is an important factor:

> They are things that are very similar to Arabic countries, and they are other things we are not used to seeing in the Middle East. I think the enjoyment really lies in both. (Interview, 2016)

Türkiye appears to have successfully localized dominant global television formats and developed them into a more relatable form, while also constructing its own cultural spaces, making them successful not only domestically but regionally, and beyond. Turkish drama serials have offered Arab audiences a feeling of living in a shared time and common experience that cannot be presented appropriately by Western popular culture, owing to the distinct lack of cultural proximity. To interpret Turkish cultural products as simply a translation of popular Western culture into a Middle Eastern context is not sufficient to understand their appeal. Similarly to Iwabuchi's argument about the success of Japanese cultural products in Asian countries,[50] the popularity of Turkish television dramas may be seen as 'Turkishness' resonating with Arab audiences' idea of modernity, and not simply a response to Western modernity. Rather, the textual appeal of Turkish dramas is closely associated with the lifestyle and social relationships of present-day Türkiye, as embodied in the storylines portrayed.

The appeal of the portrayal of women

Throughout my fieldwork, the portrayal of a strong female character in Turkish dramas was a topic that male and female study participants addressed as an essential factor in their appeal. In contrast, Arab serials were often perceived as presenting an incomplete version of Arab society: many expressed the view that the portrayal of gender roles and family relations was usually dated and unrealistic. At the same time, most participants acknowledged that the society presented in Turkish serials was far more liberal than in Qatar and other Arab countries. However, they commented that women in Qatar and other Arab regions were increasingly active in a range of sectors, and in important positions in society, but that this reality was not reflected often enough in Arab

THE IMPORTANCE OF SOCIO-CULTURAL FACTORS

television serials. In contrast, female protagonists in Turkish serials were overwhelmingly seen as critical to their success, and perceived as pursuing power and challenging the socio-cultural norms set for their gender, while at the same time searching for 'Mr Right'.

> Arab programmes are too censored and conservative, and with US ones, you feel a total disconnect. I struggle to see a woman as a strong female character who heavily drinks or has many random partners. For me, Turkish dramas offer the sweet middle. (Interview, female Palestinian serial viewer, 2016)

One of the Turkish dramas named by many study participants over the years for its popularity and appeal (other than the serials *Noor*, *Magnificent Century*, and *Resurrection: Ertugrul*) was *What Is Fatmagül's Crime?* (*Fatmagül'ün Suçu Ne?*, 2010–12, Türkiye: Kanal D). The series focuses on a young village girl who is gang-raped by a group of rich young men. Kerim, the lead male protagonist, who unlike his friends is not the son of a powerful businessman, agrees to marry Fatmagül to prevent the group from going to prison. However, Fatmagül is unaware that he was not one of the perpetrators, while he himself has no recollection of taking part in the crime, owing to having been under the influence of drugs and alcohol at the time.[51] *What Is Fatmagül's Crime?*, or *Fatma* as it is known to Arab audiences, the television adaptation of a 1986 Turkish movie of the same name, exposes a young woman's fight for justice, and her struggle, pain, and helplessness in a society that appears to have conservative values on the surface but is deeply corrupt—where wealth and connections mean that you are above the law, and the weak and vulnerable are not protected. Instead of Fatmagül being safeguarded, and the men who raped her being held accountable, she is faced with rejection and shame. While the story holds a universal appeal for women in most societies, the experience of Fatmagül is understood by Arab viewers in a Muslim cultural context, where being raped is still seen by a large portion of Turkish and Muslim society as shameful, and damaging to the honour of the family. In the Arab world, sexual violence against women is also a reality, but one that many fail to acknowledge owing to the stigma attached.[52] As this Lebanese female student stated, the character, Fatma, offers Arab viewers a female role model to aspire to, in a similar cultural context, and touching on a matter that affects many, but that most are afraid to address:

> Violence against women is a big issue. Shows like this give women in that situation hope to find courage and maybe ways to overcome and cope with the situation. Because it is not something they can talk about to anyone openly. (Focus-group discussion, 2013)

Interestingly, despite *What Is Fatmagül's Crime?* being one of the most domestically and internationally successful Turkish dramas, generating some of the highest sales revenues,[53] with the serial even adapted by Spanish media group Atresmedia in 2022,[54] it remains one of the most criticized serials in Türkiye for breaching morality and Turkish family values. The gang-rape scene, which represents the defining moment of the entire story, is believed to have been watched by over 25 million viewers when it aired in Türkiye in September 2010. It resulted in almost 3,000 viewer complaints to the Radio and Television Supreme Council (RTÜK) in less than a week.[55] During an interview with Dogan Media Group's chief executive officer at the time, Irfan Sahin (who was the producer of the enormously successful Turkish series *Gümüs*, or *Noor* in the Arab world), I asked him what he thought about *What Is Fatmagül's Crime?*, which his network was airing. In doing so they were being accused of corrupting the morals of Turkish audiences (the drama having not yet aired on Arab television). In his response, he noted that rape is a reality, and everything that is a reality can be a television serial.[56]

The enormous popularity of *What Is Fatmagül's Crime?* in Türkiye and abroad has shown that stories touching on subjects that impact people but which many shy away from, depicted in a fictional production, hold a strong appeal for viewers.[57] However, what makes *What Is Fatmagül's Crime?* even more relevant to women in the Arab world is the fact that the female protagonist had to marry one of her tormentors in order to restore her family's honour and gain acceptance in the small conservative coastal village where she was raised. Empathy, and the ability to relate to forced marriages, might not require cultural proximity, but because the topic occurs more frequently in the Muslim world, the subject resonates more profoundly with audiences. As a Tunisian woman research participant stated:

My mum and I cried when we watched the show. It is so incredibly touching. Maybe the best series I have seen.

Researcher: Why, may I ask?

Because it feels so real ... from the issue of rape to the projection of women; it all feels real.

(Focus-group discussion, 2013)

It is important to acknowledge that Turkish serials hold a level of cultural shareability for Arab viewers that, to a degree, contradicts the notion of cultural proximity.[58] Cultural shareability refers to common values, images, archetypes, and themes across cultures that permit programmes to flow across cultural boundaries. Turkish drama serials often employ archetypes that portray 'self-seeking disobedient females in a heroic struggle'—a theme with universal appeal. However, in the case of Turkish dramas, the proximity and appeal lie in the fact that the heroic struggle, such as in the case of Fatmagül, is experienced against the backdrop of a society where a strong patriarchal structure exists, and the experience of shame and honour rests on the women's shoulders.[59] In Türkiye, similar to other patriarchal societies, the norms and ideals surrounding women's appearance, behaviour, and life choices are strongly associated with the entire family's morals and honour.[60] Likewise, in the Arab world, the concept of family honour is centred on the notion that it is (primarily) the women's responsibility to behave in a way that protects the honour of the family.[61] Therefore, the fact that a serial character like Fatmagül can fight against these cultural dimensions and the crony capitalism that provides power to the rich and well-connected, where the notions of honour and shame seemingly do not apply to the wealthy, resonates with many viewers in Türkiye, the Arab world, and many parts of the Global South. Thus, it is not cultural shareability alone, but the reality of similar socio-cultural elements that attracts audiences.

Genre proximity

In looking at the final aspect of my findings, we should remind ourselves that genre proximity is an extension of cultural proximity, referring to genres that maintain similar structures, formulas, and archetypes that can reach past cultural differences and be accepted in different countries.[62] Some genres, such as melodramas, use similar forms of storytelling that have existed in many countries for centuries, so that stories may be shared across diverse cultures. My fieldwork has consistently shown that genre proximity remains one of the key factors in the appeal of Turkish programmes in the Arab world, Chile, and Israel. In the Arab world, the fact that Arabic dramas, or *musalsalāt*, have been a popular genre on regional television since the 1960s appears to have seamlessly paved the way for Turkish serials to be well received by Arab viewers.[63] The following statement by a female Lebanese viewer demonstrates the appeal and resonance of dramas that successfully weave a genre of universal appeal with cultural elements familiar across the Middle East:

> The shows are often focusing on lots of love-triangles but also on family issues. What makes it in my view engaging is the music they use and these close-ups of facial expressions. I mean there are certain things in the body language you wouldn't see in other foreign programmes; it's kind of very regional. (Focus group, 2014)

Moreover, it is important to highlight that Turkish dramas often border on the subgenre of melodrama, which places an emphasis on romance, marriage, family issues, and morality, and which is almost always accompanied by dramatic and suggestive music. The focus on personal relations, and the presence of dramatic music that is Middle Eastern in tone, have been noted as important factors in the attraction and perception of proximity in Turkish dramas.

Conclusion

The empirical data from Arab audiences in Qatar has overwhelmingly revealed that the shared history between Turks and Arabs that spans more than half a century has been a critical factor in the success of Turkish dramas. The reality that many aspects of the two cultures have become interwoven and overlapped has been established as pivotal in Turkish dramas' popularity among Arab viewers. From similar-looking ethnicities, physical appearances, and body language, to comparable customs, traditions, music, and types of food consumed—all these elements have been identified as essential factors in the appeal of Turkish serials. These important similarities have aided in the acceptance of dubbed Turkish serials by Arab viewers and have enabled Turkish dramas to enter a cultural-linguistic market that would normally require the same, or a similar, language. The findings have also illustrated that the dubbing of Turkish programmes into a colloquial Syrian dialect has provided access to broader audiences, including those who might have encountered difficulties with subtitling. The popularity of dubbed Turkish dramas also made dubbing a more widely employed method to localize foreign content, in a region that has been traditionally accustomed to subtitling. But, more importantly, the dubbing of content brought an entire country and its people closer to Arab audiences. Furthermore, the empirical data explored in this chapter has revealed that Turkish serials have successfully merged cultural and ethnic similarities, social relations, and family ties with a modern way of life that still sits recognizably in an Arab and Muslim cultural context. The ability of Arab viewers to recognize themselves or identify with 'a familiar or desired ethnic type on-screen' has contributed to the increase in the cultural proximity of Turkish programmes and their relatability among Arab viewers. But perhaps more significantly, the drama serials seem to have contributed to Turks being rediscovered by Arab viewers as people of the Middle East with a similar ethnic and cultural background.

The findings in this chapter have also illustrated that the shared religion of Türkiye and the Arab world has been a primary source of cultural capital that could intersect across nationalities and social classes. Even though the direct reference to the Islamic faith in Turkish dramas is subtle, it has influenced or mediated Arab viewers' media choices. With the realization that Turkish serials hail from a Muslim-majority country, even subtle religious elements have been experienced as vital factors contributing to their appeal. At the same time, the empirical findings have repeatedly shown that Turkish dramas focus on family values, the primary foundation of Muslim society and culture—and by maintaining these structures, irrespective of liberal storylines or of how Western female characters are dressed, they have been found to resonate highly with viewers. Therefore, the projection of a traditional family structure, set against the backdrop of a modern but Muslim society where family ties and respect for the older generation are considered essential, has been perceived as a vital factor contributing to Turkish dramas' appeal.

We have also seen that the depiction of a strong female character in Turkish dramas was experienced by Arab audiences as an essential factor in their attraction. In comparison, national and regional productions were perceived as often presenting an incomplete version of Arab society, especially with respect to the projection of gender roles and family relations. These portrayals were seen as dated and unrealistic, even though most participants recognized that the society presented in Turkish serials was far more liberal than in Qatar and other Arab countries. However, the participants noted that women in these Arab regions were increasingly active in a range of sectors and in important positions in society, but that these realities were not sufficiently mirrored in Arab television serials. In contrast, strong female protagonists in Turkish serials, who break gender norms while also searching for 'Mr Right', were overwhelmingly seen as critical to their success.

Genre proximity has also been identified as a key factor in the success of Turkish dramas. The fact that Arabic dramas (*musalsalāt*) have traditionally been a popular genre on Arab television appears to have paved the way for Turkish serials to be well received by Arab viewers. Overall, these findings have clearly demonstrated that the argument suggesting a viewer's first preference would be for material produced in their own language and within their own local or national culture does not apply here.[64] Arab viewers opt for Turkish serials irrespective of the fact that Arabic content is widely available. Cultural and linguistic elements appear to become secondary if national and regional media fail to satisfy the audience's needs. However, the findings have also demonstrated that Arab audiences actively select television content that is closest, most proximate, or most directly relevant to them in terms of culture.

In the next chapter, I will further examine the motivation of Arab women viewers, who have been identified as the primary audience of Turkish dramas—providing vital insight into why Turkish dramas are particularly entertaining and engaging for women viewers.

5 Why Turkish Dramas Resonate with Arab Women: An Analysis of the Responses of Women Viewers in Qatar

As discussed throughout this book, Turkish drama serials have become some of the most popular shows on Arab television—a phenomenon in their own right, inspiring debate and speculation about their popularity in many quarters, from critics to governments, and scholars to journalists. Women viewers over the years have been projected by Arab media as being negatively influenced by Turkish drama serials, damaging marital bliss and fuelling divorce rates in the region. Old and discredited ideas of media influence and effects have been used as a framework for understanding the viewers' attraction to Turkish drama serials.[1] This has raised an important question about women viewers' involvement with Turkish dramas. As it is an evolving phenomenon, there is still scant audience research analysing the nature of the viewing experience for Arab audiences. While there are a few exceptions to this paucity of research,[2] these serve only to raise yet further questions, thus making it even more pressing to understand the viewing motivations of Arab women. Therefore, in an attempt to contribute to an important evolving area of academic research, this chapter seeks to examine what it is about Turkish dramas that appeals particularly to Arab women. The diverse audience in the Gulf State of Qatar is used as a case study by drawing upon data gathered through interviews, focus-group discussions, surveys, observation, and informal interactions with various Arab nationals, spanning a period close to a decade.

However, to explore the viewing motivations of women audiences in Qatar meaningfully, the chapter first examines the position of women and the sociocultural structure in the country, stemming from distinctive Qatari/Arab characteristics that can determine the behaviour and attitudes of women audiences. This is followed by a brief overview of the uses and gratifications theory, which has been utilized as an analytical framework. The final section of this chapter analyses and discusses the empirical findings. The central findings in this chapter reveal that women viewers have become deeply involved with Turkish serials. Unlike the long-held argument that was repeated by most male interviewees throughout my fieldwork, the empirical data shows that this involvement cannot simply be trivialized as mindless escapism and the enjoyment of meaningless fantasy, nor can it be seen as the 'unimportant' experience of housebound women. Instead, Turkish dramas are found to fill a void on Arab screens by providing dramas of high production quality that are able to satisfy the audiences' need for entertainment, cultural proximity, and emotional realism, while at the same time exploring themes and storylines that are familiar, but generally not covered in Arab serials.

The socio-cultural structure in Qatar, and the situation of women

As women make up the primary audience of Turkish drama serials, explaining women's cultural and domestic position in Qatar is crucial. Qatar's population is highly unusual, as its citizens comprise only 11.6 per cent of the more than 2 million residents—meaning that the country holds the highest percentage of resident non-citizens in the world.[3]

Qatar is the world's second-wealthiest nation, thanks to its vast natural gas and oil reserves.[4] The largest ethnic groups are from Southeast Asia, Egypt, and the Philippines, but there are also numerous expatriates in Qatar[5] from other Arab countries.[6] As in other Gulf Cooperation Council (GCC) nations, Qatar's sponsorship law (the *kafala* system) makes it difficult for foreigners to stay in the country once their work contract has ended. With much of the Arab world afflicted by war, political conflict, or economic turmoil, Arab expatriates in Qatar are often fearful of having their work contracts (and therefore their sponsorship) terminated, the result being almost immediate expulsion from the country. Qatar's labour law requires all foreigners to be sponsored by a Qatari citizen or company, with the sponsors having control over visa status, conditions, salary, and, potentially, expulsion from Qatar. A forced return to their homeland is for many a very unwelcome prospect, usually resulting in a loss of social and economic stability and security, as the standard of living they have in Qatar is often impossible to attain in their home countries.[7]

Despite its rapid development, urbanization, and population growth, Qatar has managed to retain an extremely private culture, reflecting the Wahabi branch of Islam, which is closely associated with the Kingdom of Saudi Arabia (KSA).[8] The concept of 'honour' determines the foundation and regulation of all social interactions in Qatari and other Muslim societies, and refers to the sexual conduct of women.[9] 'A family's honour is directly related to a women's sexual behaviour and her general reputation'.[10] From early Arab societies until today, women have been in a state of subjection to their closest male relatives—their fathers, brothers, husbands, or uncles.[11] Because of an inherent fear that Qatari women and Arab women from conservative families may breach the sexual code, considered to be the most shameful action of all (or *ayb*), unmarried women (in particular) are usually permitted to leave the house only when accompanied by a family member or companion as chaperone. For a woman to enter higher education, or to work, permission is required from the male member(s) of the family.

Interestingly, greater numbers of Qatari women than men have more recently registered for higher-education courses. Qatari women are also increasingly being appointed to key positions, and across a broader range of occupations, evidencing a slow but noticeable shift in the role of women in society.[12] Arranged marriages are commonplace among Qataris and other conservative Arab nationals, with the Western customs of courtship, or spending any time together before marriage, being culturally unacceptable. Qataris are (more often than not) expected to marry a cousin, or another member of their tribe. In recent years, statistics have shown that about 40 per cent of Qatari marriages result in divorce.[13] Overall, women in Qatar face similar constraints to those experienced by women worldwide, but these are 'compounded in an Arab Middle Eastern context by religious and cultural defined attitudes and practices'.[14]

A brief overview of viewing motivations

The uses and gratifications (U&G) approach has been used as an analytical tool to examine motivations for viewing Turkish serials in Qatar. The U&G approach analyses the utilization of media, and the appeal of various types of media content to viewers. The core argument of the approach is that audiences use media to satisfy social and psychological needs.[15] According to the U&G theory, viewers actively select certain types of media content to fulfil their needs and expectations. Audiences are not interpreted as passive receivers, but as active participants, making conscious and driven attempts to seek various forms of gratification.[16] As media can serve various purposes, the outcome of the viewers' experiences can differ, even among those engaged in viewing the same (or similar) media.[17] The U&G theory does not have a single or common list of forms of the gratification obtained from media consumption. Instead, multiple lists, categories, and classification systems exist, focusing on different variables, such as entertainment, relaxation, acquisition, arousal, pastimes, diversion, escape, and sociality. Seminal research analysing the viewing of soap operas was carried out largely in the 1980s and 1990s, when television was the dominant medium.[18] However, the digital age has seen a resurgence of the U&G methodology, with a growing number of academic researchers worldwide now utilizing the theory.[19]

Even though the emergence of digital media has enabled television serials to reach a wider audience, my empirical research over the years has shown that, until the banning of Turkish television serials on the KSA and United Arab Emirates (UAE) free-to-air satellite networks, television was the most commonly utilized platform among Turkish serial audiences. This was especially true among the older generation in Qatar and across the wider MENA region.[20]

Findings

This section outlines the results of my fieldwork, which sought to uncover the reasons behind the popularity of Turkish dramas among Arab women, as well as their viewing habits and motivations. The study's key findings are presented thematically, reflecting the patterns that emerged during the analysis of the empirical data.

Entertainment

For many female viewers, Turkish drama serials are a popular source of entertainment. However, what sets these shows apart is their ability to offer a unique blend of cultural engagement that goes beyond simple distraction. Despite the argument made by some scholars that genres such as soap operas primarily serve to distract viewers from their worries and realities,[21] Turkish dramas offer a level of meaningful engagement that distinguishes them from both regional and Western productions. This sentiment is shared by many women viewers, as evidenced by a transcript from an Egyptian stay-at-home mother. Her perspective provides valuable insight into the complex interplay between the need for entertainment and various other motives:

> I'm not sure how to describe it, but Turkish shows are not just something I binge-watch to switch off, although I sometimes binge-watch. I enjoy watching them because they have so many things I can relate to. I can relax while also finding elements that are relatable and familiar to me. (Interview, 2017)

One could argue that Turkish drama serials have a unique ability to cater to multiple viewing motivations for women, thereby serving not only as entertainment, but also as an important form of cultural engagement. For women, the desire for entertainment is often intertwined with other motives. Turkish dramas fulfil these needs by offering a distinctive combination of cultural similarities (as discussed in Chapter 4) and viewing experiences that resonate on multiple levels.

The Intersection of Personal Agency and Shifting Viewing Patterns

For many women, the entertainment and pleasure gained from watching Turkish serials is also associated with the freedom of the entertainment itself. Women have the ability to consume Turkish dramas when, where, and how they want, which makes these dramas not just a source of entertainment but also a dedicated period of personal time. During these moments, husbands were often seen as disruptive, disapproving, or even dismissive of their wives' engagement with Turkish dramas. As these two transcript of viewers highlight:

> I am a mum of two young kids and there is not much time left for anything, but I enjoy watching Turkish dramas in the evening after having put the kids to bed [pause]. It is super relaxing. But because my husband doesn't

like to watch them with me, I end up watching them either in the bedroom alone, or on my laptop with headphones in the living room so at least we can still be together. (Interview, Palestinian-Qatari professional woman, 2017)

My husband often makes fun of me for watching Turkish soap operas. He thinks they are silly and have a bad influence. (Sudanese professional woman, 2017)

The experiences of women who watch Turkish drama serials alone owing to their husbands' disapproval and ridiculing of their choice highlight the fact that many Arab men consider these shows to be exclusively for women (as discussed in Chapter 4). In fact, many Arab women have reported that their husbands not only dislike Turkish dramas but are also troubled by them. Men are particularly concerned that their wives' perceptions of romance and gender relations may be negatively influenced by these shows. This concern is reflected in the following transcripts of two professional women who highlight the issue of gendered perceptions of these shows among men.

My husband thinks that Turkish soaps put the wrong expectations into women's heads. (Qatari professional woman, 2017)

He [her husband] initially disapproved because it puts men under pressure to be a certain way, but he is over it now. He avoids me when I am watching them. (Libyan professional woman, 2016)

These findings have some parallels with an earlier study by Lee and Cho which examined the experiences of university-educated Korean women in the USA who enjoyed watching soap operas. The study found that the women's husbands disapproved of their viewing choices and compared their taste to that of housemaids, who were seen as socially inferior. As a result, the women felt ashamed, and treated as if they were damaging the family image and honour.[22] However, in the case of Arab women viewers, instead of their feeling embarrassment or shame, part of the allure of watching Turkish dramas appeared to lie in doing something that is disapproved of by men. Therefore, rather than feeling apologetic for their viewing choices, Arab women were claiming their own space and leisure time, irrespective of male disapproval. Thus, watching Turkish drama serials was not only experienced as a positive activity that allowed them to allocate time for themselves amidst their busy schedules, but this feeling of reward was further elevated by the act of doing something that is not approved of by men. As the next transcript illustrates, by watching dramas alone owing to their husband's disapproval or dislike, they were able to assert their agency, and prioritize their own desires and preferences.[23]

> When I watch my Turkish shows, it's my time, and I don't care that my husband and son find them dreadful. [laughter] They can just go to a different room. (Interview, Tunisian-French professional, 2017)

Changing Viewing Patterns

Along with asserting their own preferences and desires, women viewers of Turkish drama serials have also shifted their viewing patterns, with a growing trend towards online streaming. This trend shows that these viewers not only exercise agency in what they choose to watch but also in how and when they watch it. This represents a significant departure from the findings of my earlier fieldwork, conducted via focus-group discussions and an online survey between 2013 and 2014, which indicated that Turkish serials were predominantly watched on television, especially on the MBC network, as the following transcript reveals:

> My grandmother and mum have, like, a daily routine. They watch them during breakfast and later watch a different re-run at lunch. It's, like, Turkish shows are always running in the background. (Focus-group discussion, female Qatari student, 2013)

In 2016, subsequent to my earlier fieldwork, a significant shift in the consumption patterns of Turkish serials in Qatar was observed. Turkish dramas were increasingly viewed online through various platforms, including YouTube, illegal websites offering pirated dubbed or subtitled content, Turkish-channel websites (in Turkish), and Netflix. It is noteworthy that while many female viewers preferred to watch Turkish serials at home, even while completing household chores, others had begun to watch them while running errands outside, such as during visits to the hair salon, doctor's waiting room, while shopping, and at the gym.

I have weekly appointments at the hospital—that's when I end up watching my favourite shows. Makes everything more bearable ... I end up forgetting that I am at the hospital. (Interview, female Qatari professional, 2017).

I actually love watching them when I am doing my twice-weekly ironing, or sometimes whilst cooking dinner. (Interview, Egyptian stay-at-home mother, 2017)

For women with busy schedules and multiple commitments, watching Turkish dramas through on-demand options and mobile technologies has offered a sense of autonomy, and greater opportunities for self-determination. Viewing Turkish dramas at their convenience has permitted Arab women to take further control of their leisure time.

The importance of romance: between reality and fantasy

Through my fieldwork, I have also discovered that the way romance is portrayed in Turkish dramas holds a significant appeal, and offers Arab women a rare combination of reality and fantasy, capturing both the tangible and intangible aspects of the stories and characters being depicted. By weaving together the elements of reality and fantasy, the serials offer a perspective that is grounded in truth, yet also expands beyond it. Specifically, the success of series like *Noor* (*Gümüş*, 2005–07, Türkiye: Kanal D) can be attributed not only to their emphasis on romantic storylines, but also to the fact that the lead characters had an arranged marriage—a concept that may feel foreign to Western audiences but is relatable and authentic to those in the Arab world. By reflecting the cultural values and social norms prevalent in the Muslim world, these dramas add a layer of authenticity and realism that resonates with the audience, and draws them into the storylines, making the dramas more identifiable. The same holds true for the hugely successful series *What Is Fatmagül's Crime?* (*Fatmagül'ün Suçu Ne?*, 2010–12, Türkiye: Kanal D), or *Fatma* as it is known to Arab viewers, a drama depicting the story of a gang-rape victim. While rape is not an issue exclusive to Turkish or Muslim societies, the portrayal of honour and shame, as well as the reality that women in some of these countries have to marry their rapist in order to restore and protect their family honour, is a familiar and highly relatable concept for Arab women. At the same time, the experience of fantasy for Arab women is heightened, because not only do they see more liberal gender relations, but also they see that the core values are not truly challenged. Turkish drama series may appear liberal on the surface, as they depict stories that include Western-style courtship, adultery, premarital sex, abortion, rape, alcohol consumption, and dress codes that may not be considered acceptable in Arab society. However, these themes are never truly liberal, as they are portrayed within patriarchal boundaries and storylines that are consolidated within a normative conservative framework. This framework is highly familiar to Arab viewers, making the themes and characters acceptable, relatable, and identifiable, while also providing a safe space for fantasy. It is possible to argue that fantasy becomes more impactful for Arab women when core values and ideologies are not challenged. Mumford (1995) stressed that the repetitive expression of ideology in soap opera narratives represents a significant part of the audience experience. Seeing the shared ideology recurring repeatedly becomes an integral part of viewer pleasure. Similarly, scholars such as Brunsdon have suggested that audiences are required to bring to the viewing experience 'an extra-textual familiarity', such as certain generic knowledge, knowledge specific to the serial, but also knowledge of the 'socially acceptable codes and conventions for the conduct of personal life'.[24] Thus, similar socio-cultural realities, especially those impacting women in Türkiye and the Arab world, allow Arab viewers to engage with Turkish serials meaningfully and in a way that permits them to fanatasize and reflect on their realities and positions. As these two Palestinian female students see it:

> They have things that Arabs can fully relate to. For instance, the way we feel joy, pain, or shame is similar. OK, [pause] they show a lifestyle that most of us would not agree with, but it isn't shown in a way like in a US serial. You still get a sense of the same values, like you need your parents' permission to marry someone and examples like that.

> I agree with you ... but what I wanted to add is that Turkish soaps show a lot of love stories—the women date and have boyfriends but there is still a boundary which I think makes them appreciated by people in the Arab world. You see dating but it is not sexualized like in American shows. (Focus-group discussion, 2013)

TURKISH DRAMA SERIALS

The ability of Turkish serials to present a seemingly liberal facade while upholding conservative values at their core creates an opportunity for women viewers to immerse themselves in a world that is both familiar and fantastical. This unique viewing experience harmonizes pleasure and guilt, making it particularly gratifying for viewers. For instance, a female Palestinian student's response to this phenomenon exemplifies its impact:

> Maybe it is my impression, but Turkish shows don't have this judginess. That she is a bad girl, or she has shamed our family. You get that they are Muslim, but things are more open. It's more fun to watch them, but without feeling they disrespect our culture and ignore boundaries. (Focus-group discussion, 2016)

Moreover, the cultural norms and values prevalent in Arab and Muslim societies often restrict women's roles to that of a good wife, mother, daughter, and sister, making it difficult for them to identify with characters who deviate from these prescribed roles. However, Turkish dramas offer an escape from this reality, as women viewers can relate to characters who appear to challenge norms and values without experiencing any real-life consequences, creating a distinctive, exceptionally gratifying viewing experience, as this female viewer emphasizes:

> You can watch Turkish shows without feeling that the show is trying to educate you about what is a good or bad girl. There is not this constant feeling of moral judgment and moral overload that people get in some Arab shows. (Interview, Palestinian-Qatari professional, 2017)

One could argue that Turkish drama serials offer Arab women a rare experience of utopia where problems can be solved, and feelings can be explored in ways that deviate from their own immediate realities:

> You kind of see situations and stories that we would never see, for instance, in Arab shows or even society, without being totally judged, especially as a woman. I don't know how to put this in words, but Turkish shows are maybe for Arab women, a kind of guilty pleasure where you see Muslim women have another lifestyle without it being seen as forbidden if you know what I mean. (Focus-group discussion, 2014).

Ang argues that soap operas offer women a 'play with reality' by entering a fantasy world, which can be liberating, as it is fictional.[25] This experience of fantasy allows female viewers to experiment with ideas without worrying about real-world consequences. As a result, watching Turkish drama serials allows Arab women to explore their subjectivity as a source of pleasure, suspending 'reality in parentheses', and providing a safe imaginary experience.[26] The pleasure of fantasy is achieved through a combination of cultural proximity and distance, where the known and unknown merge for women viewers. Through the characters in these shows, women appear to gain a sense of agency and self-determination that may be limited in their real lives. By presenting alternative versions of reality, Turkish dramas enable women to explore situations and storylines in a safe and non-threatening way:

> I think I like to see the different lifestyles. I like to see stories that we cannot see on Arab television. For me Turkish soaps are like a window to possibilities that are not open to us. [laughter] I mean it's not like I want that kind of life but it is quite enjoyable to see as a viewer. (Interview, Female Syrian-Palestinian postgraduate student, 2017)

> I think it's every Arab girl's dream ... no joke. All of us, especially the young ones. When we watch them, we want that life. We want to be that way. We want to be able to be that way. And we can relate to it so much because sometimes in some of these TV shows, the girl will be doing something behind her parents' back; she wouldn't want her parents to find out, and that's so relatable. And the guy, of course, but I think it's sort of like a fantasy for everyone, and that's why we watch it so much. We love it so much. We want to watch it to the end to find out what happens. (Focus-group discussion, female Jordanian student, 2013)

As these transcripts reveal, there is a dialectical tension between how the viewers live, and, at times, how they would like to live. Over the years Turkish serials have been blamed for increasing divorce rates in the Arab world, because Arab women were accused of conflating their 'real-life' romances (their marriages) with the ones projected on-screen.[27] Even though the women interviewed were never asked directly whether they gained ideas about how to conduct their personal romances from watching Turkish serials, many noted without prompting that they enjoyed the depiction of courtship, affection, and relationships in Turkish shows: they found this appealing, and lacking in Arab serials. On the other hand, the projection of courtship and romance in Western media was overwhelmingly seen as not relatable, owing to different values and moralities as illustrated by the following viewer statement:

> What women like is that Turkish series are different; they have romance, but it is not that you feel embarrassed to watch it with your daughter or your mother like American movies...there are so many things that, as a woman, you totally can relate to. They are more emotional and deeper, but it's just like feelings and worries that are very similar. (Interview, Female Qatari student, 2016)

Geraghty argued that women viewers of soap operas have the ability to recognize 'every word and gesture to understand its emotional meaning, and derive pleasure'.[28] Perhaps through feminine competencies acquired in everyday life in a patriarchal society such as Türkiye or the Arab world, Turkish dramas provide cultural cues that women viewers are more receptive to. At the same time, the appeal of Turkish serials to women viewers cannot be understood as opposition to Arab culture, or to their position in society, but rather as being situated within its cracks, in the points where meaning itself wavers, and where values are questioned.

Over the years, most study participants have criticized the projection of unrealistic male and female relations in locally- and regionally-produced serials; the depiction of family relations, such as between father and daughter, and between couples, was seen as dated and unrealistic.[29] In contrast, Turkish dramas are perceived as relatable, permitting audiences to reflect upon their own reality within the framework of daily life.

It is necessary to highlight that the viewer's vision of life in Türkiye is primarily drawn from Turkish serials, which often portray an idealized and glamorized depiction of the country rather than a realistic projection of everyday life. The focus is more on upscale neighbourhoods, and the young, attractive, and wealthy. For that reason, the authenticity experienced by viewers can be described as a 'mediated authenticity', a mediated representation of reality.[30] Still, stories and characters in Turkish dramas are considered by viewers as relatable and real, as they include boundaries familiar to viewers in Qatar. In addition, the projection of relatable human emotions becomes an essential factor in the overall viewing experience for women.

WHY TURKISH DRAMAS RESONATE WITH ARAB WOMEN

Emotional involvement and realism

Similarly to the findings of scholars who have more recently examined the transnational appeal of Danish serials among British, Japanese, and Turkish audiences,[31] my fieldwork has also shown that emotional realism is one of the most important factors in creating the appeal of Turkish serials. The ability to experience emotional realism has been an essential aspect in the viewing motivations of women viewers of Turkish drama serials. Through complex characterization and close attention to (particularly) female characters' subjective experience and emotions, Turkish serials create a perception of authenticity, and opportunities for heightened emotional realism and identification. In fact, the projection of strong female characters has been a central and essential reason for soap operas[32] and dramas[33] having great appeal. Watching a strong female character is experienced by female Arab viewers as particularly gratifying in a world where a traditional patriarchal system dominates both society and media. Turkish dramas offer female viewers stories of women overcoming challenges that are not limited to domestic life, while also searching for 'Mr Right'. The dramas serve as an outlet for emotional realism and escapism, where women can construe images of a different lifestyle as an imaginary space, against the backdrop of Muslim society. The emphasis on the emotional reality of women, but also the projection of what it means to be a mother, and the emotions that do not get explored because of being a mother in a conservative society, resonates highly with women viewers, as these two interview transcripts illustrate:

> I can't remember the show's name, but my impression is that being a mother is more important than anything else in this world. For Arabic women, there is nothing more important than your children. This aspect of Turkish shows is, for me, very important. (Interview, female Qatari-Palestinian professional, 2017)

> What women might find embarrassing to admit is that as a mother, you like seeing other mothers who also care about their children but also experience love and romance in a non-despicable way or, should I say, in a non-shameful way. (Interview, female Tunisian professional, 2017)

While the role and image of motherhood is changing in Western society and media, in Turkish dramas the position given to mothers largely remains within the traditional framework. Being a mother means being selfless and sacrificing, putting your children and family first. In some ways, one could argue that the projection of conflicts and struggles in Turkish serials reflects how the earthly world is seen in Turkish and Muslim culture. The challenges and suffering of life are seen as investments that are rewarded in the eternal world. Islamic discourse and Turkish culture attribute value to motherhood, elevating it to a sacred rank. Thus the demanding sacrifice expected from the mother becomes meaningful, and seemingly less burdensome.

So, if we summarize the significance of motherhood in Turkish serials, one could argue that it mirrors Islamic and traditional beliefs, where mothers are the guardians of the whole family. Turkish dramas are more relatable to Arab women, who experience emotional realism and fantasy simultaneously, because they not only reaffirm core values and norms about motherhood, but also explore themes of love and romance that are not typically associated with the traditional role of being a mother. Therefore, the depiction of mothers aligning with the women's worldview, as well as the portrayal of passionate romances, make these shows exceptionally appealing to women.

In soap operas and telenovelas of the 1970s, 1980s, and 1990s there were similar embedded ideological discourses that focused on the roles that women have in daily life. Scholars such as Tania Modleski have argued that the majority of soap operas possess narrative structures emphasizing the image of the 'ideal mother', where 'soaps convince women that their highest goal is to see their families united and happy, while consoling them for their inability to bring about familial harmony'.[34] Similarly to Modleski's argument about soap operas, Turkish drama serials appear to function in a rather contradictory manner: while appearing to be liberal and escapist, they simultaneously challenge and reaffirm traditional values, behaviours, and attitudes in a Muslim cultural context. Yet, intriguingly, Turkish dramas are highly appreciated for maintaining these traditional core values. For many viewers, Turkish dramas successfully find a sweet middle way, and offer the best of both worlds—tradition, and relatable contemporaneousness. In contrast, Arab productions are experienced as projecting a dated and undesirable image of women and motherhood; and Western programmes, meanwhile, are seen as dismissing traditional family values, and projecting women impossible to identify with, representing the other extreme. Therefore, the experience of emotional realism appears to be closely linked to the women viewers' pursuit of personal identity.[35] Comparable to the early findings of Livingston, whose focus was on British soap viewers,[36] it seems that Turkish serials enable women viewers to reinforce their personal values, as well as to relate to, and identify with, the stories and characters:

> I think young women like to see stories that give more power to women. I wouldn't maybe say Turkish dramas are liberating, but they offer many relatable stories. They represent a progressive step in the right direction. (Interview, female Qatari postgraduate student, 2017)

> Turkish serials show Arabs themes that are very close to home but that Arab media refuses to deal with because they think it will break our cultural norms. But to be honest, people see them with US shows anyway. Turkish shows make these subjects more appealing because they tell them from our cultural context. (Qatari, university graduate 2017)

It is important to recognize that the increased identification and involvement of viewers is not always solely dependent on cultural similarities, as people automatically respond with empathy to certain situations. Ang's seminal conceptualization of 'emotional realism', which she developed from her study on the transnational appeal of *Dallas*, revealed that, despite viewers' perception that the series' external world was not realistic, they still felt that the series was 'true-to-life'. Ang found that because viewers perceived reality in the characters' subjective experience and feelings, they were able to relate to them.[37] In the case of Arab women, while similar experiences have been described, what further intensified the women's perception of emotional realism was the shared socio-cultural realities, and the "boundaries" that were set for women, irrespective of how liberal and glamorous the lives of the female characters in Turkish dramas may appear. A similar experience is described by one female viewer:

> Turkish soaps are very emotionally charged. The feelings are often presented in such a way that it becomes so real, irrespective of how glamorous or how different their worlds are, their boundaries are similar. (Interview, female Tunisian professional, 2017)

In summary, the emotional realism in Turkish shows was greatly heightened by two important factors: firstly, through cultural proximity; and secondly, by reflecting emotions and situations that are not portrayed in Arab media and society. However, realism in itself was not seen by women viewers as a gratifying viewing experience, with many noting that realism in Arab shows was actually rather depressing. The portrayal of contemporary revolutions (the Arab Uprisings), war, and poverty were seen as unappealing, as these were realities that they already found themselves experiencing, and they did not want to see them depicted in a television serial. Ultimately, for the majority of women, Turkish serials were seen as extremely successful in drawing their viewers into the emotional world of the characters. The viewers' ability to relate to and identify with these emotional worlds was one of their most consistent motives for watching.

Turkish serials as a vehicle for engaging with Turkish modernity

Over the past decade, especially for women audiences, Turkish serials have become an established part of daily viewing. One of the most noticeable reasons for this, particularly among women viewers in Qatar, has been a desire to experience modernity. Watching Turkish serials, it seems, enables viewers to enter a world that feels familiar yet is distant enough to experience new cultural trends and the Turkish understanding of modernity. Earlier scholarly research on the soap opera genre and its viewers' motivations identified the experience and realization of modernity as central to audiences,[38] with consumer culture entrenched in the genre's origins. For instance Ang notes that the prime-time soap opera *Dallas* provided a new symbol for promoting American consumer capitalism via television.[39] At the same time, Geraghty underlines that shows such as *Dynasty* created an aspirational standard for consumer culture by projecting impressive and beautiful locations.[40] Similarly, Turkish serials appear to project a modernity that appeals to the tastes and aspirations of women viewers. While modern experiences can cut across various boundaries and unite people,[41] the appeal of Turkish modernity is that it hits upon a zeitgeist and a sense of shared time and space that is difficult to achieve in Western productions, owing to a lack of socio-cultural similarities. Nonetheless, it is important to stress that this sense of shared time and space is experienced as aspiration and possibility rather than as actual shared lifeworlds, as experienced particularly among Chilean and Israeli viewers (see Chapters 6 and

WHY TURKISH DRAMAS RESONATE WITH ARAB WOMEN

7). Many Arab women viewers interviewed over the years have been entranced by the glitzy lifestyles, beautiful settings, and attractive actors in Turkish drama serials. Women have been drawn to the portrayal of fashion, the make-up, and the hair of Turkish actresses performing in these dramas. For many, changing their hairstyles or make-up to copy the styles of these Turkish actresses, or visiting Türkiye and the prominent places in Istanbul that they had seen on-screen, was like living and consuming for themselves the glamour and urban lifestyle portrayed in these shows. The ability of television serials to function as a vehicle for consumer culture where mass audiences can forge cultural trends is not unique to Turkish dramas;[42] but the fact that this sophisticated lifestyle is set against the backdrop of a Muslim society that is different from anywhere else in the Muslim or Arab world provides Turkish serials with striking visual content. For Arab viewers, the city of Istanbul in particular represents Islamic culture meeting Western style—a true depiction of modernity, set against the backdrop of Istanbul's most desirable locations:

> Istanbul is an amazing city. It has everything from culture to shopping. It feels Western and Middle Eastern at the same time. (Interview, female Qatari, 2017)

> I just love the Bosporus, it is so magical, you can't find that anywhere else in the world ... the city is also fantastic for shopping, we got my sister's wedding dress and invitation cards from there. (Interview, female Qatari, 2017)

Similarly to the importance of the urban lifestyle to viewers of Japanese and Korean cultural products in Asia,[43] the display of urban Istanbul, Türkiye's largest metropolis, is significant in the portrayal of a Western-style modernity. Istanbul projects a uniqueness for viewers, as a place full of possibilities that cannot be replicated anywhere else in the Muslim world. Finally, yet importantly, although my empirical findings have revealed that most study participants have visited Türkiye and Istanbul on multiple occasions, the women's view of Turkish modernity is mostly shaped through images from Turkish dramas—and is in fact, as noted throughout this book, a mediated perception of modernity and everyday life in Türkiye. While this chapter has outlined specific viewing motives, it is necessary to highlight that it is the combination of all these motives that make Turkish drama serials particularly gratifying for women viewers. While some motives might be in dialectical tension with one another, combining all of them creates a unique viewing experience that only Turkish dramas are able to offer.

Conclusion

The overall discussion in this chapter has explored the most prevalent viewing motives among women audiences in Qatar. The need for entertainment has been identified as the most dominant motive. Turkish serials not only allow Arab women to enter a different world, but simultaneously provide comfort by appearing familiar and relatable. The portrayal of courtship and romance, and the ability to touch on subjects and characters that are relatable but deemed taboo in the region, hold a strong appeal. Turkish serials provide a unique level of emotional realism and personal relatability that viewers cannot experience in local, regional, and other international content. Thus, being able to relate, identify, and engage with the emotional world of Turkish characters (particularly female ones) has proved to be an important viewing motive. Turkish dramas resonate with women viewers in an exceptional way, where every word and gesture finds an emotional meaning and drives their pleasure. Despite the existence of patriarchal structures, Turkish dramas are perceived as granting women a position of power, where norms of gender are structured in such a way that women take central roles in issues related to family lives, motherhood, romance, and interpersonal relations.

At this point, I would like to reflect on one of this book's core arguments: Turkish drama's significance as a soft-power tool. Understanding the viewing motives of audiences also allows us to understand better how Turkish dramas became an essential carrier of Turkish soft power. The emotional realism women can experience by watching these programmes in turn appears to create an emotional investment and connection, not only with the serial, its characters, and its storylines, but also with Türkiye, its society, and its culture (see Chapters 3 and 4). Therefore, Turkish drama's ability to create relatable emotional realism can be seen as a core element of how the power of attraction—soft power—functions.[44]

Furthermore, the chapter has also revealed that Arab women audiences' desire to experience Turkish modernity represents an equally strong viewing motive, while the 'Turkishness' projected in serials has been perceived as highly

WHY TURKISH DRAMAS RESONATE WITH ARAB WOMEN

appealing to Arab viewers. Yet one cannot simply understand this as an audience response to Western-style modernity. Instead, the textual appeal of Turkish dramas has, for many viewers, been closely associated with the lifestyle and social relationships of urban contemporary Türkiye. One of the many pleasing elements women experienced from watching Turkish television dramas is the sense of Turkish modernity as something familiar, while still distinct, and seemingly achievable in the Muslim/Arab context; it represents a form of everyday consumerism that is compatible with their lifestyles and with the society they inhabit.

Finally, even though this chapter has identified specific viewing motives, it is imperative to recognize that it is the combination of all the viewing motives that Turkish dramas appear to satisfy that make them particularly appealing to women viewers. Turkish drama serials' ability to satisfy a range of viewing motives simultaneously is what differentiates their appeal from local, regional, and Western productions.

The following two chapters of this book utilize Chile and Israel as case studies to examine Turkish drama serials' appeal for geographically and culturally distant audiences. At the same time, they study the role of Turkish drama serials in creating a positive perception of Türkiye among Chilean and Israeli audiences.

6 Turkish Drama Serials in Chile

In this chapter and the one that follows, I examine the underlying factors facilitating the attraction of Turkish drama serials, produced for a domestic, Muslim-majority audience, to viewers outside the Muslim and Arab world. Using the Chilean audience as a departure point, we will explore how Turkish drama serials became popular among Chilean viewers without Türkiye and Chile sharing any linguistic, ethnic, historical, or religious commonalities. Thus, Chapter 6 attempts to establish whether the appeal of Turkish dramas can be studied beyond the logic of cultural proximity, by focusing on Chilean audiences' engagement with the relevance of the dramas to the viewers' lives and lifeworlds as members of a developing economy located in the Global South—like Türkiye.[1] At the same time, the chapter investigates whether geographically and culturally distant audiences still look for cultural proximity when watching Turkish dramas,[2] and what their viewing motivations are.[3] Furthermore, this chapter explores the role of Turkish drama serials in introducing and shaping audiences' perception of Türkiye. It attempts to establish whether Turkish dramas have been an equally effective soft-power tool among Chilean viewers as they have been among Arab audiences in Qatar (see Chapter 3).

The analysis and discussions in this chapter are drawn from online surveys distributed to Turkish-serial viewers and university students in Chile between winter 2019 and spring 2020,[4] as well as interviews with distribution companies and media executives in Türkiye in 2020, informal conversations with viewers and academics (in all these countries), and news articles (in Turkish, English, and Spanish).

Some of the key findings in this chapter reveal that Turkish serials aided the introduction of Turkish culture and history to a region and its people to

TURKISH DRAMA SERIALS IN CHILE

whom Türkiye was largely unknown. They appear to have positively impacted viewers' perception of what a Muslim country is like, by replacing negative impressions with an understanding of the various proximities between Türkiye and Chile. Chilean viewers have been found to relate to the same topics and themes as Turkish and Arab audiences but also to engage meaningfully with them, regardless of their cultural context.

While I reflect, in this chapter and the one that follows, on Turkish drama serials' role as a tool for soft power, and why Chilean and Israeli audiences watch them, I first need to clarify that the empirical findings examined here and in Chapter 7 do not represent how Turkish serials are generally perceived. One cannot assume that the research participants represent how all viewers in these countries perceive Turkish dramas. As already stated at the start of this book, it would be misguiding to interpret all the empirical results explored in the various chapters as the only possible reflection of the reasons for Turkish serials' appeal to viewers in Qatar, Chile, and Israel. The significance of this research is not so much about the quantitative demographic distribution of the various ways in which Turkish serials are received, but rather the question of why Chilean and Israeli viewers watch Turkish drama serials, and why they generate such appeal. Therefore, it is important to recognize that any empirical findings cannot speak for themselves, but rather should be analysed 'symptomatically'. As Ang has suggested, it is important to:

> search for what is behind the explicitly written, for the presuppositions and accepted attitude concealed within them. In other words, [the comments of viewers] must be regarded as text, as discourse people produce when they want to express or have to account for their own preference for, or aversion to, a ... piece of popular culture.[5]

Ang recommends that this is only possible by reflecting on socially available ideologies and images that illustrate the way in which a television serial (in her case, *Dallas*) acquires its overall meaning. Thus, it is necessary to examine these beliefs and images in audience response, in order to understand their viewing experiences and to unearth what really attracts audiences.

It might be somewhat challenging to attribute the appeal of Turkish serials to one motive or value, but it appears that they present stories that Chilean and Israeli audiences receive as enthusiastically as Turkish and Arab viewers.

However, the popularity of a cultural product is never a unique accomplishment, but rather is dependent on, as well as linked to, the context in which it is consumed.[6] We need to remind ourselves that global audiences—with Turkish, Latin American and Caribbean (LAC), Israeli, and Arab viewers being no exception—have become used to American television content and its production values, style, and pace, as well as its language—although in Chile and the rest of the LAC, foreign television content is traditionally dubbed. Yet dramas made in Türkiye appear to have, in some way or other, appealed in an exceptional manner to audiences in Chile. What started with the sudden and highly unexpected popularity of the drama *Las Mil y Una Noches* (*Binbir Gece/One Thousand and One Nights*, 2006–09, Türkiye: Kanal D) in 2014 transitioned into a significant and far wider development across LAC television markets. By using the audience in Chile as a case study, this chapter attempts to provide an insight into the appeal of Turkish drama serials in the LAC region.

One could argue that the popularity of Turkish television dramas is but one example of how content produced in and for one particular nation has crossed national and cultural borders and discovered audiences globally. The occurrence of travelling television content is not new, having been scrutinized by various scholars in the past.[7] But the Turkish case is the first time that television dramas from a Muslim-majority country have succeeded in attracting audiences across the globe, making our question even more urgent: what is it about Turkish serials that enables them to resonate with Turkish, Arab, Chilean, and Israeli audiences alike?

Latin American and Caribbean relations with Türkiye, past and present

The following section provides a historic overview of Turkish–LAC relations, providing the necessary context for understanding Türkiye's foreign policy in the region, which strategically combines trade, aid, and Turkish dramas. Türkiye's relationship with the LAC region dates back to the second half of the nineteenth century, when several waves of migration from the Ottoman Empire to the LAC occurred, from the 1860s until the end of the First World War.[8] These emigrants from various ethnic and religious backgrounds were collectively called 'Los Turcos', as they all had Ottoman passports.[9] Diplomatic and consular contacts between the Ottoman Empire and some Latin American countries were established at around the same time, with Chile subsequently being the first country in the region to recognize the young Republic of Türkiye.[10]

Until the 1990s, Türkiye's relations with the region had been friendly but largely stagnant,[11] mostly because of geographical distance and differences in foreign-policy priorities. Türkiye's international political, economic, and cultural presence and influence has steadily increased in recent years owing to a multi-directional and multiregional approach.[12] Under the leadership of the Justice and Development Party (Adalet ve Kalkinma Partisi, AKP), Türkiye launched a (so-called) paradigm shift in its foreign policy, which former prime minister and minister of foreign affairs Ahmet Davutoğlu named a 'Multi-Dimensional Foreign Policy'.[13] As discussed in more detail in Chapter 3, prior to the rise of the AKP in 2002, Türkiye's foreign policy, for the most part, moved within parameters that can best be described as Western-leaning and security-orientated. However, by following Davutoğlu's guidelines for foreign policy, Türkiye has since shaped new courses when it comes to international trade relations, while enhancing these new directions with humanitarian and development aid. By no longer viewing itself as a 'bridge' country, but as a central power with a unique geographic and geo-cultural position,[14] Türkiye has been able to generate an increased confidence by identifying with more than one region and culture. That in turn motivated the country to manoeuvre in, and engage with, several regions simultaneously.[15] Therefore, the LAC became another important region with which Türkiye sought to strengthen trade and diplomatic ties.

Visits by various LAC leaders to Türkiye over recent years, along with visits by Turkish officials to the LAC countries, have demonstrated Türkiye's increased prioritization of, and engagement with, the region.[16] President Erdoğan's trip to Chile, Peru, and Ecuador in 2016 as part of an official state visit was the first presence of a Turkish president in Chile in twenty years, while the visits to Peru and Ecuador represented the first ever official visits by any Turkish president to these countries.[17] With the AKP government championing the vision of a new Türkiye, reinforced by a significantly enhanced diplomatic and trade presence on the world stage,[18] Türkiye has signed economic- and trade-cooperation agreements with nineteen countries in the region (Argentina, Bolivia, Brazil, Chile, Colombia, Costa Rica, Cuba, the Dominican Republic, Ecuador, Guatemala, Guyana, Honduras, Jamaica, Mexico, Nicaragua, Paraguay, Peru, Uruguay, and Venezuela).[19]

What made the region particularly attractive to Türkiye was the high economic performance of several countries such as Chile, Brazil, and Mexico, which have joined the emerging-economies league.[20] As international relations professor Kemal Kirişci argues, behind Turkish foreign policy under the AKP government 'lies the rise of a trading state; bearing this in mind will help analysts to understand Turkish foreign policy better in regard to countries in its immediate neighbourhood as well as countries further away'.[21] Thus, LAC countries were offering Türkiye a new market,[22] with a combined population of more than 600 million people,[23] at a time when trade and political relations in the Middle East and the West had become rather unstable.

If we look at the trade volume between Türkiye and the LAC region in more recent years, we can see a significant increase: while Türkiye's trade volume with the LAC was $3.4 billion in 2006, it went on to surpass $9.2 billion by 2017.[24] The bilateral trade volume between Türkiye and Chile in 2018 amounted to almost $767 million, with $386.3 million in exports and $370.6 million in imports.[25]

In 2019, as part of an export master plan that aimed to intensify business and diplomatic engagement in LAC countries, a delegation of Turkish exporters visited Chile to meet with business executives and potential buyers from across the region (including Argentina, Bolivia, Brazil, Colombia, Ecuador, Mexico, Panama, and Uruguay). According to the head of the Turkish Export Assembly, the association accelerated efforts to strengthen the market penetration and market adhesion of exports, and the recognition of Turkish products and culture, by creating new export destinations in the region.[26] At present there are Turkish commercial offices in Argentina, Brazil, Chile, Colombia, Cuba, Ecuador, Mexico, Peru, and Venezuela. Turkish construction companies are working on building projects in Venezuela, and port construction in Ecuador. The $750-million port construction project was signed in Ecuador's capital, Quito, during President Erdoğan's visit to the country in 2016.[27] Türkiye's national carrier, Turkish Airlines, expanded its flight network to Bogotá, Buenos Aires, Caracas, Cancun, Havana, Mexico City, Panama, and São Paulo.[28] In addition, the visa requirement for most LAC countries was cancelled.[29]

Türkiye's relationship with Brazil and Mexico has been elevated to a strategic partnership. Political consultation mechanisms have also been established with seventeen LAC countries (Argentina, Bolivia, Brazil, Chile, Colombia, Costa Rica, Cuba, the Dominican Republic, Ecuador, El Salvador, Guatemala, Guyana, Mexico, Paraguay, Peru, Uruguay, and Venezuela).[30]

However, the interest and attraction hasn't been unidirectional, as the trade engagement of Türkiye with LAC countries has offered equally important benefits to the latter region, balancing the US–China binary, and enabling LAC countries more room to manoeuvre and negotiate with other suitors. Despite Türkiye's close relationship with Venezuela's disputed President Maduro, which is not seen as a favourable alliance (with most Latin American countries opposing Maduro[31]), Türkiye's trade relations in the region still have the potential to shape the geopolitical chessboard.

Moreover, Türkiye has also been increasingly recognized in the region as a development partner, providing humanitarian aid and developmental assistance, predominantly through the involvement of the Turkish International Cooperation and Development Agency (TIKA).[32] TIKA opened its first regional programme-coordination offices in Mexico City in 2015, and in Bogotá in 2016.[33] One could argue that the best way to describe Türkiye's geopolitical ambitions in the LAC is, as *Financial Times* journalists Andres Schipani and Laura Pitel defined it, 'Turkey pushing into' the Global South 'with aid, trade and soaps'.[34]

However, according to scholars such as Ariel Levaggi and Federico Donelli, Türkiye's interest in the Global South peaked during the first decade of AKP rule, when the logic of the trading state and the use of soft-power tools generated a rapid increase in political, economic, and even cultural engagement. For Levaggi and Donelli, domestic issues and the volatility around Türkiye's borders reduced the importance of Latin America on the Turkish political agenda, despite the growth in exports and investments. They argue that the region's low economic relevance, and lack of interest from the Turkish public, slowed engagement. Still, Levaggi and Donelli acknowledge that the Global South will continue to have 'a place in the Turkish foreign policy narrative, for three reasons, each of which is intertwined with domestic politics: the exploitation of anti-western rhetoric by President Erdoğan; the advancement of the domestic security agenda; and the exploration of economic opportunities'.[35]

Türkiye's multidimensional policy paved the way for Turkish drama serials to enter the LAC market

This section explores how the widened scope of Türkiye's foreign policy has created an environment conducive to the entrance of Turkish dramas into the Chilean (and later the LAC) television market, resulting in millions of people across the region watching Turkish dramas. This is similar to what happened in the Middle East and North Africa region (MENA), where diplomatic and trade relationships smoothed the way for Turkish drama serials.

As I have explored in Chapter 1, I should re-emphasize here that many leading media outlets in Türkiye are owned by large conglomerates that have interests in several other industries, such as banking, finance, tourism, automotives, construction, energy, food, and mining. Many of these conglomerates operate in regions where the Turkish government has established trade relationships. At present, over twenty companies are believed to be operating across LAC countries.[36] One could argue that a seductive combination of diplomacy, trade, and aid has created an environment conducive to Turkish serials being picked up by the Chilean channel Mega; and undeniably, conglomerates already operating in the region would have attempted to offer another core product—television serials owned by their channels. It is, however, significant that by the time that Turkish dramas entered Chile in 2014, they were already well known for having achieved enormous success in the Arab world, Balkans, Turkic-speaking countries, Russia, and South Asia. Ultimately, this made it decidedly easier for Turkish companies to market their products in the region; channel executives were at this point buying into a known and highly successful product.

Consequently, the successful penetration of Turkish serials into the LAC television market can, in many ways, also be seen as a by-product of Türkiye's economic success and the country's changing trade and diplomatic policies within the region. Yet the relationship between hard and soft power is complex and interactive, with neither being substitutable nor rigidly complementary. That said, the Turkish government implemented several initiatives to grow Turkish television exports further. For example, in 2015 the Culture and Tourism Ministry, the Economy Ministry, and the Investment Support and Promotion Agency contributed significantly to the introduction of Türkiye and Turkish TV content at MIPCOM (Marché International des Programmes de Communication/International Market of Communications Programmes) where Türkiye was also the 'country of honour' that year. This annual trade show is geared towards the television industry: representatives of television studios and broadcasters utilize the event as a marketplace to buy and sell new programmes and formats for international distribution. Incentive programmes such as this permit a significant part of Turkish TV distributors' marketing and promotion expenses to be met by the Treasury,[37] illustrating the degree to which Turkish serials and foreign policy have become intertwined—supplementing and supporting each other. In most instances, the exercise of one kind of power may enhance the other kind,[38] and this appears to be very much the case for Turkish serials. In other words, Türkiye's hard-power resources have increased the effectiveness of its soft power in the LAC region, and vice versa, as in the Arab world.

Turkish dramas entering Chilean television

This section provides a brief overview of the specific circumstances that led to Turkish serials being purchased by the Chilean channel Mega, a central moment for the arrival of Turkish dramas on the screens of LAC viewers. Telenovelas made in Latin America, which formerly dominated the region, were also hugely successful in Türkiye in the 1980s and 1990s.[39] However, since 2014, the tables appear to have been turned, with LAC audiences now watching drama serials made in Türkiye.

Patricio Hernández of Mega was the television executive responsible for introducing Turkish serials to Chilean audiences. Before joining Mega, Hernández had come across *Las Mil y Una Noches* (*Binbir Bece/One Thousand and One Nights*, 2006–2009, Türkiye: Kanal D) at an industry fair, and instantly thought that a Chilean adaptation of the story would have great potential in the country. When he returned to Chile and pitched the idea to his (then) company, it was rejected, as it was perceived as being very difficult for a Turkish story to succeed in the Chilean market. However, when Hernández joined Mega a year later, he resurrected his initial idea—but this time instead of adapting the script the whole serial was purchased, with the first two seasons almost immediately being dubbed into Spanish. It is also worth noting that when Mega decided to acquire its first Turkish serial it was facing severe financial troubles, being on the verge of bankruptcy. In fact, as scholars such as Barrios et al. have highlighted, financial troubles were then experienced by almost all Chilean television stations, including public channels.[40] The decision to broadcast a serial from a country that was (at the time) relatively unknown in the region was seen as a huge risk.[41] Unexpectedly, *Las Mil y Una Noches* became the most-watched serial in Chile, achieving success and profits that Mega could never have anticipated. In 2014, when it first aired, *Las Mil y Una Noches* achieved higher ratings than the football game between Chile and Brazil.[42]

Following this huge success, other channels started airing Turkish programmes. One of them was the Chilean Channel 13, which, after the conclusion of *Las Mil y Una Noches*, started broadcasting *El Sultán* (*Muhteşem Yüzyil*/*Magnificent Century*, 2011–14, Türkiye: Show TV, Star TV). The fact that *El Sultán* and *Las Mil y Una Noches* had the same lead actor, Halit Ergenç, created an enormous frenzy for the serial, with even fast-food chains like Burger King offering 'Ottoman burgers' at the time.[43] With Turkish serials proving enormously popular with Chilean audiences, other Chilean channels, and those in many other LAC countries, started to acquire Turkish dramas, with the dubbing being undertaken in Chile. Mega, having been the first channel to purchase Turkish dramas, subsequently obtained the rights to distribute many Turkish serials in the region, generating another income stream for the broadcaster.[44] Despite the cost of dubbing, Turkish serials have been far more economical for Mega than producing its own content. In fact, the domestic and regional success of Turkish serials has contributed to Mega becoming the most commercially successful channel in the country. At present, of all the LAC countries, Chile still broadcasts the greatest number of Turkish dramas, and has become the distribution hub for Turkish serials in the region.[45] They are widely known as 'telenovelas Turcas' to distinguish them from national and regional telenovelas.

Similarly to the phenomenon in the Arab world, where the Syrian colloquial dialect became almost the standard for Arabic dubbing, resulting in a new industry for Syria, the dubbing of Turkish dramas into Spanish in Chile has contributed to Chile becoming the dubbing centre for Turkish programmes.[46] The Chilean dubbing house Dinte was responsible for dubbing the first Turkish drama serial into Spanish; however, with the increasing demand for Turkish content, many other companies have sought to benefit.[47]

Turkish dramas have become so popular among LAC viewers in recent years that they earned the Turkish drama *Amor Eterno* (*Kara Sevda/Endless Love*, 2015–17, Türkiye: Star TV) an International Emmy Award in 2017, in the category of Best Telenovela.[48] It is worth noting that it was the first time that an award of this kind had been received by a Turkish production. Furthermore, owing to the massive success of Turkish serials in the LAC region, in 2018 the Peruvian Channel 2 (Latina Televisión) initiated the Latin Turkish Awards, voted for by viewers across the region.[49] What started as an experiment in Chile has turned into a phenomenon in the so-called cradle of telenovelas, with 'telenovelas Turcas' outperforming national and regional content in terms of popularity, despite telenovelas made in Latin America having previously dominated the region and beyond.

This engagement with Turkish dramas appears to have had another rather unexpected consequence. There have been media reports that the popularity of Turkish dramas, particularly in Chile, has contributed to parents naming their newborn children after protagonists in their favourite serials.[50] According to official state records, numerous Chilean girls born in 2016 were named Elif, a traditional Turkish name which overtook even widely popular names such as Veronica.[51] *Elif* (2014–19, Türkiye: Kanal 7) is a serial featuring a child protagonist of this name and telling the story of an abandoned girl. The serial has become the longest-running foreign drama to air on Chilean television, even surpassing the Colombian telenovela *Yo Soy Betty, La Fea* (*I am Betty, the Ugly One*, 24Horas, 2019; TVN, 2018). It is important to note that, unlike most Turkish drama serials exported internationally, *Elif* was not aired in Türkiye by a mainstream channel but rather on Kanal 7. Kanal 7, since its establishment in 1995, has been known for broadcasting Islamic content. This television drama was therefore produced for a distinctly conservative Islamic audience—making the fact that it resonated with Chilean viewers even more fascinating.

However, despite the successful and positive reception of Turkish dramas in Chile and other LAC countries, Turkish serials have also been criticized for projecting misogyny, macho behaviour, and violence against women. A Cuban journalist noted that, while he believed that Cuban audiences were enjoying Turkish serials with a critical distance, he was still worried that they might revive misogynistic and violent attitudes towards women.[52]

Findings

The following section first examines the empirical findings that reveal the role of Turkish dramas in introducing Türkiye to a geographically distant country, and their role as a soft-power tool. It then looks at viewing motivations and the reasons behind the appeal of Turkish drama serials to Chilean audiences. The responses are organized by themes that became apparent during the data analysis.

Turkish dramas introduced Chilean audiences to Türkiye

In order first to establish the importance of Turkish serials as a soft-power tool, all research participants were asked what level of knowledge they'd of Türkiye and its culture prior to watching Turkish dramas. The overwhelming majority answered that they had known close to nothing about Türkiye beforehand. Participants were also asked what they thought about Türkiye after watching drama serials: the survey participants were asked to respond in their own words. An overwhelming majority stated that they had a very favourable opinion of Türkiye. The country was often described as 'beautiful', 'modern', and a country that, 'despite being Muslim', had many perceived cultural similarities with Chile and the region. Female respondents were particularly impressed by the attractiveness of Turkish people and the Turkish lifestyle, which for many was seen as realistic and original. Owing to Türkiye being mainly unknown to Chilean viewers, the way daily life is projected in its dramas was perceived as a realistic depiction of the country and people's everyday lives. The fact that most Turkish dramas are being filmed in actual locations and real homes instead of in studios (as has often been the case in regional telenovelas) further elevated the audience's experience:

> I imagine that it must be nice living in Türkiye. Istanbul looks impressive. I haven't seen any other places like it. (Female viewer, 2020)

Participants who stated that they knew little about Türkiye before watching Turkish dramas were also asked whether Turkish serials had changed their perception of the country, to which all answered 'yes'. Participants then were also asked to elaborate on how their perceptions had changed. These respondents claimed that after watching Turkish serials, they realized that Türkiye was a beautiful country with many perceived cultural and ethnic similarities to Chile and the region. Most participants expressed a strong desire to visit and experience the locations they had seen in Turkish serials. The following two survey answers adequately summarize the overall response of most participants:

> Türkiye seems like a beautiful place. Men and women are very attractive and natural-looking. I love that people live close to the water. The architecture is very different to what we are used to seeing. I am hoping to visit Istanbul once the pandemic is over. (Female viewer, 2020)

> I knew Türkiye was Muslim, and I guess I thought it would be like Afghanistan or Saudi Arabia. I didn't realise that it was very modern and Mediterranean. I also didn't know that Turkish people are good-looking and had a Western and modern lifestyle. (Male viewer, 2020)

Participant responses clearly show that Turkish dramas contribute to a positive impression of the country—one that has the potential to generate an affirmative bias towards Türkiye, but also the prospect of changing the negative perception of Muslim countries as a whole. As the second response highlights, for many Chilean research participants, Türkiye, a Muslim-majority country, was imagined to be similar to countries such as Afghanistan or Saudi Arabia. Research participants primarily expressed an orientalist perception of Türkiye before watching these serials. For many, Türkiye was envisioned as 'backwards'. However, after watching Turkish dramas, this view was replaced by the perception of the country as a 'beautiful' and 'modern' nation. The fact that many Turkish dramas project glamorized versions of everyday life and often focus on the most desirable locations in Istanbul seems to have a powerful impact on the audiences' perception of Türkiye and Muslim societies. As scholars in the field have argued, products of popular culture can have critical importance in facilitating the construction and shaping of a country's image.[53] Turkish drama serials appear to have succeeded in adding colour, detail, and richness to the Chilean audience's imaginings of what Türkiye is like. Therefore, Turkish dramas have not only managed to introduce audiences to Türkiye and its culture: but, as Anholt stressed, cultural products—in this case, television dramas—can introduce people to a nation 'almost as well as if they'd been there'; or 'better, in fact, because the picture that's painted is often a little idealized, and all the more magical for being intangible and incomplete'.[54]

As argued throughout this book, although the appeal of Turkish serials in Chile and other LAC countries should not be seen as having the ability to influence foreign policy (as attraction does not equate to power), it should be re-emphasized that soft power reveals itself qualitatively in the shift of popular opinion, rather than quantitatively. One could argue that, perhaps, some concrete quantitative results can be found in the significant increase in visitors from LAC countries to Türkiye,[55] although the elimination of visa requirements for most countries in the region might also have influenced visitor numbers. However, as the empirical findings in this chapter reveal, the most significant tangible quantitative impact is the desire of viewers to travel to Türkiye and experience on a personal level the positive impressions they have gained through Turkish drama serials.

As already acknowledged in Chapter 3, both popular and high culture can significantly shape people's perception of a country and act as a crucial soft-power source. Joseph Nye has defined culture as 'the set of values and practices that create meaning for a society that has many manifestations'.[56] A nation's culture can be understood as a blend of things such as image, reputation, and national brand, evolved from its history, traditions, religion, values, arts, and contributions to the global community. The popular culture of a country is its music, cinema, television, other forms of art, and implicit cultural attributes.[57] According to scholars in the field,[58] popular culture specifically can hold critical importance in facilitating the construction and shaping of a nation's image. Popular culture offers the ability to generate a cultivation effect in the intended audience through the exposure to the values and messages embedded in it, which in turn can function as a tool for soft power. Hollywood is considered a prime example of a cultural industry that has effectively cultivated desirable perspectives on US positions and values in the world,[59] while the idea of 'the American dream' is another significant example of US soft power, and became familiar to people across the world through popular culture.[60] Hollywood is also seen as having played a pivotal role in influencing the global perception of other cultures, such as negative opinions of Muslims and Arabs.[61] In this context, one could argue that the soft power Turkish dramas are projecting is beneficial to Türkiye, and, more broadly, aids in creating a desirable image of Muslims that is rarely portrayed, challenging Western stereotypes. A 2021 report by the Annenberg Inclusion Initiative revealed that not only are Muslims nearly absent from episodic content, but they are still negatively stereotyped on television and in streaming content in the US, the UK, Australia, and New Zealand.[62]

Turkish drama serials thus introduce a more attractive and idealized version of Turkishness because most serials are filmed in upscale neighbourhoods, accessorized with the scenery of the Bosporus. They become central in fostering and forming a positive image of a Muslim country, culture, and society in a culturally and geographically distant region:

> I never thought that a telenovela from a Muslim country like Türkiye would be so good. I think most Turkish telenovelas don't look like they are from a Muslim country. My family is originally from Italy, and Turkish serials remind me of the Mediterranean life, which I enjoy seeing. (Female viewer, 2020)

With Turkish dramas having become a permanent fixture on Chilean and other LAC countries' screens, they have the potential to foster a long-term relationship with the region which, according to scholars in the field, is an essential component of successful public diplomacy.[63]

Nonetheless, and as argued earlier, the impact of Turkish drama serials as a soft-power tool might be difficult to measure. Yet if we look at the topic through the lens of cultivation theory, which suggests that 'the more people watch television [or any other form of media content], the more they tend to think that the real world resembles' what they see on-screen,[64] the exposure to Turkish drama serials over time is likely not only to further cultivate a desirable Turkish image but also to create an affinity for and familiarity with Türkiye in Chile and the rest of the LAC region. As scholars such as Press-Barnathan have argued, popular culture can shape 'the background knowledge of people, domestically and internationally', and prepare 'a hospitable emotional environment for certain actions, which turns popular culture into a potentially attractive soft power tool'.[65] At the same time, the consumption of a particular country's cultural products might result in the adoption of their culture, which could ultimately shape a country's cultural market and regional discourse, along with its idea of modernity, the world, the international system, and so forth.

Perhaps an example of this likely development can be found not only in the growing volume of Turkish content on LAC television, but also in the ongoing adaptations of famous Turkish drama scripts by television networks in the region. For instance, in 2020 the Mexican television giant Televisa acquired five Turkish drama scripts in order to produce adaptations. The first was *Black Money Love* (*Kara Para Aşk*, 2014–15, Türkiye: ATV) which was transformed into *Imperio de Mentiras* (*Empire of Lies*, 2020–21, Mexico: Las Estrellas), while the second adaptation was *Queen of the Night* (*Gecenin Kraliçesi*, 2016, Türkiye: Star TV), broadcast under the title *Te Acuerdas de Mí* (*I've Known You All My Life*, 18 January–3 May 2021, Mexico: Las Estrellas). Both adaptations managed to reach large audiences in both Mexico and the USA, and these are just two such examples. Given Turkish dramas' growing presence in the region, one could argue that they have a strong potential for becoming a lasting and effective mode of soft power that holds critical importance in facilitating the construction and moulding of a desirable Turkish image abroad.

Finally, the empirical data for this chapter also revealed that one of the key elements behind the appeal of Turkish drama serials to Chilean audiences, and perhaps its greatest soft power, is their ability to project a realistic-seeming modern society that still cares for traditional values and morality. The projection of a contemporary urban lifestyle and social mobility is displayed against the backdrop of Türkiye's most populous city, Istanbul, which, as one of the most inspiring metropolises, holds strong appeal.

Irrespective of how effective Turkish serials are as a soft-power tool, one thing that can be said for certain is that they have managed to enter the homes of millions of people across the LAC region. They have ignited a desire to visit Türkiye among LAC viewers, to experience for themselves what they see on the screen, while also blurring the difference between geographical proximity and distance.

Turkish serials and younger Chilean audiences

To establish whether Turkish dramas' lack of appeal to university-age individuals is limited only to young people in Qatar, I also surveyed young people in Chile. The findings have revealed that, similarly to the empirical data established for Arab audiences, Turkish serials do not appear to resonate with young Chileans as much as they do with their parents' and grandparents' generations. For the majority of young respondents, Turkish serials were not criticized for their low production values or bad acting, but were rather viewed as a genre that simply did not resonate. As with young people in Qatar, young Chileans predominantly perceived Turkish serials as a women's genre. The most common responses were that Turkish serials were 'too dramatic', 'too slow', or placed too great an emphasis on romance. For many, while these elements were seen as attributes that did not appeal to them, they were highlighted as important aspects attracting avid Turkish-serial viewers. There were also some significant similarities between the responses of young survey participants and regular viewers. The same holds true for young people surveyed in Israel, which I will reflect on in Chapter 7.

Most young Chilean respondents claimed that they rarely, if ever, watched Turkish programmes. The majority of university students surveyed stated that their mothers, older sisters, aunts, and grandmothers were regular viewers. Yet despite the vast majority of university students claiming either that they were not viewers, or that they watched Turkish serials only rarely, the majority indicated that they had watched *Las Mil y Una Noches*, while the next most-watched serials were *El Sultán*, *Elif* and *¿Qué Culpa tiene Fatmagül?*. Most notably, there was a significant similarity between the responses of students and those given by avid viewers. Again, in much the same way as I observed among audiences in Qatar and Israel, it appears that although young people are largely passive audiences, owing to Turkish shows being watched regularly by female relatives in the household, they were still able to provide similar answers to those of regular viewers when questioned about why they are so popular. The most telling differences between the two groups was that the open-ended questions were answered by serial viewers in greater detail, and were often more than a paragraph long, while the majority of university students only responded with one or two sentences. Furthermore, university students could only name one or two serials, while regular viewers could name an average of four to five.

Entertainment is the most important motive for viewing Turkish dramas

While entertainment has been identified as the most crucial viewing motive among Chilean viewers, it is essential to underline that entertainment is not something that viewers experience in isolation. The Chilean audience responses uncovered several individual motives that, in combination, appear to contribute to the positive reception of Turkish dramas. That said, entertainment was stressed by most Chilean viewers as a primary motive, as the responses by these viewers clearly articulate:

> It was my wife who started watching Turkish telenovelas, and now we watch them together in the evening when I return from work. They are relaxing to watch. We both like them a lot because the stories are new and not repetitive, and we love the places they show in the telenovelas. (Male viewer, 2020)

> I watch Turkish telenovelas because they are entertaining. I can focus on something else and take my mind off things. (Female viewer, 2019)

Scholars such as Ang have associated entertainment with pleasure,[66] and perhaps the most pressing question is: how do Turkish dramas produce pleasure among Chilean audiences? What is it about Turkish dramas that make them at times more pleasurable than national and regional content? For Spence, pleasure in the context of watching soap operas 'implies the simple possibility of a need met'.[67] This poses another question: what 'needs' do Turkish dramas meet for Chilean audiences? Perhaps a possible way of understanding the appeal of Turkish dramas to Chilean audiences is to draw, like Ang, on the Marxist idea which states:

> Because the production of culture is subject to the laws of the capitalist economy, cultural products are degraded into commodities to make as much profit as possible on the market. The capitalist market economy is only interested in the production of surplus value and as such is indifferent to the specific characteristics of goods: caring only that they are sold and consumed.[68]

This argument certainly holds true for the Turkish television market. As explored in Chapter 1, the viewership figures of a serial determine its longevity on screens, which equates to profitable advertising revenue for the television channel. However, at this point a variation on our question arises: how can Turkish serials, produced predominantly with the domestic market in mind, be entertaining and pleasurable to viewers in Chile?

As noted above, *Las Mil y Una Noches*, which aired in Türkiye between 2006 and 2009, was the first to become immensely popular in Chile, in

2014. The serial was produced at a time when Turkish producers were not aware of, or even remotely considering, international audiences. Even now, when producing serials for television, the priority is first to be successful in the domestic market (see Chapter 1). Of course, given the international success of Turkish serials in the last decade, an international audience will always be at the backs of the minds of production companies and media executives;[69] but to sell a programme internationally, it has first to be successful among Turkish television audiences before LAC TV stations will be interested in acquiring it. With broadcast and cable/satellite TV still dominating the media landscape in the region,[70] dramas that have not been tested on Turkish television are seen as too risky to be purchased by LAC channels. This takes us back to our core question: how do we explain why Turkish serials produced for a Muslim-majority country are entertaining and pleasurable to a foreign and non-Muslim audience? The findings in the next section demonstrate that experiencing entertainment and pleasure is only possible due to Chilean viewers' ability to engage meaningfully with Turkish drama serials. As Straubhaar previously argued, media choice occurs in a dynamic 'tension with other motives and attractions'.[71] Therefore, rather than establishing one aspect or motive as the key attraction of Turkish dramas, the findings in this book show that it is the combination of multiple factors that formulates Turkish drama's unique attraction to Chilean, Arab, and Israeli audiences.

The importance of perceived ethnic similarities

Most Chilean audience responses revealed that perceived ethnic similarities have been fundamental in the appeal of Turkish dramas, allowing them to feature on Chilean screens without being experienced as content from a distant unknown country. Most Chilean viewers noted that the similar appearance of Turkish actors and actresses to people in Latin America was a significant aspect of their attraction. Perceived ethnic similarities, in combination with dubbing into the Chilean dialect by Chilean voice actors, seem to have geo-localized Turkish serials and contributed to their overall positive reception. The response below from one female viewer highlights that Turkish dramas appear to have had a relatively seamless entry into Chilean television. Most viewers noted that they did not realize initially that the serial they were watching was from Türkiye and not from their own region.

> The first Turkish telenovela I watched was with my mum and both of us didn't know it was from Türkiye. We thought it was very nice and entertaining but never thought it was from a different country. (Female viewer, 2019)

Similar experiences and observations were shared by media executives working at production and distribution companies dealing with the LAC market, with ethnic similarities seen as an important factor in Turkish drama serials' success in the LAC region:

> My first take on Turkish dramas was that when I saw the first one, that I didn't know it was Turkish if that. You know they have this Latin look very similar to the look of many people in Latin America. The actors don't look very foreign to us. (Interview, 2020)

> Latin people look very similar to Turkish people. I remember in my youth when Latin telenovelas were popular in Türkiye, people here also felt that they were similar to us, and now it is basically the same thing but the other way around. (Interview, 2020)

As these responses by industry professionals and audiences show, similarities in appearance between Turks and Latin Americans have been a pivotal factor that has drawn Chilean viewers to Turkish dramas. The discovery of other proximities appears to have occurred later and also become part of the viewing experience.

The acceptance and attraction of dubbed Turkish dramas contrasts with the idea of 'cultural discount'. Cultural discount suggests that a foreign programme loses some of its value when it does not translate well into the local culture of the new market because audiences do not fully understand the settings, institutions, cultural values, and everyday life depicted. Taken together, this causes the viewers to identify less with a foreign programme. Yet, in the case of Chilean viewers, perceived ethnic similarities, in combination with dubbing, appear to have aided in bringing Türkiye and its culture closer—helping audiences discover the many similarities between them.[72]

The interplay between value proximity, thematic proximity, and similar lifeworlds

The representation of conservative values in Turkish drama serials was also mentioned by viewers as a critical factor in their appeal, while the importance given to family values was seen as highly engaging. As these two responses by female viewers reveal, Turkish dramas' depiction of several generations living together and caring for one another becomes relatable because it has significant value in proximity.

> I love that people in Turkish telenovelas live in these big mansions with large families. Like us, you get a sense that family is important; parents, grandparents, uncle and aunts are important. (Female viewer, 2019)

> Turkish culture also cares about mothers and the importance of family … I love how modern homes and their fashion looks and how traditional they are. (Female viewer, 2020)

Turkish serials' ability to project both modernity and tradition has been seen as creating an exceptionally gratifying viewing experience. Similarly to audience responses, an Istanbul-based executive director at one of Türkiye's largest conglomerates stated that, despite cultural commonalities being discovered 'accidentally', the importance given to family has resonated exceptionally with Latin American audiences. For him, positioning 'the concept of family at the heart of the content had great results' (Interview, 2020). Furthermore, according to one director at a Turkish production company, shared sensibilities and cultural commonalities between Türkiye and Latin America were pivotal to the appeal of Turkish dramas:

> Latin American audiences have a lot in common with Turkish audiences in terms of sensibilities. Unlike most of the Western world, Latin audiences value family, honour, and most of all love; like Turkish people, they also live emotions intensely. (Interview, 2020)

Intriguingly, Chilean audiences' responses also demonstrated that they primarily attributed their textual engagement with Turkish dramas to the logic of culture, where closeness exceeded the experience of distance. One could argue that shared values and parallel socio-economic realities in countries outside of the Western world, and their projection in Turkish dramas, appear to have hit upon a zeitgeist that resonates with Chileans as much as with Arab viewers. Turkish dramas are found to offer a unique balance between conservatism and Western-style modernity, despite the stories being grounded in the values and moralities of a Muslim-majority country. One could argue that because Turkish dramas do not show religion overtly, but almost always have stories that follow a conservative framework, the dramas become extremely shareable with viewers in what is a predominantly Catholic society. Therefore, regardless of differences in faith, if stories portray common values and themes, they can become transferable across cultures, and able to flow across cultural boundaries.[73]

This idea has parallels with Singhal and Udornpim's argument, which highlights the importance of shared values and themes that address and attract audiences across cultures,[74] while also offering similarities with Larkin's research that examined the popularity of Indian films among Nigerian viewers and the audience experience of a 'parallel modernity'.[75] However, it should be stressed that even Straubhaar, who has been widely credited with the elaboration of the concept of cultural proximity,[76] in his later work argued that cultural proximity should not been seen as an 'essential quality of culture or audience orientation but rather as a shifting phenomenon in dialectic relations to other cultural forces'.[77] Straubhaar summarized these other forces as being genre proximity, cultural shareability, value proximity, and thematic proximity. Genre proximity refers to familiarity with specific genres and their form of storytelling. This type of proximity is particularly relevant to Chilean and LAC audiences, as telenovelas have traditionally been the most popular genre on regional television. Value proximity refers to common values, such as moral codes. Thematic proximity relates to issues and topics, like the drive for upward mobility, or the struggle between modernity and tradition, often explored in Turkish dramas and found to resonate in an exceptional way with Chilean viewers. Shareability refers to shared values, images, archetypes, and themes across cultures, enabling cultural products to appeal beyond cultural boundaries.[78]

For the president and CEO of one Istanbul-based production and distribution company, the success of Turkish serials in the LAC region rests on the fact that Türkiye is a blend of many different cultures, allowing audiences to find something that appeals to them:

> Turkish culture has been influenced from different cultures for centuries geographically. We are in the middle of everything. We have very close connections with the middle Asian culture, Arabic culture, and on the other side, the European culture, so our culture has been influenced from everywhere. That's why our products [serials] … I mean, wherever it goes people can find something that they feel like belongs to them. (Interview, November 2020)

While one could argue that Türkiye's multilayered cultural identity enables Chilean audiences to discover and create a sense of cultural proximity with the Turkish culture despite being geographically distant, the projection of certain specific topics (thematic proximity) in Turkish serials—such as people moving to big cities from more conservative smaller communities, and all the struggles individuals and families face while trying to adapt—do appear to resonate deeply, as this Chilean respondent notes:

> I like that they focus on issues that impact people. The struggles living in a big city and all the things that felt better when we were growing up … we used to have a closer community rather than anonymity in a big city. (Male viewer, 2020)

It is important to recognize that Türkiye and Chile, but also the LAC region at large, have been economically unstable, and have encountered various domestic issues; therefore, the thematic proximity of Turkish dramas, and their relevance to Chilean viewers, is perhaps not coincidental but could be seen as a result of their socio-economic similarities.

> I miss the old telenovelas; they had innocent love stories and happy endings. It was the rich against the poor. Now people watch Turkish telenovelas because you get everything. (Female viewer, 2020)

As this female viewer describes it, Chilean audiences miss traditional telenovelas that show rags to riches stories, characters they can dream with and relate to, depicting their inner aspirations for a better life. One could argue that what made 1990s Mexican telenovelas such as *Marimar* (January–August

1994, Mexico: Televisa) and *Maria la del Barrio* (August 1995–April 1996, Mexico: Televisa) so successful, not only among LAC audiences but also across the globe including Türkiye, was that they followed this formula. Thus, Turkish drama serials that focus on social mobility, set against the backdrop of a modern-day fairy tale—where the Cinderella story receives, at times, a contemporary twist, but core conservative values remain preserved—resonate highly with Chilean viewers.

The response below from one male viewer not only summarizes the perspective offered by most serial viewers, but also demonstrates that audiences are looking for telenovelas that deal with everyday struggles while maintaining traditional values:

> In Latin America, we all grow up watching telenovelas, but they become lousy quality. The stories are never new. They show things that are not good for our society. They should show the lives and problems of real people. (Male viewer, 2019)

Arguably, the fact that both countries are part of the Global South, on the verge of industrialization, and faced with an inevitable shift from traditional to secular rational values seems to create anxieties that Turkish drama serials satisfy in a surprising manner:

> I like that Turkish telenovelas mention God and that there is a lot of romance without sex and nudity. (Female viewer, 2020)

> Turkish telenovelas are watched by many in Latin America because we are tired of shows that have poor quality and do not reflect our core values. (Female viewer, 2020)

Furthermore, *Elif* was one of the dramas that a vast majority of research participants either watched or mentioned in their responses. Unlike most dramas that have been sold internationally, *Elif* is a daytime serial that tells the story of a young girl of the same name. She becomes a foster child, placed in the care of her biological father's household, with the drama portraying the challenges she faces, including mistreatment from her biological father's wife, and the protective intervention of the housekeeper, Ayşe. Elif's struggles reveal issues related to child welfare, particularly the vulnerability of children in foster care and the potential for abuse by caregivers. The fact that *Elif* raises significant social and cultural issues has struck a chord, especially with female viewers. The presence of Ayşe as a protective figure in the girl's life goes on to highlight power and class dynamics, with the poor portrayed as caring and the rich as ruthless and cruel.

> Elif was one of the telenovelas that most of my friends and I watched. I was deeply affected by the cruelty shown towards this little girl. As a woman and a mother, it had a significant impact on me because you always worry about what will happen to your child if you die early. (Female viewer, 2020)

Themes dealing with decaying values, where the rich hold sway and the poor are mistreated, where the vulnerable are left to fend for themselves, and where crony capitalism reigns supreme, seem to resonate not only with Turkish and Arab audiences but also with Chilean viewers. This may explain why *¿Qué Culpa tiene Fatmagül?* (*Fatmagül'ün Suçu Ne?*, 2010–12, Türkiye: Kanal D) has become one of the most watched serials, and has been identified as the most popular among study participants in this book. Chilean viewers appear particularly drawn to the portrayal of power imbalances where the rich and powerful are above the law, and the poor are seemingly helpless. This theme resonates with Chilean viewers, given their country's experience with social inequality and political corruption. Therefore, it is perhaps unsurprising that dramas like *Fatmagül* and *Elif* have found a receptive audience in Chile, as they address issues that connect deeply with the lived experiences of the viewers.

> My favourite Turkish telenovela is *¿Qué Culpa tiene Fatmagül?*. I think it shows so many things that are wrong in our society. If you are rich, you rule the world. (Female viewer, 2020)

As scholars such as Inglehart and Baker note, 'economic development seems to have a powerful impact on cultural values: the value systems of rich countries differ systematically from those of developing countries'.[79] The struggle to maintain conservative values while also fighting to become successful within a capitalistic society, where the importance of material goods increasingly outweighs the value of human virtue, is a reality that resonates with Chilean audiences as much as with Turkish.

Thus, perhaps another way to understand the appeal of Turkish-serial values in Chile is to look at this question from the perspective of similar lifeworlds.

The lifeworld concept allows the consideration of viewers within a particular time–space stratification, while combining factors such as cultural practices, age, gender, or the education and intersectionality of the individual and their lifeworld. At the same time, it pays attention to the perceived reality experienced from the individual's perspective; it comprises one's experience of the world, and its material and interactional manifestations with intersubjective ideas, knowledge, norms, and values, which in turn aid in the sense-making process and individual agency. Scholars such as Neumann and Charlton stressed the importance of more permanent influences such as gender roles, but they also referred to themes that are dependent on life phases (such as becoming a parent, suffering illness, or coming of age) as trans-situational themes.[80] These are believed to steer one's social actions and guide media choices and consumption. Consequently, audiences are moved to select and consume content, influenced by and based on trans-situational contexts that become action-guiding. Chilean viewers' attraction to Turkish dramas can be understood as representing an interplay between parallel lifeworlds and cultural proximity, where value and thematic proximity hold significant positions. The role of mothers as protectors of the family resonates strongly with Chilean viewers, while the following examples demonstrate how Turkish drama serials are experienced as highly meaningful, with core values seen as under threat owing to the way they are depicted in regionally produced content.

> I think Latin telenovelas are losing their way by competing with American programmes. Turkish telenovelas always focus on real problems, on families and mothers. Telenovelas these days focus on unrealistic and repetitive stories. (Female viewer, 2020)

> I don't want to see sex, drugs and criminality. There are so many other things to show. Turkish telenovelas show traditional things that are important to many people like me. We are moving away from our Christian values. People don't like to watch telenovelas that promote ill behaviour. (Female viewer, 2019)

> It is nice to see these beautiful homes in Türkiye and women with trendy clothes and nice cars, but then you have all these traditions they maintain. It is fascinating how Turkish telenovelas can be both, and I think that is what makes them so popular. (Male viewer, 2019)

TURKISH DRAMA SERIALS IN CHILE

As these audience responses demonstrate, the ability of Turkish drama serials to package traditional values in combination with modernity and an urban lifestyle becomes highly engaging. This seductive mix, placed against the backdrop of Istanbul's most iconic locations, offers Chilean audiences a pleasurable viewing experience.

> I love Istanbul; the city looks fantastic! I am planning to travel to Türkiye as soon as the pandemic is over. It looks very different to places in Latin America. I am particularly looking forward to seeing the big mansions shown in the serials. (Female viewer, 2020)

Once more, these audience responses not only illustrate that common values become imperative in the viewing experience but also that the sensation of difference, or experiencing non-proximity, in geographic, aesthetic, stylistic elements—the aesthetics of the exotic[81]—equally attracts viewers.

The importance of romance

Most Chilean viewers noted that the way Turkish serials project romance, courtship, and the chemistry between male and female protagonists was something that they had been longing for, something that was missing in Latin American telenovelas. For these viewers it seems that rather than seeing the shows' characters acting out their physical attraction through overt and oversexualized behaviour, a far more gratifying viewing experience results from leaving everything to one's imagination through the creation of sexual tension. Similarly, Straubhaar had already described in his book *World Television: From Global to Local* more than a decade ago how women viewers of telenovelas in Brazil were opting for Mexican telenovelas because of their projection of romance, compared with the Brazilian serials which were criticized for their hyper-sexualization.[82] As this viewer describes it, Turkish serials have the ability to create physical chemistry and a spectrum of emotions, through acting and dialogue, that appear to make for very pleasurable viewing:

> Turkish telenovelas have so much passion. The body language, eyes and language is so exciting and romantic that it gets you addicted. (Female viewer, 2020)

Many viewers also noted that in a region where 'narcotelenovelas' proliferate,[83] with stories linked to drug-trafficking or featuring highly erotic content,

TURKISH DRAMA SERIALS

Turkish serials not only offer a way to escape into a different world, but also provide a much-needed alternative for audiences longing for romantic content that places an emphasis on traditional values. However, it would be wrong to misconstrue female viewers' desire for romance and traditional values as nostalgia for times gone by; rather, there is a disconnect between what audiences want to see and what television channels are interested in producing:

> Telenovelas in Chile and Mexico lost their way and forgot what we women enjoy watching … Turkish telenovelas offer you everything that others don't. (Female viewer, October 2020)

> I love the romance in Turkish telenovelas. They are a lot like the telenovelas in the 1980s and 1990s that we grew up with. (Female viewer, 2019)

Research conducted by Martín-Barbero on Latin telenovelas found that they reinforced the logic of the market by becoming increasingly transnational.[84] However, the findings of the present study reveal that these transnational tendencies appear not to resonate with viewers looking for content that projects more traditional values. Similarly, La Pastina and Straubhaar stressed that with audience reception, it is also essential to look at the local culture rather than simply the national culture. They suggest that this is necessary in order 'to see the level of proximity between a variety of television texts and the local viewers'. Therefore, 'even within a country, local viewers may not understand or identify with elements of the "national" culture as projected in national television'.[85]

This argument is undoubtedly helpful in understanding the appeal of Turkish dramas among Chilean viewers. Although Chile is an important emerging market with a young and progressive society, certain social milieus still hold conservative values and Catholic traditions. Regional telenovelas' attempt to become more transnational, and to move away from conventional norms, appears to have left viewers who appreciate these norms disconnected from their own local television dramas. Thus, one could argue that Turkish serials have successfully managed to fill this space and gratify 'needs' left unsatisfied by local and regional content.

Emotional realism

What viewer responses, particularly from female research participants, have revealed is that Turkish dramas' ability to touch on human emotions, often seen as disregarded by local or regional productions, is an important factor attracting viewers. Irrespective of how dramatic or unrealistic storylines in Turkish dramas might appear, for viewers they represent very relatable emotional realities. As Ang similarly found among viewers of *Dallas*, the 'recognition of the tragic structure of feeling, which is felt as "real" and makes sense for the viewer' has been experienced as an important aspect in their attraction.[86] As this serial viewer notes:

> *El Sultán* was the first Turkish telenovela I watched and with that one and others, what I have seen is that they always show situations or people that I have come across before. The two-facedness of people or always having someone that is mean and jealous of your achievements is true and very relatable. (Female viewer, 2020)

According to a director at one of Türkiye's leading production companies, LAC viewers are drawn to characters and stories that they can identify with:

> Stories that resonate with them always have to do with regular characters who struggle with something dramatic or even tragic, so the viewers look for characters and their stories they can empathize with. If they are able to connect and identify with the characters at the core of the stories, they become addicted and carry those series to success. (Interview, 2020)

Like the perspective offered by media professionals, Chilean viewers also stressed that they appreciated Turkish dramas' focus on, and projection of, human emotions, relationships, and characters that audiences can relate to and identify with. This in turn is seen as an important factor allowing viewers to experience pleasure. As a female viewer has described it:

> Turkish telenovelas allow you to escape into a different world that we don't find in Latin America. They are set in beautiful locations, but the issues and people are relatable. (Female viewer, 2020)

The responses of both male and female viewers also reveal that the projection of relatable emotions, in combination with good acting and the use of beautiful locations, has significantly impacted audiences' perception of realism and authenticity. It should be emphasized that emotional realism and authenticity appear to mean more than just credibility for most respondents: authenticity also means referring to, and relating to, the viewers' lifeworlds; they can identify and connect with stories and characters in Turkish dramas. Yet contrary to the emotional realism illustrated by Ang,[87] Chilean viewers of Turkish dramas are not transferring emotions from a distant world that projects the glamorous lifestyle of urban Turks in Istanbul's most prestigious locations into their own realities, but are experiencing the world depicted in these series as being similar to their own. This sense of authenticity and realism is reinforced by ethnic similarities, dubbing, and value and thematic proximity.

The importance of genre and production values

All study participants, whether they were active or passive viewers, agreed that the production values of Turkish serials are a significant aspect of their appeal, along with the attractiveness of actors, locations, lifestyles, and storylines. Turkish serials were perceived as more visually pleasing, having been primarily filmed in actual locations in Istanbul's most picturesque sites, instead of in studios, as it is often common in Latin American telenovelas. The use of real locations appears to have also influenced audiences' experience of authenticity and their mediated perception of what life is like in Türkiye.

> I like the places and homes they show in Turkish telenovelas. Everything looks so beautiful. I imagine it must be nice living in Türkiye. (Male viewer, 2020).

Furthermore, genre has been established as an equally important aspect in the success of Turkish dramas. Latin America is the cradle of telenovelas, with the genre boasting an extensive history in the region. Therefore, it is possible to argue that Turkish serials have resonated well with Chilean audiences because of their familiarity with a similar genre. This genre familiarity, combined with stories new to viewers, higher production values, and characters and locations perceived as more authentic yet also exotic, holds a strong appeal. Turkish drama serials have successfully reshaped and localized regional dramas and telenovelas into a new form of drama that has managed to attract audiences in many parts of the world. Arguably, Turkish serials are successful in Chile and other parts of Latin America not because Turkish serials are 'culturally odourless':[88] they are successful because they manage to combine a variety of elements from Western dramas and Latin American telenovelas, albeit with a Turkish twist, filling a vacuum that Western, local, and regional serials left unfilled.

Conclusion

The empirical data explored in this chapter has revealed that Turkish drama serials have played a pivotal role in establishing a favourable image of Türkiye and its people with Chilean viewers who, prior to watching Turkish dramas, knew little to nothing about Türkiye. After watching Turkish serials, respondents claimed that they realized that Türkiye was a beautiful country with many perceived cultural and ethnic similarities to Chile and the wider region. Most participants expressed a strong desire to visit and experience the locations they had seen in Turkish serials. Turkish dramas have contributed to an overall positive perception of the country that has the potential to generate an affirmative bias towards Türkiye. Although the appeal of Turkish serials in Chile and other LAC countries will not necessarily translate into influence on foreign policy (as attraction does not equate to power), as discussed earlier in the chapter, soft power reveals itself qualitatively in the shift of popular opinion, rather than quantitatively. The discussion in this chapter has indicated, however, that some tangible quantitative results can be found in the significant increase in visitors from LAC countries to Türkiye. But perhaps most importantly, Türkiye is seen in Chile as a desirable country, one that appears to have changed audiences' conceptions of what a distant Muslim country might be like.

> I was stunned to see that a Muslim country is so modern ... I did not know that these telenovelas were Turkish. (Male viewer, 2020)

As this audience response demonstrates, Turkish drama serials have effectively introduced a favourable version of Turkish culture and society to a culturally and geographically distant country. Turkish dramas have become a permanent fixture on Chilean and other LAC countries' screens. They have the serious potential for successfully fostering a long-term relationship with the region, which, according to scholars in the field, is an essential component of successful public diplomacy and soft power.[89] Turkish drama serials appear to take a pivotal role in influencing the negative perception of Muslims that

Western productions have previously established. One could argue that the soft power Turkish dramas are generating is beneficial to Türkiye and, more broadly, aids in creating a desirable image of Muslims that is rarely portrayed, challenging Western stereotypes.

Furthermore, the success of Turkish serials in Chile has not only helped Turkish culture and heritage to be introduced to a people to whom Türkiye was previously totally unfamiliar—it has also contributed to audiences being able to recognize the various proximities with a country that appears (at least at first sight) to be culturally distant. Chilean viewers were able to relate surprisingly easily to the same topics and themes as Turkish audiences, but also to engage meaningfully with them, regardless of their own cultural context. The perceived ethnic similarities between Turkish actors and Chilean viewers were an equally important factor in their appeal. These similarities, in combination with dubbing into the Chilean dialect, significantly contributed to the overall success and acceptance of Turkish serials by Chilean viewers.

For many Chileans, one of the most important appeals of Turkish dramas is the projection of romance and courtship. For many women, seeing lovers not acting on their physical attraction, but instead subtly generating sexual tension, offers a far more gratifying viewing experience than watching oversexualized content.

Despite differences in faith between Türkiye and Chile, audiences experienced significant value proximity—around the importance of family, for instance—which was highly appreciated by viewers. Turkish serials appear to offer Chilean viewers many things that they felt were increasingly lost in their society and no longer portrayed on television screens. Through the packaging of traditional values alongside modernity and an urban lifestyle, displayed against the backdrop of Türkiye's most dramatic locations, a highly pleasurable viewing experience is provided. Finally, the focus on human emotions in Turkish serials is seen as not only authentic and relatable, but also as an important factor in their appeal.

The empirical findings in this chapter have also indicated that Chilean audiences relate to storylines in Turkish dramas in a similar way to audiences in Türkiye, the Arab world, and Israel. This study has established that one of the core factors in audience interest could, to a large degree, relate back to their lifeworlds. Therefore, the attraction of Turkish dramas in Chile could be seen as an interplay between the parallels of lifeworlds and perceived cultural proximity, which make topics such as the importance of traditional values resonate with viewers in both Türkiye and Chile. The way Turkish dramas often reflect contemporary societal realities of emerging countries against the backdrop of a relatable modernity resonates greatly with viewers, and ultimately with their own emotional and societal lifeworlds. The reality that Türkiye and Chile are both rising economies in the Global South, faced with similar socio-economic pressures, in combination with their sharing of moral codes rooted in a conservative worldview (Islam and Catholicism), means that Turkish dramas are experienced not only as entertaining, but also as highly relatable and authentic.

Additionally, the production values of Turkish serials, along with the attractiveness of their actors, lifestyles, and storylines, combine to offer significant pulling power, as does offering a genre familiar to the viewers, but with stories that are new, and characters and locations that are seen as both exotic and appealing. It appears that as long as local productions fail to offer the kinds of telenovelas that audiences are longing for, where innocent romance and human emotions are set in a modern yet traditional society, with authentic characters and storylines, and which allow the viewer to enter a world that is not only highly relatable but is more glamorous or more dramatic than their own, Turkish serials will likely remain popular in the region.

Despite their limitations, the findings presented in this chapter provide a valuable insight into the transnational appeal of Turkish dramas, as well as allowing us to gain an understanding of how Turkish serials have increasingly shaped the LAC television scene and become an important soft-power tool for their country of origin.

The next chapter will examine the Turkish drama serial's appeal to Israeli audiences, and its role as a soft-power tool there.

7
Turkish Drama Serials in Israel

This chapter explores the final case study of this book, examining audience engagement with Turkish television dramas among Israeli viewers. It offers a somewhat different perspective because, unlike the circumstances in which Turkish drama serials penetrated the Arab world (see Chapter 2) and Latin America and the Caribbean (LAC) (see Chapter 6), as Türkiye's multidirectional foreign policy and trade engagement created an environment favourable for Turkish dramas to enter these regions, Turkish serials entered the Israeli television market when diplomatic relationships between the two nations had reached a critical low. However, since the first Turkish drama serial *Menekşe and Halil* (2007–08, Türkiye: Kanal D) aired in Israel in 2011,[1] Turkish dramas have managed to establish a loyal audience base, particularly among female viewers. As a result of the vast popularity of the drama *Bride of Istanbul* (*Istanbullu Gelin*, 2017–19, Türkiye: Star TV) in 2018, Turkish serials began to be picked up by mainstream Israeli broadcasters and streaming platforms. The factors facilitating Turkish drama serials' appeal to Israeli audiences remain an underexplored area, requiring further understanding. This is despite the increased attention from academic researchers[2] and media[3] on the reception of Turkish serials, and the socio-cultural and geopolitical reasons behind their success in former Ottoman territories, Türkiye's regional neighbours—and even in Latin America.

Therefore, to contribute to an evolving phenomenon, this chapter's objective is to examine the underlying factors facilitating the attraction of Turkish serials to viewers in Israel. Similarly to previous chapters, this one explores Israeli audiences' viewing motivations,[4] and examines whether Israeli viewers seek cultural proximity,[5] as do Arab and Chilean audiences when watching Turkish dramas. The chapter investigates whether the Israeli audience's engagement with Turkish drama serials can be understood beyond the theory of cultural proximity/distance, by concentrating on the dramas' relevance to the audience's specific lives and lifeworlds.[6] Finally, we will also examine Turkish serials' role as a soft-power tool by investigating their impact on Israeli audiences' perception of Türkiye, its culture, and its people.

The analysis and discussions in this chapter are drawn from online surveys distributed to Turkish-serial viewers and university students in Israel between winter 2019 and spring 2020,[7] as well as interviews with distribution companies and media executives in Türkiye in 2020, informal conversations with viewers and academics (in all these countries), and news articles (in Turkish, English, and Hebrew).

Turkish–Israeli relations, past and present

The present-day Middle East and North Africa (MENA) region, including the area then known as Palestine, was ruled by the Ottoman Empire until World War I. After that war Palestine was ruled by the British,[8] until the establishment of the state of Israel in 1948. Türkiye was the first Muslim-majority country to recognize the state of Israel, on 28 March 1949, a year after its foundation, with full diplomatic ties between the two nations established soon after.[9] However, despite this gesture, Turkish–Israeli relations remained low-profile to stagnant until the 1990s—even though intelligence and other forms of cooperation existed throughout the low-contact years, from 1950 to 1990.[10]

According to academics such as Özlem Tür, until the 1990s the Turkish–Israeli relationship had been dominated by the Arab–Israeli conflict.[11] Following the 1956 Suez Crisis and the Sinai War, Türkiye downgraded its diplomatic posting in Israel to that of chargé d'affaires, and further downgraded diplomatic relations in 1980 after the passing of the Jerusalem Act in which Israel declared that Jerusalem in its entirety was to be the capital of Israel.[12] The warming of relations between Türkiye and Israel in the 1990s was, according to international relations scholars, a development initiated by the USA, who saw this as a natural alliance, and hoped that the region's only democracies could bolster the USA's policy of containing the 'most troublesome'[13] states in the Middle East (Syria, Iraq, and Iran).[14] Consequently, during the 1990s Turkish–Israeli relations not only became more open, but they also developed in other key areas. As Altunişik argues, the emerging alliance between Türkiye and Israel at the beginning of the 1990s was perceived by many as 'the newest and at the same time the most controversial aspect of Turkish foreign policy in the post-Cold War Middle East'.[15]

The key motives behind Türkiye's alliance with Israel were security concerns and the threat from Türkiye's southern neighbours.[16] For Uzer, Arab hostility towards Türkiye, especially Syria's support of the Kurdistan Workers' Party, and neighbouring Iran's anti-secular policy, combined with Europe's half-hearted attitude towards Türkiye, all contributed to Israel's becoming an important ally. Uzer notes that it is important to recognize that despite Türkiye being a Muslim-majority country, it had a strong tradition of secularism, and favoured Western-orientated policies and identity. This was particularly prevalent among the ruling elites, intellectuals, and civilian and military bureaucracies.[17] These reactions were welcomed by Israel, which saw Syria, Iran, and Iraq as a common threat.[18]

As a symbol of the blossoming Turkish–Israeli relationship, in 1992 Türkiye commemorated the 500th anniversary of the flight of Spanish Jews to the Ottoman Empire, with Israeli president Chaim Herzog paying an unofficial visit to the country. A series of high-profile exchanges between the two countries then followed, including Israeli president Ezer Weizman's visit to the Turkish capital in 1994, and Turkish prime minister Tansu Çiller visiting Israel later that year—the first Turkish head of state ever to visit the country. The Turkish president Süleyman Demirel visited Jerusalem in 1996, not only to demonstrate the formal upgrading of bilateral relations, but also to sign two agreements: one on Military Training and Cooperation, and another on Defence Industrial Cooperation.[19] Throughout the 1990s and early 2000s the Israeli air force was frequently permitted to fly over Türkiye and to train in the country—including several annual exercises conducted between the Israeli and Turkish air forces.

For scholars in the field, the signing of agreements between the two countries not only marked a new era of strategic cooperation, but also contributed to the flourishing trade and tourism sector.[20] Israeli tourists were now flocking to Turkish beaches in large numbers to enjoy holidaying in a Muslim, yet friendly, country.[21] In a similar vein, international relations scholar Şuhnaz Yilmaz argued that, for an Israel trying to survive among a number of extremely hostile neighbours, it was highly beneficial to have an influential Muslim country as an ally, counteracting the state's isolation in the region.[22] Türkiye also offered Israel a lucrative market for the country's weapons industry; and Israel was seen by Türkiye as a reliable source of advanced military technology—which Europe and the USA were also willing to provide, but often with strict conditions attached.

To comprehend the scale of Turkish–Israeli engagement, one needs to understand that at the beginning of the 1990s, Turkish–Israeli trade was almost non-existent; by 1997, however, it had reached a volume of $1.6 billion.[23] Additionally, according to experts in the field, Türkiye was utilizing its enhanced relationship with Israel to seek help from the US Jewish lobby in order to counterbalance the influence of Greek and Armenian lobbies in Congress, who were promoting resolutions to recognize the killing of Armenians by the Ottomans during World War I as acts of genocide.[24]

Turkish–Israeli relations remained positive until late 2008. Türkiye was performing an active role as an intermediary and peace broker, having facilitated and mediated several rounds of proximity peace talks between Israel and Syria in the Turkish capital, Ankara. The negotiating teams had set out a detailed plan for Israel's return of the Golan Heights, seized in June 1967, in return for Syria altering the nature of its collaboration with Iran, and its support of terrorist groups such as Hezbollah and Hamas.[25] Arbell notes that the attendance of Israeli prime minister Ehud Olmert in Ankara on 22 December 2008 was seen as the high point of the sixteen-year partnership between Israel and Türkiye.[26]

However, as Olmert was returning to Israel from Türkiye, he indicated that he would require more time, as elections in Israel were approaching. The continuation of the Turkish-sponsored proximity talks with Syria were put on hold until the election of the next Israeli government. Only a few days after Olmert's return, Israel commenced Operation Cast Lead in Gaza. As a result of the operation (also known in the Muslim world as the Gaza Massacre).[27] Ankara withdrew permission for Israel to deploy its fighter jets from Türkiye.[28]

The incursion by Israeli forces into Gaza had taken Türkiye by surprise, which was notable considering that Turkish leaders had hosted the Israeli prime minister just a week before Operation Cast Lead began. The operation was Israel's most intense in Gaza since conquering the small strip in May 1996, and resulted in an unprecedented number of Palestinian casualties, including civilians.[29]

Sixteen years of Turkish–Israeli bilateral relations were now being profoundly tested. Not only did the operation cause the indefinite postponement of Syrian–Israeli negotiations, but it was also viewed by the governing Justice and Development Party (Adalet ve Kalkinma Partisi, AKP), and by the then prime minister and current president, Erdoğan, as an act of disrespect towards Türkiye. Erdoğan not only criticized the operation but also labelled the Israeli aggression an act against Türkiye's peace efforts, underlining that through this action Israel had slammed the door on diplomacy.[30] Erdoğan went on to become the toughest critic of Israel's military campaign.[31] The Israeli offensive in Gaza also generated waves of anger among the Turkish public, resulting in demonstrations across the country.[32] This was the point at which, on the Turkish side at least, relations took a steep downward turn, characterized by the Turkish government's harsh criticism of Israel and Israeli aggression against Palestine.

The following examples highlight some of the key incidents that have further contributed to the dramatic shift in Turkish–Israeli relations. These include Erdoğan's angry outburst at President Shimon Peres during a panel discussion at the World Economic Forum in Davos in January 2009, telling him, 'When it comes to killing, you know well how to kill'.[33] This clearly demonstrated the significant change in Türkiye's attitude towards its long-time ally. While Erdoğan's reaction at Davos created outrage in Israel, it succeeded in winning him worldwide recognition, particularly in the Arab and Muslim worlds.[34] The drama *Separation: Palestine at Love and War* (*Ayrilik: Aşkta ve Savaşta Filistin*), broadcast in October 2009 on the Turkish state broadcaster TRT1, further revealed the drastic change in the political direction of the Turkish government, along with highlighting the intertwined nature of political ideology and television content. This highly politicized drama illustrated the Turkish government's new standpoint towards Israel and the Palestine issue, contributing to further strain on Turkish–Israeli relations. The depiction of the Israeli Defense Forces as cold-blooded murderers of Arab children and civilians sparked anger among Israeli politicians and media,[35] who branded the show state-sponsored 'incitement'.[36] The Turkish government denied any involvement in the production, stating that the drama was produced by an external production company.[37]

It is interesting to note that this drama was written by a former daily columnist, Hakan Albayrak, a Turkish journalist who was later on board the *Mavi Marmara* aid flotilla.[38] The Israeli attack on the aid flotilla occurred at a time when relations between Türkiye and Israel had already reached a critically low point. One could argue that the *Mavi Marmara* incident symbolizes a significant transition that began with harsh rhetoric from the Turkish side and ended with two unfriendly and mutually opposing countries.

On 31 May 2010 the *Mavi Marmara*, a ship purchased by the IHH Humanitarian Relief Foundation (in Turkish, IHH Insani Yardim Vakfi), an NGO with Islamic sympathies, had left port to break Israel's Gaza blockade as part of a Free Gaza movement. However, while in international waters, the *Mavi Marmara* was boarded by Israeli soldiers, resulting in the deaths of nine Turkish citizens, with several more wounded.[39] Despite an apology by Israeli prime minister Benjamin Netanyahu and a $20 million compensation package for the families of those killed, diplomatic relations were slow to recover. Nonetheless, despite heated public rhetoric by leaders on both sides and the Israeli boycott of Türkiye,[40] Turkish–Israeli trade continued in the background.[41]

A decade later, and despite Türkiye's relationship with Israel having been significantly marred, it seems that a rapprochement between the two countries is now underway. One could argue that Türkiye has been motivated to re-establish ties with Israel partly as a result of the changing US administration in 2020, and partly because of the slow but steady reconciliation between Israel and certain Arab countries such as Bahrain, Morocco, Sudan, and the United Arab Emirates (UAE), who have all agreed to normalize diplomatic ties.

In an attempt to rebuild the relationship, Türkiye appointed a new ambassador to Israel in December 2020: there had been no ambassador in either country since May 2018, when Türkiye had asked the Israeli ambassador to take leave over the escalating attacks against Palestinians in Gaza. The Trump administration's decision to move the US Embassy to Jerusalem initially exacerbated the situation,[42] although in July 2021 President Erdoğan went on to congratulate Israeli president Isaac Herzog on being sworn into his new role.[43] In March 2022 Herzog was received by President Erdoğan in Ankara, the highest-level meeting of an Israeli leader in Türkiye in fourteen years.

For observers,[44] the visit of the Israeli president was seen as heralding a new era; however, any ongoing diplomatic relations are likely to depend largely on continued developments in the peace process, the Palestinian issue, and Israel's fury over the Turkish government's apparent support for Hamas and the Muslim Brotherhood.[45] Having said that, while there may be unresolvable political problems between the Turkish and Israeli governments, the empirical findings revealed in this chapter demonstrate that Turkish drama serials have managed to win the hearts of Israeli viewers, transcending diplomatic tensions.

The arrival of Turkish drama serials on Israeli television

This section will explore the entry of Turkish drama serials onto Israeli television while recognizing the exceptional political circumstances in which the first Turkish drama was offered to Israeli viewers. This came in 2011 via the Israeli television channel Viva, which specializes in the broadcasting of international telenovelas and dramas, particularly those from Latin America and Eastern Asia. When Viva announced its plans to broadcast Turkish drama serials, responses were rather sobering. It was only one year after the *Mavi Marmara* incident, and Israeli viewers were quick to express their opposition to the idea of watching content from an unfriendly nation. Yet despite negative social-media responses, Viva went ahead, albeit aware that if the Turkish drama was not well received, they would be unable to purchase further Turkish content. The channel justified its decision to proceed by arguing that it was in the business of entertainment, not politics. The drama *Menekşe and Halil* was selected to trial with its viewers, as it stars the popular Turkish actor Kıvanç Tatlıtuğ, dubbed 'the Middle East's Brad Pitt' by Turkish media.[46] The channel executives believed that because of his Western looks and softened Turkish appearance, he would appeal to, and resonate with, Israeli audiences. Not only did Viva follow through with its bold decision to broadcast *Menekşe and Halil* despite the heated political climate at the time, but the channel also scheduled the show at prime time.[47] Unexpectedly, rather than being a failure, the series was an enormous success with viewers—so much so that in 2012 Viva was rebranded as Viva Plus and became entirely devoted to serials from Türkiye and Korea.[48]

While Turkish serials may appear at first to have been popular only among viewers of Viva and Viva Plus, seen as niche channels, following the airing of the serial *Bride of Istanbul* in 2018 Turkish dramas became a nationwide sensation. What the serial *Noor* (Gümüs/, 2005–07, Türkiye: Kanal D) has been for Arab viewers, and *Las Mil y Una Noches* (*Binbir Gece/One Thousand and One Nights*, 2006–09, Türkiye: Kanal D) has been for Latin Americans, *Bride of Istanbul* became for Israeli viewers. From news programmes to satire shows, Israeli public discourse was suddenly preoccupied with the unexpected popularity of a Turkish drama serial and, for a short while at least, was less focused on the decade-long feud between the two former allies.[49]

Bride of Istanbul's enormous success resulted in other Israeli television stations following suit and acquiring and airing Turkish serials, as well as offering Turkish drama-streaming packages on their platforms.[50] Turkish serials have been so well received that *Haaretz* journalist Mika Katz even recommended them to her readers as television content to binge on during the pandemic lockdown.[51]

Findings

The following section presents the empirical findings of this chapter, beginning with the critical role that Turkish dramas play in shaping a positive perception of Türkiye among Israelis. The section then examines the reasons behind the immense popularity of Turkish dramas among Israeli viewers and delves into their viewing motivations. To provide clarity, the findings are organized thematically based on the trends that emerged during the data analysis.

Turkish serials create a positive perception of Türkiye

In order to establish the importance of Turkish serials in creating a positive perception of Türkiye, and ultimately the serials' role as a soft-power tool,[52] all research participants were asked what level of knowledge they had of

Türkiye, and of Turkish people and culture, prior to watching Turkish dramas. They were then asked whether Turkish serials had changed their perception of Türkiye, to which the vast majority answered 'yes'. Participants answering 'yes' were also asked to elaborate on how their perceptions had changed, in their own words. While most respondents claimed to have known little or almost nothing about Türkiye, what they had previously believed was overwhelmingly negative. Many respondents noted that prior to watching Turkish serials, they had seen Türkiye as a country that was 'backwards', 'primitive', 'conservative', 'religious', 'more Middle Eastern-looking', 'poor', 'hostile', a 'Third World country', 'Islamist', and where 'all women and men dressed religious'. For Israeli viewers, the realization that Turkish serials were not projecting the Turkishness that they had imagined, but instead were showing a culture and society similar to their own, was experienced as highly unexpected and surprising.

> I was expecting them to be more primitive and dress more in a way that represents their religion. (Female viewer, 2020)

> I was stunned that Turks are more like Israelis than Arabs. (Male viewer, 2020)

As was the case for viewers in Qatar and Chile, the changed perception of Türkiye was often demonstrated by research participants claiming to have visited Türkiye recently or wishing to travel to the country. Along with their perceiving Türkiye as an attractive country, viewers often expressed their eagerness to experience Istanbul's beauty for themselves. Others stated that they were fascinated by Turkish history, with some respondents using words such as 'glorious', 'impressive', or 'intriguing'. As the following response shows, period dramas appear to have played a significant role in triggering an interest in Ottoman history:

> *Magnificent Century* was one of my favourite series. I visited Türkiye to see all the historic places. I am so fascinated by the country's history. (Female viewer, 2020)

What the findings discussed throughout this chapter reveal is that the projection of everyday Turkish life in these serials has not only helped Israeli audiences to discover the many cultural and societal similarities between the two nations, but also appears to have fostered a new familiarity and affinity with the Turkish culture, people, and language among Israeli viewers. Research respondents also expressed their belief and realization that Turkish people appeared different from their portrayal in Turkish politics:

> Turkish people seem to also suffer under their government because I don't think people are the same on the ground as the government. Turkish dramas for me project a very different Türkiye to what the government is presenting. (Male university student, 2020)

While there have been scholars in recent years who have examined the politicized nature of Turkish dramas,[53] neither Israeli, Arab, nor Chilean audiences perceived Turkish dramas as politicized. Instead, they were seen as apolitical entertainment that gratified their entertainment needs and their longing for emotional realism. International relations scholars such as Galia Press-Barnathan have argued that the mostly apolitical and entertainment-orientated nature of popular culture allows it to deliver new information to audiences that might 'otherwise be quite resistant to listening'.[54] Turkish dramas have been found to cultivate new emotions of empathy towards Türkiye—a country previously perceived as 'unfriendly' in the words of several research participants. They have managed to reach audiences, and to change their perceptions to a more positive and desirable image of Türkiye—a change that might have been much more difficult to achieve through diplomatic channels. As one Israeli journalist wrote, 'Israelis may not be enthusiastic about Erdogan, but they have fallen in love with Turkish television'.[55]

Turkish dramas have been found to generate a friendlier emotional climate towards the country, and as noted earlier, are causing many viewers to express a strong desire to visit Türkiye.

> Once the pandemic is over, my wife and I are thinking of visiting Istanbul and some other touristic cities on the coast. (Male viewer, 2020)

Even though scholars have noted that cultural products can generate emotional reactions, they have equally acknowledged that emotions are difficult to quantify.[56] On the other hand, political science scholar Ty Solomon has argued that despite the creation of emotional investment and connection by cultural products (a core element of how the power of attraction functions), scholars have downplayed the emotional aspect of soft power.[57] However, as noted throughout this book, the consumption of Turkish television dramas may have implications that are not immediately apparent; but they appear to have the serious potential to foster familiarity with Turkish culture, and shape audience expectation and preference for these dramas. Otmazgin and Ben-Yari suggest that 'popular culture can potentially serve as a tool to convey a state's core values and ideology, and as its front window, selling its attractive culture abroad'[58]—while also acknowledging that this does not equate to power.

Thus, it would be problematic to assume that because Turkish serials appear to have changed the perceptions of its viewers, a country's government could now be pressured into improving relations with Türkiye. Once again, similar to my finding among the audiences in Qatar and Chile, Israeli audiences have expressed a strong desire to visit Türkiye and experience in real life the locations they have seen in dramas. In fact, visitor numbers from Israel before the start of the Covid-19 pandemic had already demonstrated a notable increase of Israeli tourists to Türkiye.[59] For instance, in 2019, 560,000 Israelis were recorded as having visited Türkiye, showing an increase of 26 per cent compared with 2018. The number of Israelis flying with Turkish Airlines has also risen by 75 per cent.[60] While it is true that Israeli nationals are exempt from any visa requirements when entering Türkiye, the sudden increase of Israeli tourists is a significant development given the decade-long dispute between the two countries,[61] and an important indication of Turkish dramas' decisive role in creating interest and motivation to get to know the country better.

Moreover, as I will further reveal in the next sections, the findings also indicate that Turkish drama serials' most significant form of soft power is their ability to transcend political differences by reminding Israeli audiences of various commonalities and shared values. Similarly to my findings in Qatar and Chile, I have discovered that Turkish drama serials are filling a void on Israeli television that local or international television dramas could not satisfy, placing them in a unique position. This position might allow them in the future to further influence and shape audience taste and perception of what a drama should be like, and, most importantly, to establish in Israel a familiarity and secondary proximity with Turkish culture.

Turkish serials and young Israeli audiences

As in the previous chapters, this section first describes the results of the comparative study focusing on the appeal of Turkish dramas to university students in Qatar, Chile, and Israel. The findings are similar across all three countries (see Chapters 3 and 6). Like the university students in Qatar and Chile, university students surveyed in Israel claimed not to be viewers of Turkish serials, but instead to be passively exposed to them by relatives (chiefly a mother) who were watching them. However, despite this claim, many admitted to having watched some episodes of *Bride of Istanbul*. Again, similarly to young respondents in Qatar and Chile, young people in Israel claimed to dislike Turkish serials because they were seen as overly dramatic and too emotional. They were also seen as a genre aimed more at 'older women' than at the younger generation. Instead, young Israelis expressed a preference for American content.

The responses of university students and of avid Turkish-serial viewers also differed in terms of the number of Turkish serials they could name. University students could only name an average of two serials, with *Bride of Istanbul* being the best known, followed by *Mother* (*Anne*, 2016–17, Türkiye: Star TV), while avid serial viewers were able to list an average of four to five dramas that they had watched. However, as with the findings in Qatar and Chile, Israeli university students were still able to provide insightful answers as to why they believed Turkish drama serials were popular among Israeli viewers, with responses similar to those of avid viewers. The most significant difference was that responses by regular viewers of serials were longer and more detailed, while university students often responded to sections of the survey that required a more descriptive answer with just a single short sentence, or single words or phrases.

The importance of cultural proximity in the experience of entertainment

The following sections explore the responses by regular viewers of Turkish dramas. The findings in this chapter, as with the findings among Arab and Chilean viewers, indicate that Israeli audiences tend to attribute their engagement with Turkish dramas primarily within the logic of cultural proximity, where cultural similarities are seen as pivotal factors in the overall appeal.

> Turks have a similar way of life to Israelis ... They show conservative values but are also super modern. That is something that I have only seen in Turkish dramas. (Female viewer, 2019)

Most audience responses indicate that Turkish drama serials offer Israeli viewers rich layers of connection, whether through perceived ethnic and cultural similarities, or relatable themes and values. While various factors have been identified as contributors to Turkish dramas being seen as entertaining and allowing Israeli viewers to engage with them meaningfully, it is important to emphasize that these factors only appear to work in connection with each other, rather than in isolation, where the audience's experience of cultural proximity becomes pivotal to Turkish dramas' overall pulling power. Scholars such as Straubhaar and Athique have linked cultural proximity to Pierre Bourdieu's concept of cultural capital: the more cultural capital, the less effective is the logic of cultural proximity, and the less cultural capital, the more effective cultural proximity becomes.[62]

Turkish drama serials started airing on Viva, an Israeli channel targeting niche audiences, where one could argue that taste formation might differ. It should be acknowledged that cultural capital is able to influence audiences' mechanisms of experiencing elements of the national and the subnational, or how the different agencies of textual relation are experienced as being effective in the audience engagement process.[63] However, with the nationwide success in 2018 of *Bride of Istanbul* on the same niche channel (Viva), Turkish dramas appear to have unearthed layers of cultural capital—or, one could argue, a hidden paradox—by reminding Israeli audiences of their many cultural and perceived ethnic similarities with Türkiye. As Israeli journalist Ariana Melamed argues, Israel has been under a 'petrifying Ashkenazi hegemony'[64]—even though the country has experienced significant waves of immigration of Sephardic and Mizrahi Jews from the Middle East and North Africa, along with immigration from Ethiopia, Latin America, and former Soviet countries, to name just a few. Ashkenazi culture has been exercising a powerful and influential position in society, enforcing a cultural superiority that has shaped all areas of life—television included.

As the following audience responses illustrate, Turkish serials are not only experienced as entertainment, which is the primary motive for watching Turkish dramas; they have also helped Israeli viewers to connect with aspects of their cultural capital and identity that were, to a degree, overlooked and not adequately represented in local productions.

> What attracted me to Turkish dramas the most were the stories and human emotions that I could relate to that I didn't find in other dramas. (Female serial viewer, 2020)

For many respondents, an important part of the pleasurable viewing experience was being able to recognize many similarities between Turkish and Israeli cultures. What appears to have surprised audiences is that Turkish people were perceived as looking similar to Israelis. Also, one of the most common responses was that audiences realized that Turks and Israelis shared a similar 'mentality'. Similarities in 'mentality' were very often mentioned by avid serial viewers. Here are the responses of two Israeli viewers which summarize the reactions of the majority of those surveyed:

> Turkish people have the same mentality as Israelis. They are warm people with a lot of fire in them, like us. (Female viewer, 2020)

> When my wife and I started watching Turkish dramas we both realized that, like us, Turks love their mothers. (Male viewer, 2020)

The discovery by Israeli audiences of their many similarities with a nation and its people that they had previously perceived not only as unfriendly towards Israel, but also as culturally and ethnically different, appears to have been seminal in the positive appeal of Turkish serials. It seems that discovering similarities is an important part of the viewing experience, along with how these similarities relate to Israeli audiences' current lives and lifeworlds, given that they remain surrounded by hostile neighbours, where differences appear to matter most. One could argue that Israeli viewers' ability to connect and relate to dramas from a Muslim-majority country, and to possess feelings of proximity, eases audience members' perceptions of being distinctly different from other nations in the region. This has converted into a pleasurable viewing experience—one that many said provided an escape into a world that is similar, but also different:

> People watch Turkish dramas because they are good for escapism. The stories and characters are very easy to relate to. Everything feels very familiar. (Male viewer, 2020)

The continual discovery of similarities appears to be an essential aspect of the enjoyable viewing experience and creates an affinity and a sense of familiarity with Türkiye and its culture.

> I realized how similar our cultures are and it made me like Turks more! (Female viewer, 2020)

Many audience responses drew comparisons between Turkish culture, as portrayed in the serials, and Israeli culture. For instance, this serial viewer highlights the similarities between the common traditional greeting among Turkish people of kissing the hands of their closest older relatives, and a tradition among Israeli Jews, who kiss the hands of their parents on Shabbat Night:

> We also kiss hands of our parents after the kiddush. Family gatherings and respect for older family members are also important to us. (Female viewer, 2020)

This resonates with Slade's work on the international popularity of telenovelas and Australasian soap operas. She found that audience pleasure does not simply lie in the viewers' ability to identify with the characters and stories of television dramas. Instead, as with Israeli viewers here, the experience of pleasure is achieved because they can see 'their own lives through the lens of similarities and differences in the lives portrayed'.[65] Furthermore, the audience's discovery that Turkish food and music has similarities to Israeli food and music also appears to have elevated the audience's experience of closeness with Turkish culture:

> Turkish serials made me look into Turkish music. I actually found out that there are many songs that have been translated from Turkish into Hebrew. (Female viewer, 2020)

One might say that Turkish serials not only remind Israelis of their commonalities with Turkish culture, but also offer them a level of cultural proximity that they were unable to obtain from local productions. The reality that a significant proportion of Israeli Jews migrated from (or were raised by parents who were born in) countries that were part of the Ottoman Empire, or countries of the Global South, appears to have significantly contributed to the audiences' appreciation and engagement with Turkish serials. As La Pastina and Straubhaar underline, 'the experience of locality is bound up with other layers of identity, such as ethnicity or language/culture'.[66] Turkish serials appeal to an important part of Israeli identity, with a deep-rooted connection to countries in the Global South—seemingly not sufficiently catered for in Israeli productions.

The importance of value and thematic proximity

The vast majority of audience responses have shown that thematic and value proximity were equally critical factors in the appeal of Turkish dramas for Israeli viewers. Despite Turkish serials focusing on Turkish society, and often prominently displaying the city of Istanbul, they are perceived as presenting widely relatable themes, values, and characters. The mediated depiction of Turkish society and culture are experienced as authentic to Israeli viewers, despite the dramas being set against the backdrop of a Muslim country and a foreign city. The following audience response demonstrates that Israeli viewers seem to be able to engage profoundly with Turkish dramas. Themes that explore the struggles between modernity and tradition, and the focus on traditional values which sits at the core of most Turkish dramas, are experienced as highly engaging:

> [The fact that in Turkish dramas] they show issues like the materialistic nature of society, and the constant push by people for wealth whilst other values stop mattering touches me the most. We are losing our culture and tradition. When I watch Turkish dramas, I enter a more traditional world, but I also like the modern life they show. (Male viewer, 2020)

However, another perspective in exploring the appeal of value and thematic proximity to Israeli viewers is to examine audience preferences within the logic of national cultures, where practical sense-making can be positioned within the social sphere and an interactionist perspective, rather than solely within culture. In other words, themes and values become meaningful topics for viewers, resonating with their life circumstances and phases, value-belief systems and attitudes, and the central themes of their lives, because these are highly relatable with the viewers' lifeworlds. This enables viewers to negotiate highly relevant topics and themes, regardless of how culturally close or distant they might feel to the way of life presented. It is important to note that while Israel transitioned from an emerging to a developing nation in 2010, it has encountered many economic and political issues in the last decade, appearing to struggle with its new status.[67] At the same time, the reality that recent migration to Israel has increasingly been from the Global South could offer another explanation for Turkish drama serials appealing to Israeli viewers and resonating with their lifeworlds.

While lifeworlds are important to consider when understanding audience behaviour, Israeli viewers have largely attributed their engagement with Turkish dramas within the notion of culture, where (similarly to Chilean viewers) cultural proximity takes a more central role than cultural distance. Audience responses have shown that Israeli viewers position themselves culturally when expressing views on Turkish dramas. Thus, one could argue that the reason for values and themes being experienced as relevant and relatable originates in a combination of shared cultural elements and common lifeworld experiences in contemporary Israel.

> I was very shocked to see that they were more like Israelis in their lifestyle than Arabic people. I felt there was a uniqueness in Turkish programmes that I was missing in telenovelas or dramas. They show traditional values, a lot of romance but also have a relatable lifestyle. (Female viewer, 2020)

Furthermore, many respondents noted that Turkish dramas' positioning of a mother as anchor of the family was remarkably relatable, with predominantly female respondents comparing the importance of mothers within Jewish culture—as the following transcript illustrates:

> Turkish and Israeli family life is similar. A Turkish mum is very much like a Jewish mum who would do anything for her children. (Female viewer, 2020)

It is crucial to highlight that mothers of Jewish faith are seen as the primary parent because they determine Jewish status, while also performing the role of the Jewish guarantor of appropriate traditional religious and cultural rearing. Many Turkish dramas have a strong and influential mother figure. Like its mediated projection in Turkish dramas, the importance of mothers in Türkiye hails from Islamic teaching, which believes that paradise lies at the feet of the mother because of the many sacrifices they must make when bearing and raising their children. One route to attaining paradise in the Islamic religion is to respect and take care of your mother. It seems that because of these similarities in the importance given to mothers, Turkish dramas become highly meaningful and engaging for Israeli viewers.

Turkish dramas seem to project a rare combination of value and thematic proximity, and relatable modernity or zeitgeist, that cannot be found in other productions. Interestingly, this experience of a shared time and space that doesn't appear to be achieved in other productions holds a strong appeal for Israeli, Chilean, and Arab audiences alike. Turkish drama serials seem to offer audiences rich layers of connection. The specific way in which daily life is portrayed in Turkish dramas makes their texts more authentic to audiences and supports viewers' engagement with topics of relevance to their lives and experiences. Arguably, Turkish dramas have succeeded in providing audiences with a multilayered textual world that presents widely relatable themes, despite focusing on Türkiye and Turkish society.

Genre proximity and emotional realism

Before discussing the significance of genre and emotional realism, we need to stress that the realization of cultural proximity between Turks and Israelis has been the most important factor in the acceptance of Turkish drama serials by Israeli viewers. The existence of various cultural similarities has helped audiences to move away from their negative preconceptions of Türkiye and Turkish people. Consequently, Turkish drama serials were able to be appreciated as a cultural product appealing to the audiences' tastes and needs, rather than as a product from an unfriendly Muslim country. Through my fieldwork, it became clear that Israeli audiences were drawn to dramas owing to the genre's emotional realism. This preference was also acknowledged by a media executive at a top entertainment and distribution company in Türkiye, which operates in both the LAC region and Israel. This executive explained that the success of dramas in both regions is largely influenced by the preference for emotionally-engaging programming. He stressed that for him some of it was also driven by the influence of Latin American migrants who brought their fondness for telenovelas to Israel. Straubhaar's concept of genre proximity also supports this idea, as he argues that audience familiarity with a particular genre is a crucial factor in understanding their preferences.[68] At the same time La Pastina and Straubhaar have also stressed that dramas and melodramas have the ability, built on underlying oral structures, formulas, and archetypes, to be shared by various cultures.[69] Responses by Israeli audiences have shown that the desire for emotionally-charged dramas has played an important role in the positive reception of Turkish drama serials. For most Israeli viewers, good dramas are associated with emotionally-impactful content. However, many viewers have expressed the view that such content is currently lacking on Israeli television, as this comment by a male viewer demonstrates:

> I think Israeli television is not producing meaningful dramas, which is why my wife and I watch Turkish dramas. While stuck at home during the pandemic, we discovered them and now find them more interesting than other shows. (Male viewer, 2020)

Turkish drama serials have been praised for their ability to provide viewers with high levels of emotional realism—which is experienced as one of their primary appeals. The emotional resonance of Turkish dramas is regarded as a vital element in allowing Israeli viewers to engage with them meaningfully, resulting in a satisfying viewing experience. For many audiences, this is achieved through the use of well-crafted characters, relatable storylines, family structures, and nuanced performances that effectively connect with them on a personal level. The significance of emotional realism and authenticity in engaging Israeli viewers with Turkish dramas is illustrated by the following three comments from viewers:

> I think people love tear-jerking drama in Israel. The Turkish shows are giving people exactly that. (Male student, 2020)

> The way they show the love of a mother for her child, the importance of family bonds, or the two-faced nature of people is something I cannot find in other dramas. (Female viewer, 2020)

> I love how Turkish shows create so much emotional tension with minimal actions, and the way people are portrayed as never being as they seem makes them feel very real to me. (Female, viewer, 2020)

For many viewers, Turkish dramas offered a level of authenticity and realism that was seen as absent in other productions. The following two audience responses serve as examples of how Turkish drama serials portray emotions that are not explored in alternative content:

> I watch Turkish dramas because they are more real in the sense of people's feelings and family relations. I think many people like that they show the fears and struggles of people that are not given much attention. I like that the characters are normal, that normal family structures are shown, and that there is still romance and sexual energy without unnecessary explicit scenes (Male viewer, 2020)

> Turkish people, like Israelis, are very passionate and express their emotions freely. We are not reserved people, which is why we appreciate Turkish dramas, as we can relate to the emotions and actions of the characters. The connection we feel with the characters is because they display the same passion and emotional expression that we do. (Female viewer, 2020)

It could be argued that the significant cultural and mental similarities between Israelis and Turks enable Turkish dramas to forge a deeply personal connection with Israeli viewers. Human emotions, whether they are joy, pain, envy, etc., are seen as being conveyed in a credibly authentic manner. This experience of relatable emotional authenticity is so powerful that many viewers have reported crying while watching Turkish dramas. The following responses of a female viewer demonstrate the importance of emotional realism in the viewer's ability to relate to the characters' emotional spheres:

> Turkish programmes have so much emotional depth, it is very hard with some of them not to cry. You feel instantly connected to the story and characters ... you can relate to their feelings. I think Israeli and international shows are shying away from this. The trend is more action, more sci-fi, more nudity... (Female viewer, 2020)

Even though many respondents stressed their initial astonishment about their ability to identify with the worries and joys of characters originating from a 'Muslim country', many responses have revealed that Turkish dramas allow viewers to engage with them not only symbolically or as fantasies, but by offering meaningful connections to their own lives. As the following two responses summarize, human emotions, interpersonal relations, and social realities in Turkish dramas are seen as not only relatable but also recognizable to viewers in Israel:

> I am a single mom, and even in Israel, it can be tough raising children. I find that many of the struggles portrayed by female characters in Turkish dramas are relatable to my own experiences. (Female viewer, 2020)

> I think the way corruption and injustice are portrayed in Turkish dramas makes them feel familiar to me, as these are issues we deal with every day. I believe that the rich often get away with everything, which is very frustrating. Turkish dramas show these issues in a way that makes them entertaining instead of just depressing reality. (Male viewer, 2020)

Israeli viewers seem to perceive the narratives and emotions in Turkish serials as authentic and relatable, projected by authentic characters who behave, feel, and even look rather like themselves. Ang's study in the Netherlands established that, despite *Dallas*'s external world being perceived as not very realistic, viewers still felt that it was 'true-to-life'. For Ang, viewers attributed realness to the characters' subjective experiences and feelings, to which they could relate.[70] However, unlike with the emotional realism described by Ang, Israeli viewers did not view Turkish dramas as projecting emotions and realities from a distant world into their reality: instead, they perceived the world portrayed in Turkish shows as similar to their own, making it relatable to their own life experiences. By paying attention to emotions and human relations that were increasingly neglected in national and international productions, Turkish dramas have occupied a space that was previously unfilled for many viewers, as the next audience response demonstrates:

> I feel that Turkish dramas pay attention to stories and emotions that are often dismissed by American or Israeli producers as too traditional or conservative. To me, these shows portray real-life situations that should be more frequently included in our programming. Unfortunately, in our attempt to be too progressive, we are losing our audience to foreign shows because people will always gravitate toward the content they want to see. (Male viewer, 2020)

Interestingly, unlike viewers in Qatar or Chile, Israeli viewers did not overly focus on the fact that Turkish serials are dramas which contain a great deal of romance and romantic storylines. Instead, the focus was much more on the projection of human emotions and relationships, as well as their authenticity and relatability, which they did not find in local and other international content—one of those elements being the projection of traditional family values, and another being the role of mothers, as highlighted above.

Subtitling instead of dubbing

The empirical findings in Qatar and Chile have shown that the dubbing of Turkish dramas into the local language has geo-localized Turkish content and made it accessible to a broader audience, avoiding a significant degree of 'cultural discount'.[71] However, in the case of Israel, Turkish serials have succeeded in entering the Israeli television market without being dubbed—because unlike in the Arab world and Latin America, in Israel foreign content is traditionally subtitled. Israeli audiences were asked how they felt about hearing the Turkish language, and whether they would prefer Turkish dramas to be dubbed into Hebrew. Unexpectedly, a significant number of respondents stated that they found the Turkish language pleasant and appealing to the ear, rather than unfamiliar and unappealing. Several respondents went so far as to include a Turkish word or sentence to show their appreciation of the language:

> The Turkish language sounds familiar, *evet* ['yes' in Turkish]. I love Turkish dramas. (Female viewer, 2020)

> I watched Turkish dramas before on the Russian channel. *Cok guzel, Turkiye cok guzel*. ['Very beautiful, Türkiye is very beautiful.'] (Male viewer, 2020)

The fact that Israeli viewers do not understand Turkish did not seem to impede their engagement with the dramas as, similarly to viewers in the English-speaking world, Israeli viewers are accustomed to consuming foreign content that is subtitled rather than dubbed. However, some respondents noted that they watched dubbed Turkish content on Russian and Argentinian television.

The importance of production values

What the majority of study participants have agreed on in Israel, Chile, and Qatar is that Turkish serials are perceived as content with high production values, and suspenseful and engaging storylines. The quality of the acting and the physical appearance of the actors were seen as significant factors in their appeal, with many claiming to be struck by Türkiye's ability to produce high-quality dramas, while also having actors that many described as 'very attractive' or 'model-like'.

> I was so surprised that Turks know how to do a good drama. They have very talented and very good-looking actors. The country looks quite beautiful—not what I had expected at all. (Female viewer, 2020)

Respondents (women in particular) emphasized their appreciation not only of the physical appearance of the actors, but also of the beautiful locations where Turkish serials were filmed.

> I had no idea that Istanbul was so beautiful and had such interesting architecture. I expected something underdeveloped. (Male viewer, 2019)

Therefore, the combination of high production values, engaging storylines, good acting, and attractive actors and appealing locations, represents another important factor in the appeal of Turkish dramas.

Conclusion

The empirical data analysed in this chapter has shown that the existence of various cultural similarities between Türkiye and Israel has contributed to audiences moving away from their negative preconceptions about Türkiye and its people, allowing Turkish serials to be appreciated as a cultural product appealing to the audiences' tastes and needs, rather than as a product, from an opposing Muslim country, that should be rejected. One could argue that Turkish serials have been successful not only because they are simply dramas which have a transnational appeal, but also, significantly, because they have the distinctive ability to exhibit human emotions and storylines within a cultural framework that is not only relatable but also highly identifiable for viewers in Israel. Additionally, Turkish serials are appreciated for their high production values, 'suspenseful' and 'engaging storylines', and great acting. They appear to have generated a familiarity and affinity with the Turkish culture, people, and language among Israeli viewers that most likely could not be achieved by any diplomatic initiative. It also seems that the version of Turkish society and culture projected in the serials holds a strong appeal because Türkiye is seen as a Mediterranean country with a Western-style modernity, while also greatly valuing conservative traditions. The constant interaction between modernity and tradition deeply resonates with the lifeworlds of Israeli viewers. This has influenced viewers to change their negative preconceptions of Türkiye, with many even expressing an increased desire to visit the country to experience its culture, historic sites, and the locations where Turkish serials have been filmed. It would not be incorrect to say that Turkish serials not only show Israelis their numerous similarities, but also encourage them to realize that they can be at home in various cultures. Israel's diverse population results from the country's being located in the Middle East, with a population that has migrated from many corners of the world.

Turkish–Israeli relations may now be on the mend: whether relations will ultimately improve or not remains to be seen. However, irrespective of geopolitics, Turkish serials have managed to win the hearts of an extensive Israeli audience, and (for serial viewers at least) the feeling of opposition towards Türkiye appears to have transformed into one of warmth and genuine interest in the country and its people. While the attraction of Turkish cultural products may not translate into policy goals, it seems that Turkish serials are likely to have a continued impact on the audience's expectation of what a good drama should be, while changing the perception of a Muslim society and allowing a recognition of the many similarities Türkiye and Israel share, rather than focusing on their differences.

Summary and Conclusion

This book set out to examine a significant development in global television that started with Turkish dramas taking Arab screens by storm and led to their expansion across the world. While the book acknowledges that traveling television serials have been studied by scholars in the past,[1] and that this phenomenon is not limited to Turkish productions, it highlights a significant shift. For the first time, drama serials from a Muslim-majority country have successfully captured the attention of audiences beyond their cultural and linguistic region. This book has argued that the triumphant entry of Turkish drama serials onto Arab television represents a pivotal moment, paving their way to becoming internationally popular serials. The unprecedented success of Turkish dramas across the Arab world was met with huge interest among Arab and international media alike, who reported on the Arab viewer's passion for Turkish programmes, which subsequently generated attention and curiosity across other parts of the globe. In order to explore this evolving phenomenon, we have examined the pressing question: what is it about Turkish dramas that resonates with Arab, Chilean, and Israeli audiences alike, and at times allows them to even surpass national, regional, and Western productions in popularity?

It is essential to emphasize that the first Turkish dramas to achieve international success were produced solely for the Turkish domestic television market. Even after the onset of their global appeal, Turkish dramas produced for television are still required to be successful first among Turkish viewers before becoming marketable for international buyers. Therefore, by taking an audience-centric approach, this book examined qualitative and quantitative audience data gathered in Qatar, Chile, and Israel, and adopted a multi-theoretical perspective, drawing on concepts such as cultural proximity, uses

SUMMARY AND CONCLUSION

and gratifications, lifeworld, and soft power, to analyse this evolving development in television.

Thus, **Chapter 1** critically examined the factors that contributed to the transition of the Turkish television industry, from dependency on foreign content for television serials to becoming the world's second-highest exporter of scripted TV dramas. This chapter revealed that along with economic imperatives, the availability of trained creative professionals contributed to the rise of the Turkish television industry. On the one hand, there was the migration of an established and experienced pool of film and theatre talent over to television, and the subsequent utilization of their professional expertise, which played a significant role in the development of the television production sector. On the other hand, we witnessed the rising popularity of university degrees in media, communication, film, and drama, and their social acceptance as professions for both women and men in what is a Muslim-majority country, which further contributed to the availability of skilled cultural-industry professionals—providing Türkiye with the necessary foundation to become a significant global player. One could argue that this aspect has been one of the Turkish television industry's most significant advantages when compared to other Muslim-majority countries, where professions in the film and television sector are still largely perceived as culturally unacceptable, and even more so for women.

At the same time, positive economic developments in Türkiye in the 2000s, along with changes in foreign policy and trade relationships, saw the country transition away from predominantly Western-orientated relations and policies, aiding Türkiye's economic advancement and its diplomatic and economic rapprochement with the Arab world. The fact that many leading Turkish media outlets are owned by large multi-sector conglomerates who directly benefited from these new trade partnerships further fuelled growth in the national television sector. Trade between Türkiye and the Arab world's most powerful nation, the Kingdom of Saudi Arabia (KSA), gained significant momentum between 2002 and 2008. While Turkish–Saudi trade volume sat at $8.3 billion between 1996 and 1997, it went on to reach $20.3 billion by 2008. Therefore, the period leading up to the acquisition of the first Turkish serial *Gümüs* (*Noor* in the Arab world) by the Saudi-owned MBC network in 2007 was characterized by several historic political, economic, security, and bilateral cultural agreements between Türkiye and KSA. This increased diplomatic and economic engagement provided the necessary framework for Turkish drama serials to enter the Saudi Arabian television market along with other products and services. Thus, the penetration of Turkish drama serials into Arab television represents a vital interplay between economic and political integration and signifies a pivotal moment that allowed Turkish dramas to transition from being successful nationally, within their geo-linguistic region (Turkic-speaking countries), and among Turkish diasporic audiences, to becoming internationally-popular television serials. Yet perhaps even more crucially, this development exemplified the success of foreign-policy efforts and the broadening of trade relationships by the Turkish state in the 2000s.

Chapter 1 also revealed that with the growing international demand for Turkish serials and persistently growing domestic competition, production companies in Türkiye have been under constant pressure to meet the needs of audiences, channel executives, and government regulators, with serials having become an essential commercial platform. In addition to growing domestic rivalry, the sector has been faced with the entry of foreign production houses. However, despite the challenges, increasing rivalry in the sector also generated positive outcomes. It has contributed to Turkish serials achieving a high production quality, allowing them to compete effectively in the international television market. The establishment of domestic streaming platforms and the entry of international giants such as Netflix, Amazon Prime, and Disney+ have denoted a gradual but essential shift in how Turkish audiences consume content, with younger Turkish television viewers in particular starting to supplement traditional terrestrial and satellite content consumption with streaming services. Recognizing the significant profit to be made, Turkish and international streaming platforms have more recently focused on producing original content specifically tailored towards these streaming services. Turkish and international viewers who were not previously drawn to the drama/romance formula of Turkish serials, and Western audiences who remained immune to the charms of Turkish dramas, have been increasingly targeted by content produced exclusively for streaming. However, the intersection between television and streaming platforms still presents a blend of the two in Türkiye, rather than one medium replacing the other.

SUMMARY AND CONCLUSION

The analysis in Chapter 1 also discussed how new Turkish platforms—such as Dramax, launched in 2021 by Demirören Media (part of Türkiye's largest conglomerate), and Türkiye's national broadcaster TRT's YouTube channel (to name but two examples)—are now offering content in a multitude of languages. This increased investment, along with the rapid growth of digital media in Türkiye, illustrates a noteworthy development in the Turkish television industry. It demonstrates that the industry is positioning itself to reach international audiences away from traditional export routes, instead targeting these audiences directly. In other words, by cutting out the middleman, the television production industry in Türkiye is accessing new revenue streams, bypassing geopolitical constraints such as those that caused the cancellation of Turkish serials from 2018 to 2022 on the Arab world's largest media network, the MBC Group. The ability to reach broader audiences nationally and internationally, along with the ability to move away from restrictive ratings systems, fierce competition, and the limitation of only focusing on one particular genre (drama-romance), clearly presents a highly beneficial model for the production sector in Türkiye.

Chapter 2 aimed to provide the reader with an overview of, and necessary context to understand, the various factors that permitted the paths of Turkish serials and the Arab world's most influential media group MBC to cross, resulting in Turkish dramas appearing on the screens of millions of Arab viewers in the MENA region and beyond. Therefore, this chapter first gave an insight into the structure of the television markets in the Arab world starting from the 1990s, which saw the restructuring and privatization of the Arab media landscape. The chapter examined the markets' socio-political, economic, and cultural dynamics, their ownership and affiliations, and illustrated their dependence for funding on oil-rich Gulf monarchies. The latter possess significant influence and control over content production—while at the same time, the preferences of Saudi audiences have been the benchmark for what content is deemed successful, owing to the country's economic power and population size. By paying particular attention to the establishment of Saudi-owned MBC in the 1990s until the present, it has been possible to demonstrate how the media outlet evolved to become the region's most influential media organization and the first broadcaster to introduce Turkish serials to Arab audiences.

While Chapter 1 examined the dynamics that led to the entry of Turkish dramas into the Arab world when diplomatic and trade relations were at a high point from the Turkish perspective, this chapter outlined the developments from the Arab perspective, coupled with prevailing circumstances that a decade later led to declining diplomatic ties and the cancellation of Turkish dramas in 2018 for a period of four years. Together, Chapters 1 and 2 have shown that the 2000s represented a period where Turkish–Arab relations reached a historic peak, creating vital conditions for Turkish serials to enter the Arab media space. The introduction of the first dubbed Turkish drama *Noor* (*Gümüş*) during Ramadan 2008 was a bold but decisive move by MBC. It permitted the network to trial a Turkish drama with potentially the largest television audience across the Arab world. Following on from the success of *Noor*, other Arab channels started to broadcast Turkish dramas across the region. In fact, the acquisition of Turkish dramas has become a win–win for Arab networks, firstly because Turkish dramas have been found to have the potential to draw in large audiences and generate desirable advertising revenue, and secondly because Turkish dramas had already been successfully tested on Turkish television. Therefore, in contrast to traditional Ramadan series where channels buy a concept, idea, or script, Turkish television dramas have been offered as a finished product, making it significantly easier for television stations to foresee their success.

Moreover, the analyses in Chapter 2 also demonstrated that despite the ban of Turkish serials on Saudi and Emirati free-to-air satellite channels owing to diplomatic tensions, Turkish drama serials have continued to be offered to viewers across the region via pay-TV and subscription video-on-demand (SVOD) services. Similarly, an online survey of over 300 (mostly female) respondents on Arabic fan sites for Turkish serials on social media, shortly after the ban of Turkish dramas in 2018, yielded empirical findings showing that the majority of Arab viewers who had previously watched Turkish dramas on television were now opting to watch them online with either English or Arabic subtitles (such as on YouTube or illegal websites), or they were visiting the official websites of Turkish TV networks to view the content in the Turkish language. Meanwhile, older viewers were searching for free-to-air satellite channels that still aired Turkish dramas.

SUMMARY AND CONCLUSION

Consequently, whether viewers can afford pay-TV and/or streaming services, or access free Turkish content on YouTube, catch-up TV on Turkish channel websites, or opt for other free-to-air Arab channels, the study shows that Arab audiences actively seek content that best serves their needs, even when faced with restrictions and censorship. The findings underscore the importance of catering to viewers' preferences in a way that is accessible and accommodating.

Despite television still being the most prominent medium in the MENA region,[2] these findings have shown that the new media landscape, along with cheaper and faster internet connectivity, has permitted Arab audiences to select media content they would like to engage with, rather than being forced to consume what the state or media corporations believe they should be watching. Furthermore, the recent growth in SVOD services in the Arab world and Türkiye has enabled Turkish dramas to expand their presence in Arab media markets without a reliance on broadcast networks. These parallel developments in the Arab and Turkish media landscape demonstrate how the advent of the digital era, and a pro-business approach, have led to persistence prevailing over politics. The fact that Turkish dramas are still finding Arab audiences on MBC's streaming platform Shahid, despite their being banned on their free-to-air channels, is a clear example of financial interest becoming more important than political tensions. Therefore, whether it is down to StarzPlay Arabia having signed a partnership with BluTV in 2021, or Shahid acquiring a sizeable catalogue of Turkish content, the analysis in Chapter 2 has demonstrated that Turkish dramas cannot simply be removed from screens across the Arab world by government-imposed bans. That said, with the diplomatic relationship between Türkiye, KSA, and the United Arab Emirates (UAE) being back on the mend, Turkish serials have now returned to free-to-air satellite stations after a hiatus of almost four years.

Lastly, Chapter 2 also illustrated a development in Arab serial production that could have an important impact on the region's production industry. The MBC-affiliated and Istanbul-based O3 Productions has adopted the Turkish style of serial production. In 2019, when Turkish serials were banned on free-to-air satellite television, O3 produced an Arabic adaptation of its internationally successful serial *Bride of Istanbul* (*Istanbullu Gelin*, 2017–19,

175

Türkiye: Star TV), renaming it *The Bride of Beirut* (2019–20, MBC). However, rather than dubbing Turkish content, or filming the adaptation of *Bride of Istanbul* in the Arab world, O3 Productions used its expertise in producing Turkish dramas, shooting the serial using Turkish production staff but utilizing Arab actors mainly in locations across Türkiye. With diplomatic relations normalized between Türkiye and KSA since the summer of 2022, MBC Group signed in October 2022 a five-year agreement with Turkish production companies Medyapim and Ay Yapim. The five-year partnership will see a host of Turkish content shared exclusively with the MBC Group via 'first look' and volume deal agreements, along with original Arabic-language content produced for the MENA market. The usage and adaptation of Turkish production methods and expertise may ultimately signal the next phase of content production in the Arab world, where Turkish influence in the cultural sphere manifests itself in a rather unusual way: rather than only exporting serials, they may instead produce them specifically for the Arab world.

While Chapters 1 and 2 provided overviews of the Turkish and Arab television industries, and examined factors that contributed to Turkish drama serials entering the broadcast schedule of the Arab world's largest media network, MBC, **Chapter 3** studied how the growth in diplomatic and economic ties between Türkiye and the Arab world since the turn of the century has coincided with the enormous surge in popularity of Turkish television dramas in the MENA region. By drawing on audience data from various Arab nationalities residing in Qatar, the chapter examined whether the growing awareness and more positive perception of Türkiye among Arabs should be attributed to Turkish foreign policy, or to exposure to Turkish dramas. This is a notable area of study, as Turkish political influence and growing economic strength and engagement have intersected with the success of Turkish serials in the Arab world. In order to examine this research question, the chapter first explored historical, political, economic, and cultural factors that were found to be decisive elements contributing to Türkiye's prestige and confidence, and the country being seen as a significant soft-power nation in the MENA region. The discussions covered in Chapter 3 showed that Türkiye's so called neo-Ottomanist foreign policy under the ruling Justice and Development Party (Adalet ve Kalkinma Partisi, AKP) government since 2002 has enabled the country to expand its diplomatic ties, which purposefully went hand in hand

SUMMARY AND CONCLUSION

with trade relations, and away from its traditional Western-centric approach. However, the chapter also demonstrated that Türkiye's drive as a trading state and its rapprochement with the Arab world was, in fact, not unidirectional. On the contrary, key events such as Türkiye starting to negotiate with the European Union in 2005 to become a full member only increased interest from Türkiye's Arab neighbours. The country was now seen as a stabilizing figure in the region, with access to economic prospects that would benefit the Arab world. At the same time, I examined key factors that appear to have caused the Turkish–Arab relationship to fluctuate rather than remain consistent. I analysed central geopolitical conflicts and crises such as the Arab Uprisings starting in 2010, and the Qatar diplomatic crisis in 2017, that saw the Muslim world's two most influential nations, Türkiye and KSA, hold opposing political views. The chapter ultimately revealed that these fundamental differences in political standpoints have become critical factors in the fluctuation of Turkish soft power and its impact across the Arab world, albeit mostly with respect to the ruling elites in KSA and the UAE, who started to become wary of Türkiye's political and cultural influence.

The discussion in Chapter 3 also demonstrated that despite being unplanned, the international success of Turkish dramas has fallen nicely into the soft-power strategy of the Turkish government. Following the enormous success of Turkish drama serials throughout the MENA region, the Turkish government started to use these serials strategically, focusing on improving the country's image through soft power, particularly in the Arab world. Turkish drama serials were now recognized as highly effective platforms by which to promote the country's cultural persona and the Turkish way of life, which in turn deliver positive impacts on other industries, such as tourism. Furthermore, the Turkish government understood that they had entered an era where the traditional metrics of power were no longer the sole and ultimate determiners of a country's influence. Instead, historical connections, cultural similarities, and television serials could represent an equally important framework for Türkiye's soft-power capacity in its former Ottoman territories. The empirical findings in Chapter 3 have shown that Turkish drama serials have significantly contributed to the rise of Türkiye's soft power, even though the drama sector's initial expansion, growth, and penetration into the MENA region was linked to Türkiye's hard power.

For many Arab study participants, the awareness and interest surrounding Türkiye was first triggered by their exposure to Turkish dramas, ultimately prompting both them and their families to visit the country. Television serials appear to have helped to transform the Turkish identity into a consumable commodity in the form of Arab tourism. But most interestingly, the perception of Türkiye on-screen, compared with the experience of Türkiye in reality, was often seen as an accurate and generally authentic depiction of the country. The present study has acknowledged that tourists still typically visit only the most popular areas and do not experience the whole reality that is Türkiye—however, for many Arab study participants, Türkiye's real shortcomings were experienced as simply making the country more relatable. As Nye suggests, it all depends on 'who relates to whom under what circumstances'.[3] Many study participants, when talking about Türkiye, often compared it to other countries in the Arab and Muslim world, Türkiye being perceived as more 'advanced', 'organized', 'Westernized', and 'progressive'.

It is important to highlight that despite the fieldwork in this book and chapter having been conducted during a period when Türkiye was shaken by nationwide anti-government protests, various corruption scandals, conflicts with Kurdish minorities, the imprisonment of a large number of Turkish journalists, social-media bans, multiple terrorist attacks, coup attempts, forced closures of media outlets, an economic downturn, a declining relationship with the EU, Türkiye's military intervention in Syria and Libya, and worsening relationships with Egypt, KSA, and the UAE, study participants were quick to overlook these, continuing instead to focus solely on the positive attributes associated with Türkiye. Thus, while scholars in the field have argued that these developments signify the decline of Turkish soft power, the empirical findings have revealed that the perception of Türkiye had been transformed in a matter of only a few years and remained positive despite these domestic, economic, and diplomatic challenges. The findings go on to establish that Türkiye's unique soft-power resource is its 'demonstrative effect', which has led to Türkiye being seen as a 'work in progress', enabling Arab countries to both see themselves in Türkiye's imperfections and experience a different societal model. Türkiye's culture, political theories, and policies have come to be seen as attractive, which is the essence of soft power. At the same time, Türkiye's unstable relations with the EU, KSA, the UAE, and Egypt, along

SUMMARY AND CONCLUSION

with its domestic political issues and economic shortfalls, are perceived as acceptable rather than damaging to Türkiye's new-found image as a model nation, peace broker, and defender of Muslim interests.

Chapter 3 also revealed that the country's imperial past was no longer seen as a period of Arab oppression. Instead, study participants emphasized their admiration for Ottoman history, which they perceived as a period when not Ottomans or Turks but *Muslims* collectively mattered. Television dramas dealing with Türkiye's Ottoman past have been found to have a pivotal impact in creating a desirable perception of Ottoman history among Arab participants. Instead of perceiving Turkish period dramas as glorifying Türkiye's imperial past, viewers saw them as depicting a period where the Muslim world held significant influence and when the East was important and stood for glory. Therefore, the findings in Chapter 3 have illustrated that Ottoman period dramas hold a rare soft power. Audiences are fascinated by the reality that a Muslim empire was once powerful. The fact that the serials are depicted by actors who look like people of the Middle East and are the heroes instead of the villains represents a strong appeal. Furthermore, the audience's realization that a Muslim country, such as Türkiye, can produce high-quality content has equally created a sense of admiration.

The empirical findings also revealed that Turkish serials enable Arab audiences to satisfy their curiosity about living a secular and more Western lifestyle, against the backdrop of a Muslim society. Türkiye's ability to provide a rare balance between modernity and Islam was established as one of the core reasons for its positive perception. One could argue that one of Turkish dramas' most significant soft powers is their ability to touch on subjects considered taboo in the Arab world. They have aided in projecting Türkiye as a nation where people have a choice between a liberal or conservative lifestyle—an ideal fusion of democracy and Islam, of modernity and tradition.

While Turkish serials have been the most significant catalyst for creating a positive perception, interest, and awareness of Türkiye among study participants, the focus-group and interview responses also showed that Türkiye's economic and military achievements have been an equally important source of soft power, resonating particularly with Arab males. Türkiye's hosting of more Syrian refugees than all of the Arab nations combined, and its vocal support of the Palestinian cause, have aided in elevating its status in the minds of research participants, who increasingly perceive the country to be a defender of Muslim interests. The data revealed in Chapter 3 has also shown that the Turkish president himself has become a source of soft power for many in the Arab world. Recep Tayyip Erdoğan has been seen as an inspirational Muslim leader with the power and authority to stand up to the West. For male research participants, he is perceived as directly responsible for strengthening political Islam, aided by the country's economy and military. President Erdoğan's popularity among young Arabs has become a soft-power source in itself. Chapter 3 showed that in the minds of Arab research participants, Türkiye's achievements are conceived of as accomplishments for the greater good of the Muslim world, rather than simply a Turkish achievement. One could argue that these findings are in line with public diplomacy scholar Nicholas Cull's argument that 'the management of the international environment through making [a country's] cultural resources and achievements known overseas and/or facilitating cultural transmission abroad' is a significant element of cultural diplomacy and soft power.[4] The findings of this chapter revealed that this is precisely what Turkish drama serials appear to be doing so well.

Finally, the analysis in this chapter demonstrated how foreign policy and cultural influence through Turkish television dramas have become crucial interrelated factors, both aiding Türkiye to gain soft power. However, Türkiye's unstable relationships with the most powerful Gulf monarchies, such as KSA and the UAE, demonstrate that the ruling elites remain wary of Turkish cultural influence in the region. Chapter 3 questioned whether the attractiveness of Turkish drama serials to Arab audiences should be seen as automatically equating to influence on foreign policy. The ban of Turkish drama serials from KSA and UAE free-to-air satellite channels validated the findings that Turkish serials are a powerful instrument in creating not only a positive perception of the country among Arab audiences, but also an affinity and familiarity with Türkiye, its culture, and its history, that would be difficult to achieve with other public diplomacy incentives. Ironically, it was MBC that first ignited the fever for Turkish serials on their free-to-air satellite channels and who later extinguished their existence on Arab screens, replacing them until 2022 with regional productions—albeit due to political influences rather than commercial motivations. The more recent reconciliation of Ankara, Abu Dhabi, and Riyadh resulted in the signing of various bilateral agreements

SUMMARY AND CONCLUSION

spanning different sectors and commitments for investment in Türkiye, and also the reintroduction of Turkish drama serials on KSA and UAE free-to-air satellite stations. This recent development confirms that diplomatic and trade relations have been pivotal in allowing Turkish drama serials to enter the Arab television market.

Recent scholarly arguments regarding soft power, or the power of attraction, have emphasized the importance of establishing emotional investments and connections as a core element in how soft power functions. Thus, while the attraction of Turkish television dramas may not directly translate into policy goals, they generate a level of emotional investment with a genuine sense of admiration, interest, warmth, and closeness towards Türkiye and its culture. The continued consumption of Turkish cultural products with the growth of Turkish dramas on streaming and pay-TV platforms also has the potential to greatly influence how the Arab world perceives modernity, and to shape the overall cultural market. Furthermore, with the rising exposure to Turkish visual aesthetics, it is possible that these aesthetics could become the new standard in the region.

Building on the key finding of Chapter 3, which revealed that Turkish drama serials have had a decisive impact on creating interest and awareness of Türkiye by establishing a desirable perception of the country and its people, and its historical and cultural elements, thus wielding significant influence, **Chapter 4** further examined how the cultural and historical relationship between Arabs and Turks, spanning more than half a century, including a common culture and heritage, similar ethnic types, and a common religion, played an important role in the pulling power of Turkish drama serials in the MENA region. By utilizing the diverse audience of the Gulf State of Qatar as a departure point, the chapter explored socio-cultural factors that facilitated the attraction of Turkish television dramas among Arab viewers. The empirical data overwhelmingly revealed that a shared history between Turks and Arabs has been a critical factor in the success of Turkish dramas. The reality that many aspects of the two cultures overlap, and have become interwoven, was established as pivotal. From similar-looking ethnicities, physical appearance, and body language, to comparable customs and traditions, along with similarities in the type of food consumed and music played—all of these elements have been identified as essential factors in the appeal of Turkish serials. These parallels have aided in the acceptance of dubbed Turkish serials by Arab viewers and enabled Turkish dramas to enter a cultural-linguistic market that would normally require the same, or a similar, language in order to avoid encountering cultural discount.

This chapter's findings also showed the importance of the dubbing of Turkish programmes into a colloquial dialect, which has provided access to a more diverse audience, including those who might have encountered difficulties with subtitling. The popularity of dubbed Turkish dramas ultimately saw dubbing applied more widely as a way to localize foreign content in a region that has been traditionally accustomed to subtitling. More importantly, the dubbing of content brought an entire country and its people closer—a country and people that many in the Arab world were unaware were so proximate. This allowed audiences to better recognize themselves or identify with 'a familiar or desired ethnic type on-screen', contributing to the increase in the cultural proximity of Turkish programmes and their relatability among Arab viewers. Significantly, the drama serials seem to have contributed to Turks being rediscovered by Arab viewers as people of the Middle East with a similar ethnic and cultural background.

Chapter 4 also illustrated that the shared religion between Türkiye and the Arab world has been a primary source of cultural capital that could intersect across nationalities and social classes. The subtle references to the Islamic faith in Turkish dramas has influenced or mediated Arab viewers' media choices. The empirical findings have repeatedly shown that Turkish dramas focus on family values, the primary foundation of Muslim society and culture, and by maintaining these structures, irrespective of liberal storylines or of how Western the dress of female characters is, the dramas profoundly resonate with viewers. The projection of a traditional family structure, set against the backdrop of a modern but Muslim society where family ties and respect for the older generation are considered essential, is a vital factor contributing to Turkish dramas' attraction. For most viewers, Turkish serials are experienced as having successfully merged cultural and ethnic similarities, social relations, and family ties with a modern way of life that is still recognizable in the Arab and Muslim cultural context.

The empirical data has also shown that the depiction of strong female characters in Turkish dramas was experienced as an equally essential factor in

SUMMARY AND CONCLUSION

their attraction. In contrast, national and regional productions were perceived as often presenting an incomplete version of Arab society, especially when it came to the projection of gender roles and family relations, which were often seen as dated and unrealistic. Most participants recognized that the society presented in Turkish serials was much more liberal than in Qatar and other Arab countries; however, the participants often stressed that women in Qatar and other Arab regions were increasingly active in a range of sectors, and in important positions in society, but that these realities were not sufficiently mirrored in Arab television serials. In contrast, strong female protagonists in Turkish serials who break gender norms while also searching for 'Mr Right' were overwhelmingly seen as critical to their success.

Moreover, Chapter 4 established that Turkish drama serials held a level of cultural shareability for Arab viewers that, to a degree, opposes the notion of cultural proximity. Turkish drama serials often employ archetypes of self-seeking, headstrong females in a courageous struggle—a theme with universal appeal. However, in the case of Turkish dramas, this heroic struggle of women protagonists is depicted against the backdrop of a Muslim society, where a strong patriarchal structure exists and the experience of shame and honour rests on the women's shoulders. The fact that women protagonists often fight against these cultural dimensions and the crony capitalism that provides power to the wealthy and well-connected, where the notions of honour and shame seemingly do not apply to the rich, resonates with many viewers in the Arab world. Thus, Chapter 4 revealed that it is not cultural shareability alone, but the reality of similar socio-cultural elements that are universal to the Muslim and Arab world which attracts audiences.

Genre proximity is identified in this chapter as another key factor in the success of Turkish dramas. The fact that Arabic dramas (*musalsalāt*) have traditionally been a popular genre on Arab television appears to have seamlessly paved the way for Turkish serials to be well received by Arab viewers. Once more, the findings demonstrate that the argument whereby the viewer's first preference would be for material produced in their own language and local or national culture does not hold among Arab, Chilean, or Israeli viewers.[5] Arab viewers have been opting for Turkish serials irrespective of the fact that Arabic content is widely available. Cultural and linguistic elements appear to become secondary if national and regional media fail to satisfy the audience's needs, while viewers still actively select television content that is closest, most proximate, or most directly relevant to them in terms of culture.

Finally, the empirical findings on university-level students in Qatar have shown that the younger generation were not the primary audience of Turkish drama serials. For the most part, university students underlined that they were only occasional viewers or passive audiences of Turkish dramas because their female relatives watched the serials in their households. Turkish drama serials were perceived as a women's genre, tailored particularly towards older women viewers, with serials being experienced as often too lengthy and overly dramatic. However, an overwhelming majority of female and male students believed that Turkish serials had surpassed local and regional television content in terms of production values and were comparable with content from the USA.

Chapter 5 examined why Turkish drama serials resonate with Arab women viewers, and what it is about Turkish dramas that satisfies their needs. It investigated female audiences' viewing motivations and patterns. In order to provide the reader with meaningful context, the chapter first critically examined the position of women in Qatar and the socio-cultural factors stemming from distinctive Qatari/Arab characteristics that can determine the behaviour and attitudes of women audiences. The empirical data analysed in the chapter revealed that Turkish serials are no longer consumed at the end of the day but at convenient times throughout the day, at home, often while completing household tasks, or while running errands. The findings established that the gratification gained from watching Turkish serials was also associated with the freedom of entertainment, because women viewers have been increasingly able to watch Turkish dramas online, via YouTube, on illegal websites providing pirated content with dubbed or subtitled Turkish dramas, on Turkish-channel websites (in Turkish), on Netflix, or via regional over-the-top (OTT; set-top) platforms. These platforms have removed the significance of broadcasting slots and have permitted viewers the flexibility to consume Turkish dramas wherever and however they want, and at a time convenient to them. These developments are in stark contrast to the empirical data collected (in focus-group discussions and an online survey) between 2013 and 2014, when Turkish drama serials were mainly watched on television and most commonly on MBC.

Chapter 5 revealed that the primary motive for Arab women to watch Turkish dramas is to seek out meaningful entertainment and an escape from

SUMMARY AND CONCLUSION

their daily lives. Turkish serials are able to provide a unique form of entertainment that not only allows women to escape from their everyday realities but also offers a sense of connection to the stories and characters portrayed in the shows. By immersing themselves in these shows, women can experience a different world that feels both familiar and relatable. The findings presented in this chapter showed that a unique combination of cultural proximity and distance, glamour, attractive actors, and strong female characters have made the viewing experience of Turkish serials highly gratifying. But perhaps most significantly, the portrayal of courtship and romance, not acceptable in the Arab world, and the ability to encroach on subjects and characters that are relatable but deemed taboo, hold a strong appeal. Thus, Turkish serials are found to provide an exceptional level of emotional realism and personal relatability that women viewers expressed they could not experience via local, regional, or other international content. Turkish dramas resonate with women viewers in an exceptional way, where every word and gesture finds an emotional meaning and drives their pleasure. Women viewers are able to relate to, identify, and engage with the emotional world of Turkish characters (particularly female ones), something that has been identified as a vital viewing motive. Moreover, despite the existence of patriarchal structures, Turkish dramas are perceived as granting women a position of power, structuring gender norms in such a way that women take central roles in issues related to family lives, motherhood, romance, and interpersonal relations. At the same time, Arab audiences' desire to experience Turkish modernity has been found to offer a strong viewing motive, with the 'Turkishness' projected in serials being perceived as highly appealing.

However, the findings equally demonstrated that an interest in Turkish modernity is not simply an audience response to Western modernity. Instead, the textual appeal of Turkish dramas has, for many viewers, been closely associated with the lifestyle and social relationships of urban contemporary Türkiye. One of the many gratifications women received from watching Turkish television dramas was the experience of Turkish modernity as familiar and still different (yet achievable in the Muslim/Arab context), featuring everyday consumerism.

Lastly but most importantly, even though this chapter identified several key viewing motives, it is imperative to recognize that it is the combination of all these various motives that Turkish dramas appear to satisfy, and which makes them particularly attractive to women viewers. Turkish drama serials' ability to gratify a range of needs simultaneously is what differentiates them from local, regional, and Western productions.

The main objective of **Chapter 6** was to examine the underlying factors facilitating the attraction of Turkish serials for viewers in Chile, who unlike Arab audiences do not share linguistic, ethnic, historical, or religious commonalities with Türkiye. Examining Chilean audiences as a case study has been particularly significant to this book because the country was the first nation in Latin America and the Caribbean region (LAC) to broadcast dubbed Turkish serials. The successful entry of Turkish dramas onto Chilean television represents a landmark moment that catapulted them into an entirely new market, ultimately reaching millions of television viewers across the LAC region. What the Chilean station Mega started in 2014 as an experiment transformed into a region-wide trend.

In an attempt to understand the appeal of Turkish dramas to Chilean audiences, and whether audience engagement could be considered beyond the logic of cultural proximity/distance, the study in Chapter 6 also focused on audience engagement within the notion of a serial's relevance to the audience's specific lives and lifeworlds, located as they are in the Global South. This chapter also set out to examine whether Chilean viewers were still seeking cultural proximity when watching Turkish dramas, and what their viewing motivations were. At the same time, it explored whether Turkish dramas had an influential role in generating awareness and/or a more positive perception of Türkiye and, therefore, could be seen as a critical soft-power tool for introducing and promoting Türkiye.

However, to provide readers with additional background, Chapter 6 commenced with a brief overview of Turkish diplomatic and economic relations with LAC countries. The chapter offered the reader an overview of these relations, past and present, to provide the necessary context to understand Türkiye's foreign policy and its significant changes under the ruling AKP government. The critical examination of Turkish–LAC relations identified that Türkiye's multidirectional foreign policy, which strategically combined trade and aid, created an environment that was highly conducive for the entry of Turkish drama serials. Along with many other products and services, Turkish dramas first penetrated the Chilean and later the rest of the LAC market.

SUMMARY AND CONCLUSION

Moreover, the empirical data from Chilean audiences revealed that Turkish drama serials played a pivotal role in establishing a favourable image of Türkiye and its people with Chilean viewers, who, prior to watching Turkish dramas, knew little or nothing about Türkiye. After watching Turkish serials, respondents realized that Türkiye was a beautiful country with many perceived cultural and ethnic similarities to Chile and the wider region. Most viewers expressed a strong desire to visit and experience the locations they had seen in Turkish serials. Turkish dramas contributed to an overall positive experience of the country, with the potential to generate an affirmative bias towards Türkiye. Although the appeal of Turkish serials in Chile and other LAC countries will not necessarily translate into influence on foreign policy, as discussed throughout this book, soft power reveals itself qualitatively in the shift of popular opinion, rather than quantitatively. Throughout this chapter we have seen that there are tangible, quantitative results that can be attributed not only to the significant increase in visitors to Türkiye from LAC countries but also to the empirical findings presented here. These findings indicate that Turkish dramas have a decisive impact on viewers' perception of Türkiye, making them more interested in visiting the country.

The findings analysed in Chapter 6 also showed that Turkish drama serials have successfully introduced a mediated version of Turkish culture and society to a culturally and geographically distant country. With Turkish dramas having become a permanent fixture on Chilean and other LAC countries' screens, they possess the potential to foster a long-term relationship with the region, contributing to a significant familiarity and secondary proximity with Turkish culture. Equally, Turkish drama serials hold a pivotal role in influencing the negative perception of Muslims that Western productions previously established. Therefore, one could argue that the soft power Turkish dramas are generating is beneficial to Türkiye and, more broadly, aids in creating a desirable image of Muslims that is rarely portrayed, challenging Western stereotypes.

Once more, the success of Turkish serials in Chile has not only aided in introducing Turkish culture and heritage to a region and its people to whom Türkiye was previously unfamiliar, but it has also contributed to audiences recognizing the various proximities between their own culture and a country that appears (at least at first sight) to be culturally distant. Chilean viewers were able to relate with surprising ease to the very same topics and themes as Turkish audiences, but also to engage meaningfully with them, regardless of their own cultural context. The perceived ethnic similarities between Turkish actors and Chilean viewers was an important factor in their appeal. These similarities, in combination with the dubbing into the Chilean dialect, significantly contributed to the overall success and acceptance of Turkish serials by Chilean viewers.

For many Chileans, one of the important appeals of Turkish dramas has been the projection of romance and courtship. For many women, seeing lovers not acting on their physical attraction, but instead subtly generating sexual tension, offers a far more gratifying viewing experience than watching over-sexualized content.

Furthermore, despite differences in faith between Türkiye and Chile, audiences experienced significant value proximity—around, for instance, the importance of family—which was highly appreciated by viewers. Turkish serials appear to be offering Chilean viewers many things that they felt were increasingly lost to their society and no longer presented on television screens. Successfully packaging traditional values with modernity and an urban lifestyle, displayed against the backdrop of Türkiye's most iconic locations, generated a highly pleasurable viewing experience.

The focus on human emotions in Turkish serials is seen as not only authentic and relatable, but also as an important factor in their appeal. Chilean audiences relate to stories in Turkish dramas in a similar way to audiences in Türkiye, the Arab world, and Israel. This study has established that one of the core factors in audience interest could, to a large degree, relate back to their lifeworlds. Therefore, the attraction of Turkish dramas in Chile could be seen as an interplay between the parallels of lifeworlds and cultural proximity that make topics such as the importance of traditional values resonate with viewers in both Türkiye and Chile. The way Turkish dramas often reflect the contemporary societal realities of emerging countries against the backdrop of a relatable modernity resonates greatly with viewers, and ultimately with their own emotional and societal lifeworlds. The reality that Türkiye and Chile are both rising economies in the Global South, faced with similar socio-economic pressures, combined with their shared moral codes rooted in conservative worldviews (Islam and Catholicism), has resulted in Turkish dramas being experienced by Chilean viewers as not only entertaining but also highly relatable and authentic.

SUMMARY AND CONCLUSION

Additionally, the production values of Turkish serials, along with the attractiveness of their actors, lifestyles, and storylines, combine to offer significant pulling power—as does offering a genre familiar to the viewers, but with stories that are new, along with characters and locations that are seen as both exotic and appealing. It would appear that while local productions continue to fail to offer the kinds of telenovelas that audiences are longing for, where innocent romance and human emotions are set in a modern yet traditional society with authentic characters and storylines, and which allow the viewer to enter a world that is not only highly relatable but is more glamorous or more dramatic than their own, Turkish serials will likely remain popular in the region.

Finally, the empirical findings in Chapter 6 also established that, as in Qatar, Turkish drama serials did not appear to resonate with university students in Chile as much as with their parents' and grandparents' generations. However, for the majority, Turkish serials were not criticized for their low production values or bad acting but were rather viewed as a genre that simply did not resonate. As with young people in Qatar, young Chileans predominantly perceived Turkish serials as a women's genre. The most common responses were that Turkish serials were 'too dramatic', 'too slow', or placed too great an emphasis on romance. For many, while these elements were seen as attributes that did not appeal to them, they were highlighted as important aspects attracting avid Turkish-serial viewers.

Chapter 7's primary objective was to examine the underlying factors contributing to the attraction of Turkish serials to viewers in Israel. As in Chapter 6, Chapter 7 attempted to discover whether the audience's engagement with Turkish drama serials could be understood beyond the theory of cultural proximity/distance by also concentrating on the dramas' relevance to the audience's specific lives and lifeworlds. This is considered notable owing to the reality that a significant proportion of Israeli Jews migrated from (or were raised by parents who were born in) countries that were part of the Ottoman Empire, or countries of the Global South. At the same time, despite Israel joining the ranks of developed economies over a decade, it has experienced economic and political turmoil. Bearing these important realities in mind, the chapter explored the viewing motivations of Israeli audiences while also seeking to establish if Israeli viewers were still looking for cultural closeness when watching Turkish dramas. Furthermore, I analysed the role of Turkish drama serials in creating soft power by investigating their impact on the audience's perception of Türkiye, its culture, and its people. Once more, to offer the reader a broad picture, the chapter first examined Turkish–Israeli relations from the establishment of the state of Israel to the present day. Turkish–Israeli relations have been particularly significant to this study as Turkish drama serials entered the Israeli television market in 2011, when diplomatic relations between the two nations had reached an unprecedented low. This was in stark contrast to the circumstances in which these serials penetrated Arab and LAC television markets, where Türkiye's multidirectional foreign policy and trade engagement had created an environment favourable for Turkish dramas to succeed. However, the empirical data analysed in this chapter showed that the existence of various cultural similarities between Türkiye and Israel contributed to audiences moving away from their negative preconceptions about Türkiye and its people, allowing Turkish serials to be appreciated as a cultural product that appeals to audiences' tastes and needs, rather than as a product from an unfriendly Muslim country. At the same time, the serials were found to generate a familiarity and affinity with the Turkish culture, people, and language among Israeli viewers.

The findings presented in this chapter showed that Turkish serials have been successful not only because they are simply dramas that have a transnational appeal, but significantly because Turkish serials have the distinctive ability to exhibit human emotions and storylines within a cultural framework that is not only relatable but also highly identifiable for viewers in Israel. For Israeli viewers, relatable dramas were found to be increasingly absent in local and Western productions. Thus, Turkish drama serials were experienced not only as entertainment (the primary motive for watching Turkish dramas), but they also helped Israeli viewers to connect with aspects of their cultural capital and identity that were, to a degree, suppressed under the Ashkenazi cultural hegemony. Turkish drama serials were found to appeal to a part of Israeli identity that holds a deep-rooted connection to countries in the Global South, seemingly not sufficiently catered for in Israeli productions. Therefore, an important part of the pleasurable viewing experience for Israeli audiences has been their ability to recognize similarities between Turkish and Israeli culture. The discovery by Israeli audiences of their many similarities with a nation and its people that previously were not only believed to be unfriendly towards

SUMMARY AND CONCLUSION

Israel, but were also seen as culturally and ethnically different, appears to have been seminal in the reception of Turkish serials. It seems that discovering similarities is an important part of the viewing experience, and we considered how these similarities could relate to Israeli audiences' current lives and lifeworlds given that they remain surrounded by hostile neighbours, where differences appear to matter more than commonalities. Thus, Israeli viewers' ability to connect and relate to dramas from a Muslim-majority country, while generating feelings of proximity, has removed the audience members' perception of being distinctly different to Turkish people and culture. This has converted into a pleasurable viewing experience, and one that many said provided an escape into a world that is similar but also different.

It also seems that the version of Turkish society and culture projected in the serials holds a strong appeal because Türkiye is seen as a Mediterranean country with Western-style modernity, while also greatly valuing conservative traditions. The constant interaction between modernity and tradition deeply resonates with the lifeworlds of Israeli viewers. This was established as having influenced viewers to change their negative preconceptions of Türkiye, with many even expressing an increased desire to visit the country to experience its culture, historic sites, and the locations where Turkish serials have been filmed.

Additionally, findings in Chapter 7 revealed that Turkish serials are appreciated for their high production values, 'suspenseful' and 'engaging storylines', and great acting. And as with Chilean viewers, the fact that Turkish dramas are mainly filmed in real locations and Istanbul's most picturesque settings was experienced by viewers as very visually pleasing.

Turkish–Israeli relations appear to be now on the mend, with the Israeli president having visited Türkiye in March 2022 for the first time in fourteen years, and a new US government that has encouraged Turkish–Israeli relations. However, whether relations will ultimately improve or not remains to be seen. Nevertheless, irrespective of geopolitics, the empirical findings have shown that Turkish serials managed to win the hearts of many Israeli audiences and, for serial viewers at least, the feeling of enmity or opposition towards Türkiye appears to have transformed into one of warmth and genuine interest in the country and its people. While the attraction of Turkish cultural products may not directly transform into policy goals, it seems that Turkish serials are likely to have a continued (positive) impact on the audience's expectation of what a good drama should be, while changing the perception of Muslim society.

Lastly, like the university students in Qatar and Chile, university students surveyed in Israel claimed not to be viewers of Turkish serials, but instead to be passively exposed to them by relatives (chiefly a mother) who watched them. However, despite this claim many admitted to having watched some episodes of *Bride of Istanbul*. Again, similarly to young respondents in Qatar and Chile, young people in Israel claimed to dislike Turkish serials because they were overly dramatic, and too emotional. They were also seen as a genre aimed more at 'older women' than at the younger generation. Instead, young Israelis expressed a preference for American content.

Final remarks

This book set out to examine what specifically made Turkish serials appealing to Arab viewers in Qatar, and equally to viewers in Chile and Israel. It established that viewers in each of these countries enjoy Turkish dramas and engage with them for predominantly similar reasons. Turkish serials hold a strong allure for viewers owing to cultural proximity, common lifeworld experiences, and similar values. Audiences have developed an affinity for Turkish drama serials based on emotional realism, their balancing of modernity and conservatism, their emphasis on family values, and their realistic characters, strong acting, good-looking actors, and original stories presented with an appealing technique in eye-catching and authentic settings. The empirical findings explored throughout this book have revealed that the existence of a multi-layered mix of cultures and identities in the Arab world, Chile, and Israel has been pivotal in terms of audience engagement and the viewer's underlying experience when it comes to entertainment and pleasure. Notably, the struggle between modernity and tradition, and the challenge of adapting to a world in which materialism often outweighs human virtue, results in culturally relatable stories with common traditional values and themes, and an emphasis on the family and motherhood that transcends differences in language, religion, and culture. These characteristics meaningfully distinguish Turkish serials from Western, domestic, and regional serials, and have satisfied viewers' longing for earlier times, when traditional values still mattered.

SUMMARY AND CONCLUSION

The lack of hypersexualization, with instead a focus on emotional realism and human relationships, is considered key for Qatari, Chilean, and Israeli viewers, no matter how unrealistic the plots might be. That said, for Qatari viewers, the portrayal of romance and courtship is still perceived as more progressive and liberal than they are accustomed to. Yet despite the patriarchal values portrayed, Turkish drama serials resonate with women, who are enabled to fantasize with no sense of threat. The serials, unlike local or international content, allowed viewers in all three countries to experience emotions that they might not otherwise be permitted to enjoy in everyday life, providing both comfort and gratification. Turkish drama serials' emphasis on interpersonal relations, and the introduction of a wide range of characters who do not simply represent good or evil forces within a family or community but are three-dimensional and realistic, holds strong appeal.

The notion of cultural proximity has proved helpful in understanding the pulling power of Turkish dramas among Arab audiences in Qatar, and most Chilean and Israeli viewers who have culturally situated themselves towards Turkish dramas and their perceived or imaginary conception of the Turkish culture by attributing their interest and engagement primarily within the logic of cultural proximity. The concept has aided in establishing how socio-cultural similarities and common lifeworld experiences intersect and generate a meaningful viewing experience.

For Chilean and Israeli viewers, a relatable and common lifeworld has contributed to Turkish dramas becoming highly engaging. For these viewers, the socio-economic realities depicted were perceived as relatable, while for Arab viewers, they were experienced as aspirational and a window into achievable alternative modernity. At the same time, perceived cultural or value similarities appear to have permitted Chilean and Israeli audiences to negotiate specific themes relevant to the viewers' personal experiences and circumstances. Turkish dramas are seen as highly relatable—something that is not sufficiently offered by national and international serials. Even though Turkish dramas project an idealized version of Turkish society that showcases the glamorous lifestyles of the rich and beautiful, these are often juxtaposed with the lives of the poorer and less fortunate. The projection of luxury and poverty, upward mobility, and migration from a small town to a big city to seek a better life have meaningful relevance to Arab, Chilean, and Israeli audiences.

TURKISH DRAMA SERIALS

Turkish drama serials appear to offer audiences a multi-layered textual space that, while focusing on Turkish society and life in its largest metropolis, Istanbul, is experienced as presenting values and widely relatable themes seen as ignored by national and international content producers. Turkish drama serials appear to have succeeded in providing viewers with layers of connection that intersect cultural and national boundaries. What started as a trial on the Arab world's biggest media network, MBC, has accidentally hit a zeitgeist and a sense of common time and space with viewers, where family values still matter, and a constant battle between modernity and tradition is experienced as an authentic depiction of everyday life. A society projected as a melting-pot of various cultures, and a key example of a country located in the Global South struggling economically while fighting to maintain a balance between Western-style modernity and tradition, is perceived as highly authentic and relatable to Arab, Chilean, and Israeli viewers. Therefore, irrespective of the fact that Turkish dramas emanate from a Muslim-majority country, the level of engagement these shows generate demonstrates that if television content becomes relevant to viewers, it can transcend cultural differences. Turkish dramas have managed to offer viewers a rare combination of elements from Western dramas and Latin telenovelas, with a Turkish twist, that now fill a significant gap that has not been satisfied by Western, domestic, or regional programming.

Interestingly, outside Türkiye, the dramas resonate less with young and/or male viewers, proving instead to be more popular with women. The fieldwork in Qatar, Chile, and Israel has shown that Turkish drama serials did not resonate with young university-age individuals. They did not appeal to the tastes of young viewers and were viewed as a genre aimed at older women. The length of Turkish dramas and their emphasis on romance were especially identified as key factors contributing to the lack of appeal for this audience group in all three countries.

The book also set out to examine the importance of Turkish drama serials as a source of soft power by reviewing their role in creating a positive perception of Türkiye. The empirical findings from Qatar, Chile, and Israel revealed that Turkish drama serials provide an important source of Turkish soft power, enabling both a reconnection with the Arab world and, in Chile and the rest of the LAC region, an introduction to Turkish culture. Turkish drama serials

SUMMARY AND CONCLUSION

in Israel have directly (positively) affected viewer's perceptions of Türkiye, helping to cement a strategic shift from an attitude of opposition to a recognition of cultural similarities. Turkish serials have succeeded in projecting Türkiye as a beautiful, exciting country with a rich history—an example of a modern nation that still retains its core traditional values. One common impact that Turkish dramas have had among those audiences surveyed is an increased interest in visiting Türkiye, resulting from the way everyday life is projected on-screen. Yet perhaps more significantly, the soft power generated by Turkish dramas appears to be beneficial not only to Turkiye: it also possesses the potential to create a more positive image of Muslims as a whole, who are rarely portrayed as challenging Western stereotypes. At the same time, one could argue that the adaptation of Turkish serials, and the Turkish expertise in drama productions in the Arab world, is ultimately the next phase of Turkish influence on the region's cultural industry. In the LAC region, Turkish scripts are increasingly being adapted for production in the cradle of telenovelas, while often surpassing local and regional productions in popularity. Moreover, these developments demonstrate how Turkish drama serials have significantly influenced audience expectations regarding a drama's visual aesthetic and emotional impact.

These developments reveal that Turkish drama serials have already had a direct impact on local productions in determining what an audience expects from a drama—how it looks, and how it makes one feel. Political science scholar Ty Solomon argued that 'soft power stems not only from its cultural influence or narrative construction, but more fundamentally from audiences' affective investments in the image of identity that it produces'.[6] As Press-Barnathan noted, the unique potential value of popular culture originates from its ability to reach a large number of people while creating emotions that impact viewers' perceptions of both friend and enemy.[7] Joseph Nye, who developed the concept of soft power, has himself argued that soft power originates from several sources, of which one key characteristic is attraction, which he described as a quintessential soft-power feature. Nye outlined that official policy, along with a society's culture, can aid in nurturing a state's attractiveness.[8] Therefore, the ability of Turkish drama serials to foster a familiarity, interest, admiration, and affinity with Turkish culture and history might not immediately translate into concrete policy goals. However, the

195

continued consumption of Turkish drama serials may result in an emotional investment by viewers, ultimately leading to a more positive perception of Türkiye in the long run. This suggests that the soft power projected by Turkish dramas could have a lasting impact on shaping global perceptions of the country, its culture, and its people.

Finally, this book has revealed that all three regions were drawn to Turkish drama serials' ability to project traditional values on a backdrop of modern society, maintaining norms and values that have been lacking in international and local productions. That said, future research should investigate whether the growing investment and expansion of Turkish serials produced for streaming platforms (often edgier and more sexualized) generate the desired interest and engagement with younger, and perhaps Western, audiences—or whether this trend will result in Turkish drama serials losing their core audience, who have appreciated their lack of sexuality and nudity, and their strong focus on traditional values.

Notes

Introduction

1. Bhutto, 2019; Melamed, 2019; Schipani & Pitel, 2021; Tali, 2016.
2. Al Jazeera Turk, 2014; Hürriyet Daily News, 2014; Vivarelli, 2017.
3. DTVE-Report, 2016.
4. Daily Television, 2019; Gusman, 2019; Martinez, 2021; Terranova, 2021.
5. Anaz, 2014; Arda, Aslan, & Mujica, 2021; Aslan, 2019; Berg, 2017a; Kaptan & Algan, 2020; Khan & Rohn, 2020; Kraidy & Al-Ghazzi, 2013; Özalpman & Sarikakis, 2018; Yanardağoğlu & Karam, 2013.
6. Ang, 1985; Katz, 1993; La Pastina & Straubhaar, 2005; McCabe & Akass, 2012; Straubhaar, 1991, 2007.
7. Salamandra, 2012.
8. Al-Sweel, 2008; Kimmelman, 2010.
9. Al-Sweel, 2008; Bhutto, 2019; Butler, 2009; Kimmelman, 2010.
10. Tokyay, 2017.
11. Baños, 2020.
12. Ashley, 2019.
13. Ang, 1985.
14. Marcus et al., 2017.
15. Braun & Clarke, 2019.

1. The Turkish Television Industry: From National to Transnational

1. Hürriyet Daily News, 2019b; Strait Talk, 2021.
2. Hürriyet Daily News, 2019b; Strait Talk, 2021.
3. Kurban & Sözeri, 2012.

4   TRT, 2023.
5   Kale, 2019.
6   Kale, 2019.
7   Kocabaşoğlu, 2010.
8   Sümer & Taş, 2020.
9   Kaptan & Algan, 2020.
10 Kale, 2019.
11 Bozkus, 2017; Ustuk, 2019.
12 Kaptan, 2018; Kaptan & Algan, 2020; Yesil, 2005.
13 CNNTürk, 2010, 2016; Milliyet, 2017.
14 Kaptan, 2018.
15 İlaslan, 2014.
16 Yesil, 2015.
17 Algan, 2003; Bariş, 2005; Y. Kaptan, 2020; Kaptan & Algan, 2020; Kaya & Çakmur, 2010.
18 Kaya & Çakmur, 2010.
19 Kaya, 1994; Kaya & Çakmur, 2010.
20 Founded by Cem Uzan and Ahmet Özal in 1989 as Magic Box, the channel started its test broadcasting in May 1990. For a brief period in the early 1990s, it was called Star Magic Box owing to the name Star 1 being copyrighted by another media organization.
21 Bariş, 2005; Kaya & Çakmur, 2010.
22 Sümer & Adakli, 2010; Waldman & Caliskan, 2017.
23 Öncü, 2005.
24 Çarkoğlu & Yavuz, 2010; Cetin, 2014; Kaptan & Algan, 2020; Kaya, 1994; Sönmez, 1996; Waldman & Caliskan, 2017.
25 Kaya & Çakmur, 2010.
26 Kejanlioğlu, 2004; Sümer & Adakli, 2010.
27 Cetin, 2014; Kaptan & Algan, 2020; Kurban & Sözeri, 2012; Saran, 2014; Sümer & Adakli, 2010.
28 Bryant & Hatay, 2013; Yanatma, 2016, 2021.
29 Mutlu, 1999.
30 RTÜK has been criticized for being politically influenced and not functioning as an independent regulatory body. Critics argue that the council is not free from political pressure and influence, which undermines its ability to regulate the broadcast media in an impartial manner (Kejanlıoğlu, Adaklı, & Çelenk, 2001).
31 Kaptan & Karanfil, 2013.
32 Hürriyet Daily News, 2019a; Öztürk, 2019; Yanardağoğlu & Turhalli, 2020.
33 RATEM, 2018.
34 Kaptan & Karanfil, 2013; Soysal, 2018.
35 Bryant and Hatay, 2013; Çetin, 2012; Gürzel, 2014.

NOTES

36 Szigetvári, 2019.
37 Cetin, 2014.
38 Hoskins, McFadyen, & Finn, 1997; Straubhaar, 1991.
39 De Sola Pool, 1977.
40 Soysal, 2018; Yesil, 2015.
41 Cetin, 2015; Cetin, 2014; Yesil, 2015.
42 Yesil, 2015.
43 Takvim, 2021.
44 Deloitte, 2014.
45 Cetin, 2014.
46 Yesil, 2015.
47 Deloitte, 2021; Ergocun, 2021.
48 Cetin, 2015.
49 Deloitte, 2014.
50 Algan, 2019; Cetin, 2014.
51 Alankuş & Yanardağoğlu, 2016; Vivarelli, 2017.
52 CNNTürk, 2014.
53 MedyaRadar, 2016; Yolculuk, 2018.
54 Takvim, 2018.
55 CNNTürk, 2021.
56 Deloitte, 2014.
57 Soysal, 2018.
58 Alankus & Yanardagoglu, 2016.
59 Deloitte, 2014.
60 Alankuş & Yanardağoğlu, 2016; Kaptan & Algan, 2020.
61 Vivarelli, 2017; https://variety.com/2017/tv/markets-festivals/turkish-tv-reaches-more-viewers-abroad-1202591287/.
62 Algan, 2019; Cetin, 2014; Hurtas, 2015; Karakartal, 2018; Yörük & Vatikiotis, 2013.
63 Prensario Internacional, 2018.
64 Hürriyet Daily News, 2019b.
65 Daily Sabah, 2019b; Uştuk, 2019.
66 Thussu, 2006.
67 An over-the-top media service offers viewers access to content directly via the internet.
68 Hürriyet Daily News, 2020.
69 Daily Sabah, 2021.
70 Eurostat, 2019.
71 Interview, December 2020.
72 Vivarelli, 2021.
73 Hürriyet Daily News, 2021.

74 Reuters, 2018.
75 Cumhuriyet, 2022.
76 Özdemir, 2022.
77 Oğuzlu, 2008; Sözen, 2010.
78 Bryant & Hatay, 2013; Gürzel, 2014.
79 Oğuzlu, 2008; Sözen, 2010.
80 Kutlay, 2011.
81 Türk, 2009.
82 Ataman, 2009.
83 Reuters, 2007.
84 Khan, 2006.
85 See Chapter 3 for more on Turkish–Arab rapprochement and Turkish serials' role as a tool for soft power.

2. Turkish Drama Serials in the Arab World

1 Kimmelman, 2010.
2 Yanardağoğlu & Karam, 2013.
3 Al-Sweel, 2008; Bhutto, 2019; Kimmelman, 2010; Williams, 2013.
4 Arab World Data (2023). World Bank. Retrieved from https://data.worldbank.org/region/arab-world; O'Neill, 2021.
5 Buccianti, 2016; Khalil, 2015.
6 The report included countries such as Jordan, Saudi Arabia, the UAE, Tunisia, Lebanon, Egypt, and Qatar. (Dennis, Martin, & Hassan, 2019.)
7 Khalil, 2020.
8 Alkebaisi, 2019; Buccianti, 2016; Khalil, 2020.
9 Apple TV+, Disney+, Amazon Prime Video, MBC Shahid, Viu, StarzPlay Arabia, Icflix, Istikana, Cinemoz.
10 Digital TV Research, 2020.
11 Khalil, 2020; Khalil & Kraidy, 2017.
12 Buccianti, 2016; Khalil, 2015; Khalil & Kraidy, 2017; Sakr, Skovgaard-Petersen, & Della Ratta, 2015.
13 Khalil & Kraidy, 2017; Sakr, 2007.
14 Khalil & Kraidy, 2017; Sakr et al., 2015.
15 Kaptan & Algan, 2020.
16 Pintak, 2010; Sakr, 2007.
17 McPhail, 2010; Pintak, 2010; Rugh, 2004.
18 Pintak, 2010.

NOTES

19 Ayish, 1997; Rubin, 2015; Sakr, 2007.
20 Khalil, 2020.
21 Khalil & Kraidy, 2017.
22 Ayish, 1997; Khalil & Kraidy, 2017.
23 Khalil & Kraidy, 2017; Rugh, 2004.
24 Rugh, 2004.
25 Khalil & Kraidy, 2017.
26 Mellor, Rinnawi, Dajani, & Ayish, 2011.
27 Khalil & Kraidy, 2017; Pintak, 2010; Rugh, 2004.
28 Khalil, 2019.
29 Yaakoubi, 2021.
30 Khalil & Kraidy, 2017.
31 Khalil & Kraidy, 2017; Mellor, 2013; Sakr, 2007.
32 Sakr, 2007.
33 Khalil, 2020, p. 439.
34 Khalil & Kraidy, 2017.
35 Khalil & Kraidy, 2017.
36 CIA, 2023.
37 Buccianti, 2016; Khalil & Kraidy, 2017.
38 Fahim, 2021; Khalil & Kraidy, 2017.
39 Khalil & Kraidy, 2017.
40 Buccianti, 2016.
41 Tamimi, 2012.
42 Tamimi, 2012.
43 Tamimi, 2012.
44 Khalil, 2020; Khalil & Kraidy, 2017.
45 Cordesman, 2020.
46 Kraidy & Al Ghazzi, 2013, p. 19.
47 Bhutto, 2019; Masrawy, 2018.
48 Kerr, 2018.
49 Masrawy, 2018.
50 See Chapter 3 for more details on deteriorating relationships between the two countries.
51 Khalil & Zayani, 2020.
52 Digital TV Research, 2020.
53 Hürriyet Daily News, 2016a; Khalil & Zayani, 2021.
54 Arab News, 2021.
55 See Chapter 1.
56 Saudi 24 News, 2020.

3. Fluctuating Turkish–Arab Relations and the Soft Power of Drama Serials

1. Akgun & Gündogan, 2012; Altunişik & Ellabbad, 2011.
2. Focus-group discussion and interviews were conducted in English.
3. Altinay, 2008; Aras, 2009; Benhaïm & Öktem, 2015; Benli Altunişik, 2008, 2011; Berg, 2017b; Bhutto, 2022; Bryant & Hatay, 2013; Ekşi & Erol, 2018; Çevik, 2019a; Juburi, 2015; Kalin, 2011; Oguzlu, 2007; Tol, 2018; Tweissi, 2011; William, 2013; Yörük & Vatikiotis, 2013; Zaman, 2011.
4. Al-Ghazzi & Kraidy, 2013; Altunişik, 2010; Bryant & Hatay, 2013; Çevik & Seib, 2016; Demiryol, 2014; Kraidy & Al-Ghazzi, 2013.
5. Altinay, 2008; Altunişik, 2011; Bryant & Hatay, 2013; Kirişci, 2011; Oğuzlu, 2007; Rousselin, 2013.
6. Bryant & Hatay, 2013; Çetin & Gallo, 2012.
7. Altunişik, 2010.
8. Sydney Morning Herald, 2002; UPI, 2002.
9. NTV, 2003.
10. Altinay, 2008; Altunişik, 2008, 2010.
11. Altunişik, 2010.
12. Çevik & Seib, 2016; Yörükoğlu & Atasoy, 2010.
13. Çevik, 2019a.
14. Kimmelman, 2010; Reuters, 2008.
15. Al Arabiya, 2008a, 2008b; Buccianti, 2010; Moussley, 2008; Salamandra, 2012.
16. Bilbassy-Charters, 2010; Deniz, 2010; Elhusseini, 2018; Kimmelman, 2010.
17. Çevik & Seib, 2016; Kirişci, 2012.
18. Yilmaz, 2012.
19. Altunişik, 2008; Yalvaç, 2012.
20. Parris, 2019; Walker, 2010.
21. Birand, 1996; Bryant & Hatay, 2013; Çevik, 2019a; Kraidy & Al-Ghazzi, 2013.
22. Bengio & Özcan, 2001.
23. Karaosmanoglu, 1985.
24. Dal, 2012, p. 247.
25. Jung, 2005, p. 7.
26. Carley, 1995; Jung, 2005; Kayali, 2014; Tol, 2012.
27. Aydin, 2000; Hale, 2012; Robins, 2003.
28. Jung, 2005; Kürkçüoğlu, 1980.
29. Jung, 2005.
30. Hale, 2012.

NOTES

31 Kaya, 2004.
32 Haarmann, 1988.
33 Haarmann, 1988; Jung, 2005.
34 Nachmani, 2003.
35 Nachmani, 2003, p. 23.
36 Altunişik, 2010; Bengio & Özcan, 2001.
37 Mardin, 2015; Sözen, 2010.
38 Demir, 2015.
39 Oğuzlu, 2008.
40 Sözen, 2010; Yörük & Vatikiotis, 2013.
41 Raxhimi, 2011; Reuters, 2014.
42 Davutoğlu, 2001.
43 Davutoğlu, 2001, 2010.
44 Oguzlu, 2008.
45 Salem, 2011.
46 Yalvac, 2012.
47 Yalvaç, 2012, p. 165.
48 Çevik & Seib, 2016.
49 Bryant & Hatay, 2013; Çevik & Seib, 2016; Gürzel, 2014.
50 Daily Sabah, 2021b; Tokyay, 2021. Türkiye is ranked as the world's third-largest humanitarian donor state (Çevik, 2015).
51 Çevik & Seib, 2016; Kalin, 2011.
52 Altunişik, 2008; Bryant & Hatay, 2013; Ergec, 2014; Sharma, 2017.
53 Demiryol, 2014.
54 Nye Jr, 2004, 2008, 2016; Nye, 1990, 2011.
55 Nye, 2004, p. 5.
56 Nye, 2004, p. 11.
57 Nye, 2004, p. 16.
58 Altunişik, 2008; Altinay, 2008; Oguzlu, 2007.
59 Aras, 2009.
60 Kalin, 2011.
61 Kalin, 2011.
62 Ergec, 2014.
63 Economist, 2011; Quamar, 2018.
64 See for example Bryant & Hatay, 2013.
65 Bryant & Hatay, 2013.
66 A wave of demonstrations and civil unrest began in Türkiye in late May 2013, originally opposing the development plan for Istanbul's Taksim Gezi Park. The protests were set off by outrage at the violent eviction of a sit-in at the park protesting the government's

203

urbanization plan. A barrage of supporting protests and strikes took place across Türkiye, protesting against a wide range of issues, at the core of which were questions of freedom of the press, expression and assembly, as well as concerns over allegations that the AKP government was planning on dissolving Türkiye's secularism.

67 Cerami, 2013; Çevik, 2019a; Kirişci, 2016; Strohecker, 2018; Tol & Başkan, 2018.
68 Çevik, 2019a.
69 Cengiz, 2020
70 Ataman, 2009
71 Khan, 2006
72 Cengiz, 2020
73 Celik, 2020; Cengiz, 2020
74 Al Jazeera, 2020; BBC News, 2017.
75 Euronews, 2018.
76 Daily Sabah, 2016.
77 Al-Masri, 2016.
78 Kose, 2018.
79 BBC, 2018.
80 Gulf News Saudi Arabia, 2018.
81 Al-Nar, 2019, MBC.
82 Bhutto, 2020.
83 Gellner, 1981.
84 Halawa, 2013; Tamimi, 2012.
85 Daily Sabah, 2021b; Reuters, 2021a.
86 Ataman, 2022; Reuters, 2022.
87 Navani, 2022.
88 Hürriyet Daily News, 2012.
89 Hürriyet Daily News, 2012.
90 Akyol, 2014; Duvar, 2019.
91 Habibi, 2015.
92 Hürriyet Daily News, 2012.
93 Algan & Kaptan, 2021.
94 Nye, 2004, p. 12.
95 Kunczik, 1997.
96 Anholt, 2007, p.100.
97 Otmazgin, 2008.
98 Press-Barnathan, 2012, p. 37.
99 Otmazgin & Ben-Yari, 2012, p. 31.
100 Fuller, 2013; Seymour, 2013.
101 Schönwälder, 2014.

NOTES

102 Çevik, 2019b.
103 Berg, 2017b.
104 For accuracy and conformity with the updated nomenclature, all references to Turkey have been amended to Türkiye.
105 An 'active' viewer in this context has been categorized as one who watches Turkish drama serials regularly, by choice, while a 'passive' viewer is subjected to the content involuntarily, owing to other members of their household being regular viewers.
106 Kirişci, 2011, p. 40.
107 Nye, 2004, p. 16.
108 Anholt, 2007.
109 Berg, 2022.
110 BBC News, 2019.
111 Seib, 2013.
112 Seib, 2013.
113 Kraidy & Al-Ghazzi, 2013.
114 Press-Barnathan, 2011.
115 Solomon, 2014.

4. The Importance of Socio-Cultural Factors in the Appeal of Turkish Serials among Arab Viewers

1 Salamandra, 2012.
2 Yanardağoğlu & Karam, 2013.
3 Kraidy & Al-Ghazzi, 2013.
4 Bhutto, 2019; Tokyay, 2017.
5 Hamid, 2018.
6 Abu-Nasr, 2019; Jabbour, 2015.
7 Annahar, 2021.
8 Ar Al Mokhtsa.
9 Bhutto, 2019; Kaptan, 2020; Sayin, 2021.
10 Khalil, 2020; Khalil & Ziyani 2022; Salem, 2017.
11 Focus-group discussions, semi-structured interviews, and online surveys were conducted in the English language.
12 Straubhaar, 1991, p. 51.
13 Sinclair, 1999.
14 La Pastina & Straubhaar, 2005.
15 The term 'expatriate' or 'expat' refers to workers who stay much longer than a typical short-term contract and try to create a new life away from their country of origin.

205

16 Straubhaar, 1991.
17 De Sola Pool, 1977; La Pastina & Straubhaar, 2005; Straubhaar, 2003.
18 Sinclair, 2009.
19 Straubhaar, 2007, p. 237.
20 Ksiazek & Webster, 2008; La Pastina & Straubhaar, 2005; Straubhaar, 2003.
21 La Pastina & Straubhaar, 2005; Straubhaar, 1991, 2003, 2007.
22 La Pastina & Straubhaar, 2005
23 Iwabuchi, 2001; Leung, 2008.
24 Straubhaar, 2007.
25 Bourdieu, 1984.
26 La Pastina & Straubhaar, 2005.
27 Maluf, 2003.
28 Statistics, 2013.
29 Bhutto, 2019.
30 Salamandra, 2012.
31 Salamandra, 2012.
32 Khalil, 2020.
33 Hoskins & Mirus, 1988.
34 Straubhaar, 2007.
35 La Pastina & Straubhaar; Yanardagoglu & Karam, 2013.
36 Straubhaar, 2007, p. 205, and 2005.
37 Iwabuchi, 2004.
38 Jung, 2005.
39 Onar, 2009; Taşpinar, 2011.
40 Bhutto, 2019.
41 Gellner, 1981.
42 Al-Ghazzi & Kraidy, 2013.
43 Barbero, 1993.
44 Straubhaar, 2007, p. 222.
45 Sinclair, 1998.
46 Qureshi, 2007, p. 295.
47 Qureshi, 2007.
48 Algan, 2019; Athique, 2014; Khorana, 2013.
49 Kraidy, 2005, p. 5.
50 Iwabuchi, 2002.
51 Williams, 2013.
52 Saleh, 2021.
53 Hürriyet Daily News, 2016b.
54 Bozkus, 2017; Uştuk, 2019.

NOTES

55 The Turkish state agency for monitoring, regulating, and sanctioning radio and television broadcasts.
56 Interview, December 2010.
57 Flores, 2022.
58 Singhal & Udornpim, 1997, p. 171.
59 Cihangir, 2013; Cooney, 2014; Simga, 2019.
60 Cihangir, 2013; Cooney, 2014.
61 Douki, Nacef, Belhadj, Bouasker, & Ghachem, 2003; Mosquera, Manstead, & Fischer, 2002.
62 La Pastina & Straubhaar, 2005.
63 Buccianti, 2016.
64 De Sola Pool, 1977; Straubhaar, 1991, 2003, 2007.

5. Why Turkish Dramas Resonate with Arab Women: An Analysis of the Responses of Women Viewers in Qatar

1 Al Arabiya, 2008a; Emirates 24/7, 2012; Salamandra, 2012.
2 Alardawi et al., 2021; Anaz, 2014; Aslan, 2019; Barrios et al., 2021; Berg, 2017a, 2022; Khan & Rohn, 2020; Özalpman & Sarikakis, 2018; Yanardağoğlu & Karam, 2013.
3 CIA, 2023.
4 CIA, 2023.
5 Owing to Qatar's demographic diversity, it was possible to conduct qualitative research not only with Qataris but also with nationals from various other Arab countries who reside there. The majority of research participants were from, or had identified their heritage as originating from, Algeria, Bahrain, Egypt, Iraq, Jordan, Lebanon, Libya, Morocco, Palestine, Saudi Arabia, Sudan, Syria, Tunisia, and Yemen.
6 Gengler, 2012; Snoj, 2019.
7 Lay, 2005.
8 Gengler, 2012.
9 Nydell, 2006.
10 Lay, 2005, p. 183.
11 Lay, 2005.
12 AlMuftah, 2018.
13 Teller, 2014.
14 Metcalfe, Hutchings, & Cooper, 2009.
15 Rosengren & Windahl, 1972; Rubin & Rubin, 1985.
16 McQuail, 1987; Anderson, 1987.
17 Anderson, 1987.
18 Allen & Allen, 1995; Ang, 1985; Geraghty, 1991; Livingstone, 1988; Rubin, 1985; Spence, 2005.

19 Choi et al., 2004; Chung & Kim, 2009; Grellhestl & Punyanunt-Carter, 2012; Leung, 2001, 2013; Leung & Wei, 2000; Roy, 2009; Rubin, 2009; Ruggiero, 2000; Shin, 2009; Sundar & Limperos, 2013.
20 Northwestern University-Qatar report, 2014, 2016, 2018.
21 Ang, 1985; Dyer, 2002.
22 Lee & Cho, 1990.
23 Ang, 1985; Horna, 1988.
24 Mumford, 1995; Brunsdon, 1981, p. 36.
25 Ang, 1985, p. 134.
26 Ang, 1985, p. 135.
27 Al Arabiya, 2008a; Emirates 24/7, 2012.
28 Geraghty, 1991, p. 43.
29 Berg, 2022.
30 Enli, 2015.
31 Eichner, 2020; Jacobsen, 2020; Kaptan, 2020.
32 Iwabuchi, 2002; Modleski, 1979; Singhal & Udornpim, 1997.
33 Eichner, 2020; Jacobsen & Jensen, 2020.
34 Modleski, 1979, p. 14.
35 McQuail, 1987.
36 Livingston, 1988.
37 Ang, 1985.
38 Abu-Lughod, 2005; Ang, 1985; Baran, 2017; Huat, 2004; Kraidy & Al-Ghazzi, 2013; Samandra, 2012.
39 Ang, 1985.
40 Geraghty, 1991.
41 Berman, 1983.
42 Hobson, 2003; Matelski, 1999.
43 Iwabuchi, 2004; Ko, 2004; Ming & Leung, 2004.
44 Leonhard, 2009; Nye, 2004; Ty, 2014.

6. Turkish Drama Serials in Chile

1 Habermas, 1984; Schutz & Luckmann, 1973.
2 La Pastina & Straubhaar, 2005; Straubhaar, 1991.
3 Katz, Blumler, & Gurevitch, 1973; Livingstone, 1988; Ruggiero, 2000; Swanson, 1977.
4 The surveys were distributed in Spanish and later translated into English. The interviews with media professionals in Türkiye were conducted in English.
5 Ang, 1985, p. 11.

NOTES

6   Ang, 1985.
7   Ang, 1985; Katz, 1993; La Pastina & Straubhaar, 2005; McCabe & Akass, 2012; Straubhaar, 1991, 2007.
8   Karpat, 1985.
9   Klich & Lesser, 1996.
10 Ministry of Foreign Affairs.
11 Sochaczewski, 2015.
12 Ministry of Foreign Affairs.
13 Davutoğlu, 2001.
14 Bilgin, 2007.
15 Sözen, 2010.
16 Haber Turk, 2009; Levaggi, 2013.
17 IHA, 2016.
18 Kalin, 2011.
19 Ministry of Foreign Affairs.
20 Önis, 2011.
21 Kirişci, 2009, p. 53.
22 Levaggi & Donelli, 2021.
23 Worldometer, 2021.
24 Ministry of Foreign Affairs.
25 Daily Sabah, 2019c.
26 Daily Sabah, 2019b.
27 Munyar, 2016.
28 Daily Sabah, 2019a.
29 BBC News, 2017.
30 Ministry of Foreign Affairs.
31 Reuters, 2019.
32 Akilli & Donelli, 2016.
33 Daily Sabah, 2019a.
34 Schipani & Pitel, 2021.
35 Levaggi & Donelli, 2021, p. 1123.
36 Levaggi & Donelli, 2021
37 Varol, 2016.
38 Gallarotti, 2011.
39 Sinclair, 2009; Varol, 2016.
40 Barrios et al., 2021.
41 Chamy, 2014.
42 Ashley, 2019.
43 Abramovich, 2014.

TURKISH DRAMA SERIALS

44   Ashley, 2019.
45   Baños, 2020.
46   Ashley, 2019; Pontificia Universidad Católica De Chile, 2015.
47   Augusto, 2019.
48   NTV, 2017.
49   Prensario Internacional, 2019.
50   Añez, 2015; TRT Español, 2020.
51   Yavuz, 2017.
52   Del Rio, 2020.
53   Anholt, 2007; Van Ham, 2005; Kunczik, 1997; Nye, 2004.
54   Anholt, 2007, p. 100.
55   Hürriyet Daily News, 2018; Mourenza, 2020.
56   Nye, 2004, p. 11.
57   Leonard, Stead, & Sweming, 2002.
58   Cull, 2009; Kunczik, 2016.
59   Melissen, 2005.
60   Press-Barnathan, 2011.
61   Kunczik, 2016.
62   Khan et al., 2021.
63   Anholt, 2007; Kunczik, 1997; Leonard, 2002, Nye, 2004; Zaharna, 2010.
64   Gans-Boriskin & Tisinger, 2005, p. 100.
65   Press-Barnathan, 2017, p. 160.
66   Ang, 1985.
67   Spence, 2005, p. 167.
68   Ang, 1985, p. 18.
69   Interviews conducted in December 2020 with media executives in Istanbul.
70   Straubhaar et al., 2019.
71   Straubhaar, 2007, p. 201.
72   McFadyen et al., 2000.
73   Singhal & Udornpim, 1997.
74   Singhal & Udornpim, 1997.
75   Larkin, 2008.
76   Straubhaar, 1991.
77   Straubhaar, 2007, p. 196.
78   Singhal & Udornpim, 1997.
79   Inglehart & Baker, 2000, p. 29.
80   Neumann & Charlton, 1988.
81   Athique, 2014.
82   Straubhaar, 2007.

NOTES

83 Giraldo, 2015; Ordóñez, 2012.
84 Martín-Barbero, 2002.
85 La Pastina & Straubhaar, 2005, p. 274.
86 Ang, 1985, p. 87.
87 Ang, 1985.
88 Iwabuchi, 2002.
89 Anholt, 2007; Kunczik, 1997; Leonard, 2002, Nye, 2004; Zaharna, 2010.

7. Turkish Drama Serials in Israel

1 NTV, 2011.
2 Aslan, 2019; Buccianti, 2010; Kaptan & Algan, 2020; Kraidy & Al-Ghazzi, 2013; Arda, Aslan, & Mujica, 2021; Yanardağoğlu & Karam, 2013.
3 Bhutto, 2019; Emirates 24/7, 2012; Hürriyet Daily News, 2018; Kimmelman, 2010.
4 Katz, Blumler, & Gurevitch, 1973; Livingstone, 1988; Swanson, 1977.
5 La Pastina & Straubhaar, 2005; Straubhaar, 1991, 2007.
6 Habermas, 1984; Schutz & Luckmann, 1973.
7 While the interviews were conducted in English, the surveys were administered in Hebrew and later translated into English.
8 Hathaway, 2019.
9 Yilmaz, 2010.
10 Uzer, 2013.
11 Tür, 2012.
12 Inbar, 2001.
13 Yilmaz, 2004.
14 Uzer, 2013; Ş. Yilmaz, 2004.
15 Altunişik, 2000, p. 172.
16 Altunişik, 2000; Tür, 2012.
17 Uzer, 2013.
18 Altunişik, 2000; Uzer, 2013.
19 Arbell, 2014; Sofuoglu, 2016.
20 Arbell, 2014.
21 Uzer, 2013.
22 Yilmaz, 2004.
23 Yilmaz, 2004.
24 Arbell, 2014; Uzer, 2013; Yilmaz, 2004.
25 Amos, 2011.
26 Arbell, 2014.

27 Schulte, 2010.
28 Y. Katz, 2010.
29 Aytürk, 2009.
30 Milliyet, 2008.
31 Inbar, 2011.
32 Kardas, 2009.
33 Bennhold, 2009.
34 BBC News, 2009.
35 AbuToameh, 2010.
36 Reuters, 2009.
37 Watson & Comer, 2009.
38 Hürriyet, 2010.
39 Booth, 2010.
40 Efron, 2018.
41 Efron, 2018; Heinrich, 2017; Kershner & Timur, 2022; Zimet, 2014.
42 Al Jazeera, 2020.
43 Luxner, 2021; Reuters, 2021; Times of Israel, 2021.
44 Kreshner & Timur; Kirişci & Arbell, 2022.
45 Soylu & Inanc, 2022.
46 Butler, 2009.
47 NTV, 2011.
48 Byron, 2018.
49 Melamed, 2019; Spiro, 2019.
50 Seńal News, 2020; TTV News, 2020.
51 M. Katz, 2020.
52 Nye Jr, 2004, 2008.
53 Carney, 2018; Cetin, 2014; Çevik, 2020.
54 Press-Barnathan, 2017, p. 176.
55 Friedman, 2018.
56 Bar-Tal, Halperin, & De Rivera, 2007; Bleiker, 2015; Press-Barnathan, 2011.
57 Solomon, 2014.
58 Otmazgin & Ben-Yari, 2012, p. 31.
59 Spingold, 2019.
60 Melamed, 2019; Spingold, 2019.
61 Shapira, 2020.
62 Athique, 2016; Straubhaar, 2007.
63 Athique, 2017, p. 1236.
64 Melamed, 2019.
65 Slade, 2010, p. 59.

NOTES

66 La Pastina & Straubhaar, 2005, p. 277.
67 Solomon, 2010.
68 Straubhaar, 2007.
69 La Pastina & Straubhaar, 2005.
70 Ang, 1985.
71 Hoskins & Mirus, 1988.

Summary and Conclusion

1 Ang, 1985; Katz, 1993; La Pastina & Straubhaar, 2005; McCabe & Akass, 2012; Straubhaar, 1991, 2007.
2 Northwestern University in Qatar, 2018.
3 Northwestern University in Qatar, 2018.
4 Nye, 2004, p. 16.
5 Cull, 2009, p. 19.
6 de Sola Pool, 1977; Straubhaar, 1991, 2003, 2007.
7 Solomon, 2014, p. 270.
8 Press-Barnathan, 2017.
9 Nye, 2004.

References

24Horas (2019). Elif se corona como la teleserie más larga emitida en Chile. Retrieved from https://www.24horas.cl/tendencias/espectaculosycultura/elif-se-corona-como-la-teleserie-mas-larga-emitida-en-chile—3478572.

Aaron, L., Robinson, J., & Smothers, S. (2002). Convergence, defined. *Presstime* May, 18.

Abramovich, P. (2014). Telenovelas turcas causan furor en Chile y van a la caza de América Latina. *El Nuevo Herald*. Retrieved from https://www.elnuevoherald.com/noticias/mundo/americalatina/article5251011.html

Abu-Lughod, L. (1995). Movie stars and Islamic moralism in Egypt. *Social Text*, 42, 53–67. https://doi.org/10.2307/466664

Abu-Lughod, L. (2005). *Dramas of Nationhood: The Politics of Television in Egypt*. Chicago: University of Chicago Press.

Abu-Nasr, D. (2019). Saudis can't resist Turkey's cultural invasion. Retrieved from https://www.bloomberg.com/news/features/2019-08-25/saudi-arabians-can-t-resist-turkey-s-cultural-invasion.

Abu Toameh, K. (2010). Anti-Israel TV show angers Palestinians. *Jerusalem Post*. Retrieved from https://www.jpost.com/jewish-world/jewish-news/anti-israel-tv-show-angers-palestinians.

Akilli, E., & Donelli, F. (2016). Reinvention of Turkish foreign policy in Latin America: The Cuba case. *Insight Turkey*, 18(2), 161–81.

Akyol, R.A. (2014). Arab buyers boost Turkish real estate market. *Al-Monitor*. Retrieved from https://www.al-monitor.com/originals/2014/04/arabs-buy-turkey-property.html.

Al Arabiya (2008a). Turkish soap star sparks divorces in Arab world. Retrieved from https://english.alarabiya.net/articles/2008/06/29/52291.

Al Arabiya (2008b). Turkish soap 'Noor' takes Arab world by storm. Retrieved from https://english.alarabiya.net/articles/2008/08/25/55419.

Algan, E. (2019). The transnationalization of Turkey's television industry. In S. Shimpach, ed., *The Routledge Companion to Global Television*. New York & London: Routledge. 445. https://doi.org/10.4324/9781315192468-43

Algan, E., & Kaptan, Y. (2021). Turkey's TV celebrities as cultural envoys: the role of celebrity diplomacy in nation branding and the pursuit of soft power. *Popular Communication*, 19(3), 222–34. https://doi.org/10.1080/15405702.2021.1913494

REFERENCES

Al-Ghazzi, O., & Kraidy, M.M. (2013). Turkey, the Middle East & the media | Neo-Ottoman cool 2: Turkish nation branding and Arabic-language transnational broadcasting. *International Journal of Communication*, 7, 2341–2360.

AlHumiri, S. (2020). Cult Saudi series 'Takki' has finally landed on Netflix. *Cosmopolitan*. Retrieved from https://www.cosmopolitanme.com/life/cult-saudi-series-takki-has-finally landed-on-netflix.

Al Jazeera (2020). Turkey appoints ambassador to Israel after two years: report. Retrieved from https://www.aljazeera.com/news/2020/12/14/turkey-selects-new-ambassador-to-israel-report.

Al Jazeera Turk (2014). Türk dizilerinin rekoru. Retrieved from http://www.aljazeera.com.tr/al-jazeera-ozel/turk-dizilerinin-rekoru.

Alkebaisi, M. (2019). The Gulf region. Retrieved from https://global-internet-tv.com/the-gulf-region/

Allen, R.C. (ed.) (1995). *To Be Continued...: Soap Operas around the World*. London: Routledge.

Al-Malki, A., Kaufer, D., Ishizaki, S., & Dreher, K. (2012). *Arab Women in Arab News: Old Stereotypes and New Media*. A&C Black.

Al-Masri, A. (2016). Turkish–Saudi relations: a burgeoning relationship. Ankara: Anadolu Agency. Retrieved from https://www.aa.com.tr/en/economy/turkish-saudi-relations-a-burgeoning-relationship/656010.

Al Muftah, H. (2018). Human development in Qatar. In A. Farazmand (ed.), *Global Encyclopedia of Public Administration, Public Policy, and Governance*. Cham: Springer. https://doi.org/10.1007/978-3-319-31816-5_3205-1

Al-Sweel, F. (2008). Turkish soap opera flop takes Arab world by storm. Retrieved from https://www.reuters.com/article/us-saudi-soapopera-idUSL633715120080726

Altinay, H. (2008). Turkey's soft power: an unpolished gem or an elusive mirage? *Insight Turkey*, 10(2), 55–66.

Altunışık, M. (2000). The Turkish–Israeli *rapprochement* in the post-Cold War era. *Middle Eastern Studies*, 36(2), 172–91. https://doi.org/10.1080/00263200008701313

Altunışık, M.B. (2008). The possibilities and limits of Turkey's soft power in the Middle East. *Insight Turkey*, 10(2), 41–54.

Altunışık, M.B. (2010). *Turkey: Arab Perspectives*. Turkish Economic and Social Studies Foundation.

Altunışık, M.B. (2011). Challenges to Turkey's soft power in the Middle East. *TESEV Policy Brief*, I, 1–4.

Altunisik, M., & Ellabbad, M. (2011). *Arap Dunyasinda Turkiye Algısı* [Turkey's Perception in the Arab World]. 11. Istanbul: TESEV Dış Politika Programı. Retrieved from https://scholar.google.com/scholar?hl=en&as_sdt=0%2C5&q=Altunisik%2C+M.%2C+%26+Ellabbad%2C+M.+%282011%29.+Arap+Dunyasinda+Turkiye+Alg%C4%B1s%C4%B1+&btnG=#d=gs_cit&t=1677597675749&u=%2Fscholar%3Fq%3Dinfo%3A_8XAQY5D16sJ%3Ascholar.google.com%2F%26output%3Dcite%26scirp%3D0%26hl%3Den

Amos, D. (2011). *Eclipse of the Sunnis: Power, Exile, and Upheaval in the Middle East*. New York: Public Affairs.

Anaz, N. (2014). The geography of reception: why do Egyptians watch Turkish soap operas? *The Arab World Geographer*, 17(3), 255–74.

Anderson, J.A. (1987). *Communication Research: Issues and Methods*. New York: McGraw-Hill.

Añez, P.C.S. (2015). ¿Por qué los latinoamericanos están bautizando a sus hijos con los nombres turcos 'Onur' y 'Sherezade'? *GlobalVoices*. Retrieved from https://es.globalvoices.org/2015/04/09/por-que-los-latinoamericanos-estan-bautizando-a-sus-hijos-con-los-nombres-turcos-onur-y-sherezade/.

Ang, I. (1985). *Watching Dallas: Soap Opera and the Melodramatic Imagination*. London: Routledge.

Anholt, S. (2007). *Competitive Identity: The New Brand Management for Nations, Cities, and Regions*. New York: Palgrave Macmillan.

Annahar (2021). After years of boycott… 'Dubai' channel returns to showing Turkish drama. Retrieved from https://www.annahar.com/arabic/section/6-%D9%81%D9%86-%D9%88%D9%85%D8%AC%D8%AA%D9%85%D8%B9/01102021100458924 [Link no longer available.]

Arab News. (2021). StarzPlay strengthens Turkish content offering with BluTV add-on. Retrieved from https://www.arabnews.com/node/1842886/media.

Aras, B. (2009). Turkey's soft power. *The Guardian*, 14 April. Retrieved from https://www.theguardian.com/commentisfree/2009/apr/13/turkey-middleeast

Arbell, D. (2014). *The US–Turkey–Israel Triangle*. Brookings: Center for Middle East Policy, Analysis Paper 34.

Arda, Ö., Aslan, P., & Mujica, C. (eds). (2021). *Transnationalization of Turkish Television Series*. Istanbul: Istanbul University Press. DOI: 10.26650/B/SS18.2021.004

Ashley, J. (2019). Chilean television on shifting terrain: movement toward a postnetwork era. *Television & New Media*, 20(5), 476–91. DOI: 10.1177/1527476418776416

Aslan, P. (2019). Uluslararasi iletişim ve popüler kültür üzerine: Latin Amerika'daki Türk televizyon dizileri üzerinden bir araştırma. *Connectist: Istanbul University Journal of Communication Sciences*, 57, 25–50. https://doi.org/10.26650/CONNECTIST2019-0052

Ataman, M. (2009). Türkiye–Suudi Arabistan ilişkileri: temkinli ilişkilerden çok-taraflı birlikteliğe. *Ortadoğu Analiz*, 1(9), 72–81. Retrieved from https://www.orsam.org.tr/d_hbanaliz/8muhittin.pdf.

Ataman, M. (2022). A new page in Turkey–Saudi relations. *Daily Sabah*, 6 July. Retrieved from https://www.dailysabah.com/opinion/columns/a-new-page-in-turkey-saudi-relations.

Athique, A. (2014). Transnational audiences: geocultural approaches. *Continuum*, 28(1), 4–17. https://doi.org/10.1080/10304312.2014.870868

Athique, A. (2017). *Transnational Audiences: Media Reception on a Global Scale*. Hoboken, New Jersey: John Wiley & Sons.

Agusto, B.C. (2019). Turcas, series y películas: ellas son las mujeres detrás de los doblajes de voz. *Neuva Mujer* (Chile), 4 September. Retrieved from https://www.nuevamujer.com/chile/2019/09/04/dobles-de-voz-entrevista.html

REFERENCES

Aydin, M. (2000). Determinants of Turkish foreign policy: changing patterns and conjunctures during the Cold War. *Middle Eastern Studies*, 36(1), 103–39.

Ayish, M.I. (1997). Arab television goes commercial: a case study of the Middle East Broadcasting Centre. *Gazette (Leiden, Netherlands)*, 59(6), 473–94.

Aytürk, İ. (2009). Between crises and cooperation: the future of Turkish–Israeli relations. *Insight Turkey*, 11(2), 57–74.

Baños, J.J. (2020). Las telenovelas turcas: el fenómeno mundial que nadie vio venir. *La Vanguardia*, 9 August. Retrieved from https://www.lavanguardia.com/television/20200809/482739613619/las-telenovelas-turcas-el-fenomeno-mundial-que-nadie-vio-venir.html.

Barbero, J.-M. (1993). Latin America: cultures in the communication media. *Journal of Communication*, 43(2), 18–30. DOI: 10.1111/j.1460-2466.1993.tb01259.x

Barrios, L.A., Andrada, P., & Mujica, C. (2021). Digital transformation and the impact of Turkish telenovelas in Chile: back to melodrama. In Ö. Arda, P. Aslan, & C. Mujica (eds), *Transnationalization of Turkish Television Series*, 27. Istanbul: Istanbul University Press. https://doi.org/10.26650/B/SS18.2021.004.002

Bar-Tal, D., Halperin, E., & De Rivera, J. (2007). Collective emotions in conflict situations: societal implications. *Journal of Social Issues*, 63(2), 441–60. https://doi.org/10.1111/j.1540-4560.2007.00518.x

BBC News (2009). Arabic press praises Erdogan. Retrieved from http://news.bbc.co.uk/2/hi/middle_east/7860328.stm.

BBC News Mundo (2017a). Por qué Turquía le importa cada vez más a América Latina. 17 April. Retrieved from https://www.bbc.com/mundo/noticias-internacional-36827436.

BBC News (2017b). Qatar crisis: what you need to know. 19 July. Retrieved from https://www.bbc.co.uk/news/world-middle-east-40173757

Bengio, O., & Özcan, G. (2001). Old grievances, new fears: Arab perceptions of Turkey and its alignment with Israel. *Middle Eastern Studies*, 37(2), 50–92. https://doi.org/10.1080/714004395

Benhaïm, Y., & Öktem, K. (2015). The rise and fall of Turkey's soft power discourse: discourse in foreign policy under Davutoğlu and Erdoğan. *European Journal of Turkish Studies: Social Sciences on Contemporary Turkey*, 21. https://doi.org/10.4000/ejts.5275

Bennhold, K. (2009). Leaders of Turkey and Israel clash at Davos panel. *New York Times*, 29 January. Retrieved from https://www.nytimes.com/2009/01/30/world/europe/30iht-30clash.19795420.html?searchResultPosition=1

Berg, M. (2017a). The importance of cultural proximity in the success of Turkish television dramas in Qatar. *International Journal of Communication*, 11, 3415–30.

Berg, M. (2017b). Turkish drama serials as a tool for Soft Power. *Participations: Journal of Audience & Reception Studies*, 14(2), 32–52.

Berg, M. (2022). The interplay between authenticity, realism and cultural proximity in the reception of Turkish drama serials among Qatari audiences. *Journal of Popular Television*, 10(1), 21–40. https://doi.org/10.1386/jptv_00068_1

Berman, M. (1983). *All That is Solid Melts into Air: The Experience of Modernity*. New York & London: Verso.

Bhutto, F. (2019). How Turkish TV is taking over the world. *The Guardian*. 13 September. Retrieved from https://www.theguardian.com/tv-and-radio/2019/sep/13/turkish-tv-magnificent-century-dizi-taking-over-world.

Bhutto, F. (2020). How Turkey's soft power conquered Pakistan. *Foreign Policy*., 5 September. Retrieved from https://foreignpolicy.com/2020/09/05/ertugrul-turkey-dizi-soft-power-pakistan/.

Bielby, D.D., & Harrington, C.L. (2008). *Global TV: Exporting Television and Culture in the World Market*. New York: New York University Press.

Bilbassy-Charters, N. (2010). Leave it to Turkish soap operas to conquer hearts and minds. *Foreign Policy*, 15 April. Retrieved from https://foreignpolicy.com/2010/04/15/leave-it-to-turkish-soap-operas-to-conquer-hearts-and-minds/.

Bilgin, P. (2007). 'Only strong states can survive in Turkey's geography': the uses of 'geopolitical truths' in Turkey. *Political Geography*, 26(7), 740–56. DOI: 10.1016/j.polgeo.2007.04.003

Birand, M.A. (1996). Is there a new role for Turkey in the Middle East? In Henri Barkey (ed.), *Reluctant Neighbor: Turkey's Role in the Middle East*, 172. Washington DC: United States Institute of Peace Press.

Bleiker, R. (2015). Pluralist methods for visual global politics. *Millennium*, 43(3), 872–90. https://doi.org/10.1177/0305829815583084

Booth, R. (2010). Israeli attack on Gaza flotilla sparks international outrage. *The Guardian*. Retrieved from https://www.theguardian.com/world/2010/may/31/israeli-attacks-gaza-flotilla-activists.

Bourdieu, P. (1984). *Distinction: A Social Critique of the Judgement of Taste*. Cambridge, Massachusetts: Harvard University Press.

Boyd, D.A. (1999). *Broadcasting in the Arab World: A Survey of the Electronic Media in the Middle East*. Ames: Iowa State University Press.

Bozkus, F. (2017). Dizi ihracatımız çok hızlı yükseliyor. *Ekonomist*, 11 January. Retrieved from https://www.ekonomist.com.tr/medya/dizi-ihracatimiz-cok-hizli-yukseliyor.html.

Braun, V., & Clarke, V. (2019). Reflecting on reflexive thematic analysis. *Qualitative Research in Sport, Exercise and Health*, 11(4), 589–97. https://doi.org/10.1080/2159676X.2019.1628806

Brock, T.C., & Livingston, S.D. (2004). The need for entertainment scale. In L.J. Shrum (ed.), *The Psychology of Entertainment Media: Blurring the Lines between Entertainment and Persuasion*, 255–74. Mahwah, New Jersey & London: Lawrence Erlbaum Associates.

Browers, M. (2009). *Political Ideology in the Arab World*. Cambridge Middle East Studies 31. Cambridge: Cambridge University Press.

Brunsdon, C. (1981). 'Crossroads' notes on soap opera. *Screen*, 22(4), 32–37.

Bryant, R., & Hatay, M. (2013). *Soft Politics and Hard Choices: An Assessment of Turkey's New Regional Diplomacy*. Report 2/2013. Oslo: Peace Research Institute.

REFERENCES

Buccianti, A. (2010). Dubbed Turkish soap operas conquering the Arab world: social liberation or cultural alienation? *Arab Media and Society*, 10, 4–28.

Buccianti, A. (2016). Arab storytelling in the digital age: from musalsalāt to web drama? In M. Hagener, V. Hediger, & A. Strohmaier (eds), *The State of Post-Cinema: Tracing the Moving Image in the Age of Digital Dissemination*, 49–70. London: Palgrave Macmillan.

Butler, D. (2009). Turkey's 'Brad Pitt' stirs wide Arab interest. Retrieved from https://de.reuters.com/article/us-turkey-mideast-soaps-idCATRE52A06Y20090311.

Byron, B. (2018). ההיסטריה מאיסטנבול ('The hysteria from Istanbul). TVBee. Retrieved from https://www.mako.co.il/tvbee-tvbee-weekend/Article-59a98ab1ec2f661006.htm.

Carley, P. (1995). *Turkey's Role in the Middle East*. (Peaceworks No. 1.) Washington, DC: United States Institute of Peace: Washington DC. Retrieved from https://www.usip.org/publications/1995/01/turkeys-role-middle-east

Carney, J. (2018). Resur(e)recting a spectacular hero: Diriliş Ertuğrul, necropolitics, and popular culture in Turkey. *Review of Middle East Studies*, 52(1), 93–114.

Celik, H. (2020). ANALYSIS—Saudi establishment wary of desires of young crown prince. Anadolu Agency. Retrieved from https://www.aa.com.tr/en/analysis/analysis-saudi-establishment-wary-of-desires-of-young-crown-prince/1771611

Cengiz, S. (2020). Turkey: between the EU and GCC. *Gulf State Analytics*. Retrieved from https://gulfstateanalytics.com/turkey-between-the-eu-and-gcc/

Cerami, C. (2013). Rethinking Turkey's soft power in the Arab world: Islam, secularism, and democracy. *Journal of Levantine Studies*, 3(2), 129–50.

Cetin, K.B.E. (2014). The 'politicization' of Turkish television dramas. *International Journal of Communication*, 8, 2462–83 .

Çevik, B.S. (2015). The benefactor: NGOs and humanitarian aid. In B.S. Çevik & P. Seib (eds), *Turkey's Public Diplomacy*, 121–52. New York: Palgrave Macmillan. DOI: 10.1057/9781137466983_7

Çevik, B.S., & Seib, P. (2016). *Turkey's Public Diplomacy*. New York: Palgrave Macmillan. DOI: 10.1057/9781137466983_7

Çevik, S.B. (2019a). Reassessing Turkey's soft power: the rules of attraction. *Alternatives*, 44(1), 50–71. DOI: 10.1177/0304375419853751

Çevik, S.B. (2019b). Turkish historical television series: public broadcasting of neo-Ottoman illusions. *Southeast European and Black Sea Studies*, 19(2), 227–42. https://doi.org/10.1080/14683857.2019.1622288

Çevik, S.B. (2020). The empire strikes back: propagating AKP's Ottoman Empire narrative on Turkish television. *Middle East Critique*, 29(2), 177–97. https://doi.org/10.1080/19436149.2020.1732031

Chamy, C.H. (2014). Cómo Turquía está cambiando el mercado de las teleseries de A. Latina. *BBC Mundo*, 3 September. Retrieved from https://www.bbc.com/mundo/noticias/2014/09/140903_cultura_telenovelas_turcas_conquistan_america_latina_ch.

Chung, M.Y., & Kim, H.S. (2015). College students' motivations for using podcasts. *Journal of Media Literacy Education*, 7(3), 13–28. Retrieved from http://hdl.handle.net/11603/24022

CIA (2023). *CIA, The World Factbook*. Retrieved from https://www.cia.gov/the-world-factbook/

Cihangir, S. (2013). Gender specific honor codes and cultural change. *Group Processes & Intergroup Relations*, 16(3), 319–33. https://doi.org/10.1177/1368430212463453

Clarke, S. (2019). Netflix launches 'Justice,' its first series from the UAE. *Variety*, 23 January. Retrieved from https://variety.com/2019/tv/news/netflix-justice-first-series-united-arab-emirates-1203115437/

CNNTürk. (2016). Bir zamanlar Türk televizyonlarında fırtınalar estirmiş pembe diziler. 22 October. Retrieved from https://www.cnnturk.com/fotogaleri/kultur-sanat/sinema/bir-zamanlar-turk-televizyonlarinda-firtinalar-estirmis-pembe-diziler?page=1

Cooney, M. (2014). Family honour and social time. *The Sociological Review*, 62(2), Suppl., 87–106. https://doi.org/10.1111/1467-954X.12193

Cordesman, A.H. (2020). *Greater Middle East: From the 'Arab Spring' to the 'Axis of Failed States'*. Washington DC: Center for Strategic and International Studies (CSIS).

Cull, N.J. (2009). *Public Diplomacy: Lessons from the Past*. 12. Los Angeles: Figueroa Press.

Cumhuriyet (2022). Disney Plus Türkiye'de: Netflix ve televizyon kanallarının rekabeti dizi sektörünü nasıl değiştiriyor? Retrieved from https://www.cumhuriyet.com.tr/dunya/disney-plus-turkiyede-netflix-ve-televizyon-kanallarinin-rekabeti-dizi-sektorunu-nasil-degistiriyor-1946876.

Daily Sabah. (2016). Business Forum to lead way to Turkish-Saudi FTA. 15 April. Retrieved from https://www.dailysabah.com/business/2016/04/15/business-forum-to-lead-way-to-turkish-saudi-fta

Daily Sabah (2019a). Turkey to further develop relations with Latin America. Retrieved from https://www.dailysabah.com/diplomacy/2019/05/23/turkey-to-further-develop-relations-with-latin-america.

Daily Sabah (2019b). Turkish exporters intensify efforts to stimulate business in Latin America. Retrieved from https://www.dailysabah.com/economy/2019/09/14/turkish-exporters-intensify-efforts-to-stimulate-business-in-latin-america.

Daily Sabah. (2019c). Popular Turkish TV series raise exports of goods, services. 10 November. Retrieved from https://www.dailysabah.com/business/2019/11/10/popular-turkish-tv-series-raise-exports-of-goods-services

Daily Sabah. (2020). Turkish BluTV leaves Netflix behind as top streaming platform in Q1. 20 April. Retrieved from https://www.dailysabah.com/business/tech/turkish-blutv-leaves-netflix-behind-as-top-streaming-platform-in-q1

Daily Sabah. (2021a). Eid aid: Turkish donors deliver charity to the world. 19 July. Retrieved from https://www.dailysabah.com/turkey/eid-aid-turkish-donors-deliver-charity-to-the-world/news

Daily Sabah (2021b). Saudi imports of Turkish goods hit new low amid informal boycott. 25 March. Retrieved from https://www.dailysabah.com/business/economy/saudi-imports-of-turkish-goods-hit-new-low-amid-informal-boycott.

REFERENCES

Daily Television (2019). Exitoso drama turco Fatmagül tendrá su remake español. Retrieved from https://www.thedailytelevision.com/articulo/contenidos/telenovelas/exitoso-drama-turco-ifatmaguli-tendra-su-remake-espanol.

Dal, E.P. (2012). The transformation of Turkey's relations with the Middle East: illusion or awakening? *Turkish Studies*, 13(2), 245–67. https://doi.org/10.1080/14683849.2012.685257

Davutoğlu, A. (2001). Stratejik derinlik: Türkiye'nin uluslararası konumu. *Middle East Journal*, 55(4), 693–4. Retrieved from https://scholar.google.com/scholar?hl=en&as_sdt=0%2C5&q=Stratejik+derinlik%3A+T%C3%BCrkiye%27nin+uluslararas%C4%B1+konumu+davutoglu&btnG=

Davutoğlu, A. (2010). Turkey's zero-problems foreign policy. *Foreign Policy*, 20(5). Retrieved from https://foreignpolicy.com/2010/05/20/turkeys-zero-problem-foreign-policy/

Deloitte (2021). *Türkiye'de Tahmini Medya ve Reklam Yatırımları 2020 Raporu*. April. Retrieved from https://www2.deloitte.com/content/dam/Deloitte/tr/Documents/technology-media-telecommunications/medya-ve-reklam-yatirimlari-2020-raporu.pdf.

Del Rio, J.C. (2020). Telenovelas turcas demuestran misoginia, machismo y violencia doméstica. *Ciber* (Cuba), 24 January. Retrieved from https://www.cibercuba.com/noticias/2020-01-25-u80279-e80279-s27315-telenovelas-turcas-demuestran-misoginia-machismo-violencia.

Demir, V. (2015). Historical perspective: Ottomans and the Republican era. In B.S. Çevik & P. Seib (eds), *Turkey's Public Diplomacy*, 43–65. New York: Palgrave Macmillan. DOI: 10.1057/9781137466983_3

Demiryol, T. (2013). Poverty of soft power: evidence from Turkish foreign policy in the Middle East. *European Journal of Research on Education*, 2014 Special Issue: International Relations, 6–11.

Deniz, A.Ç. (2010). Gümüş dizisinin Arap kamuoyuna etkileri bir sosyal medya incelemesi. *Uşak Üniversitesi Sosyal Bilimler Dergisi*, 3(1), 50–67.

Dennis, E., Martin, J., & Hassan, F. (2019). *Media Use in the Middle East, 2019: A Seven-Nation Survey*. Northwestern University in Qatar.

Dennis, E., Martin, J., & Wood, R. (2018). Media use in the Middle East. In *Entertainment*. https://www.mideastmedia.org/survey/2018/

de Poli, B. (2017). Arab television channels: the image of women between local and global trends. In E. Maestri & A. Profanter (eds), *Arab Women and the Media in Changing Landscapes*, 13–33. London: Palgrave Macmillan.

de Sola Pool, I. (1977). The changing flow of television. *Journal of Communication*, 27(2), 139–49.

Digital TV Research. (2020) Middle East & North Africa OTT TV and Video Forecasts. Retrieved from https://www.digitaltvresearch.com/products/product?id=213

Douki, S., Nacef, F., Belhadj, A., Bouasker, A., & Ghachem, R. (2003). Violence against women in Arab and Islamic countries. *Archives of Women's Mental Health*, 6(3), 165–71. DOI 10.1007/s00737-003-0170-x

DTVE-Report (2016). France and Turkey join biggest programme exporters. *Digital TV*. Retrieved from https://www.digitaltveurope.com/2016/04/15/france-and-turkey-join-biggest-programme-exporters/.

Duvar (2019). Arabs bought over 11 million square meters of real estate in last 16 years in Turkey. Retrieved from https://www. english.com/domestic/2019/12/20/arabs-bought-over-11-million-square-meters-of-real-estate-in-last-16-years-in-turkey-report.

Dyer, R. (2002). *Only Entertainment*. New York: Routledge. https://doi.org/10.4324/9780203993941

Economist (2011). The Turkish model: A hard act to follow. Retrieved from https://www.economist.com/briefing/2011/08/06/a-hard-act-to-follow.

Efron, S. (2018). *Future of Israeli–Turkish Relations*. Santa Monica, California: Rand Corporation. DOI: https://doi.org/10.7249/RR2445

Eichner, S. (2020). Lifeworld relevance and 'practical sense making'—audience engagement with Danish TV drama series. In P.M. Jensen & U.C. Jacobsen (eds), *Reconsidering Audience Proximities: the Global Travel of Danish Television Drama*. Gothenburg: Nordicom, University of Gothenburg. 107–23.

Ekşi, M., & M.S. Erol. (2018). The rise and fall of Turkish soft power and public diplomacy. *Gazi Akademik Bakış*, no. 23. 15–45.

El Nazer, S. (2020). Competition rising: video streaming in Mena. *Wamda*, 5 March. Retrieved from https://www.wamda.com/2020/03/competition-rising-video-streaming-mena.

Elouardaoui, O. (2013). The crisis of contemporary Arab television: has the move towards transnationalism and privatization in Arab television affected democratization and social development in the Arab world? *Journal of Arab & Muslim Media Research*, 6(1), 51–66. Retrieved from https://escholarship.org/uc/item/13s698mx

Eluniverso (2021). ¿Por qué gustan tanto las telenovelas turcas? Retrieved from https://www.eluniverso.com/larevista/sociedad/por-que-gustan-tanto-las-telenovelas-turcas-nota/.

Emirates 24/7 (2012). Turkish soap opera blamed for UAE divorces. Retrieved from https://www.emirates247.com/news/emirates/turkish-soap-opera-blamed-for-uae-divorces-2012-04-04-1.452235.

Enli, G. (2015). *Mediated Authenticity*. New York: Peter Lang.

Ergec, N.E. (2014). To creation discourse by the press: neo-Ottoman discourse. *European Journal of Research on Social Studies* 1 (Special Issue 1), 141–45.

Ergocun, G. (2021). Turkey: Investments in media, advertising hit $2.5B. *Anadolu Agency*. 8 April. Retrieved from https://www.aa.com.tr/en/economy/turkey-investments-in-media-advertising-hit-25b/2202248.

Euronews (2018). Mısır'da konuşan Suudi prens Türkiye, Katar ve İran için 'şeytan üçgeni' dedi. Retrieved from https://tr.euronews.com/2018/03/06/m-s-r-da-konusan-suudi-prens-turkiye-katar-ve-iran-seytan-ucgeni.

Eurostat. (2019). Individuals using the internet for watching TV, videos or movies. Retrieved from https://ec.europa.eu/eurostat/statistics-explained/index.php?title=Individuals_using_the_

REFERENCES

internet_for_watching_TV,_videos_or_movies#Watching_TV.2C_videos_or_movies_on_the_internet [Link no longer working].

Fahim, J. (2021). Ramadan TV: seven things we learned from the 2021 shows. *Middle East Eye*. Retrieved from https://www.middleeasteye.net/discover/ramadan-arab-tv-review-seven-things-learned.

Ferjani, R. (2010). Religion and television in the Arab world: towards a communication studies approach. *Middle East Journal of Culture and Communication*, 3(1), 82–100. https://doi.org/10.1163/187398609X12584657078367

Flores, K. (2022). '¿Qué culpa tiene Fatmangül?', la serie turca que inspira el drama español 'Alba' en Netflix. *Nacionflix*. Retrieved from https://www.nacionflix.com/netflix/Que-culpa-tiene-Fatmangul-la-serie-turca-que-inspira-el-drama-espanol-Alba-en-Netflix-20220728-0008.html.

Frau-Meigs, D. (2006). Big Brother and reality TV in Europe: towards a theory of situated acculturation by the media. *European Journal of Communication*, 21(1), 33–56. https://doi.org/10.1177/0267323106060988

Friedman, A. (2018). 'לא נשמתי מרוב בכי": סדרות טורקיות הן ההתמכרות החדשה'. 'I did not breathe from crying': Turkish series are the new addiction. *Ynet*. Retrieved from https://www.ynet.co.il/articles/0,7340,L-5374204,00.html.

Fuller, G.E. (2013). Turkey's growing pains. *New York Times*, 13 June. Retrieved from https://www.nytimes.com/2013/06/14/opinion/global/turkeys-growing-pains.html?searchResultPosition=1

Gallarotti, G.M. (2011). Soft power: what it is, why it's important, and the conditions for its effective use. *Journal of Political Power*, 4(1), 25–47. https://doi.org/10.1080/2158379X.2011.557886

Galtung, J., & Ruge, M.H. (1965). The structure of foreign news: the presentation of the Congo, Cuba and Cyprus crises in four Norwegian newspapers. *Journal of Peace Research*, 2(1), 64–90. https://doi.org/10.1177/002234336500200104

Gans-Boriskin, R., & Tisinger, R. (2005). The Bushlet administration: terrorism and war on the West Wing. *Journal of American Culture*, 28(1), 100–13.

Gellner, E. (1981). *Muslim Society*. Cambridge University Press.

Gengler, J. (2012). The political costs of Qatar's Western orientation. *Middle East Policy*, 19(4), 68-7. DOI: j.1475-4967.2012.00560.x.pdf

Geraghty, C. (1991). *Women and Soap Opera: A Study of Prime Time Soaps*. Cambridge: Polity Press.

Ghareeb, E. (2000). New media and the information revolution in the Arab world: an assessment. *The Middle East Journal*, 1 July, 395–418.

Giraldo, I. (2015). Machos y mujeres de armas tomar. Patriarcado y subjetividad femenina en la narco-telenovela colombiana contemporánea. *La manzana de la discordia*, 10(1), 67–81.

Grellhest, M., & Punyanunt-Carter, N.M. (2012). Using the uses and gratifications theory to understand gratifications sought through text messaging practices of male and female undergraduate students. *Computers in Human Behavior*, 28(6), 2175–81. http://dx.doi.org/10.1016/j.chb.2012.06.024

Gulf News (2018). MBC drops all Turkish programmes. Retrieved from https://gulfnews.com/world/gulf/saudi/mbc-drops-all-turkish-programmes-1.2182733.

Gurzel, A. (2014). Turkey's role as a regional and global player and its power capacity: Turkey's engagement with other emerging states. *Revista de Sociologia e Política*, 22, 95–105. https://doi.org/10.1590/1678-987314225007

Gusman, S. (2019). Le 5 soap Turche che hanno conquistato il pubblico Italiano. *ComingSoon.*, 20 December. Retrieved from https://www.comingsoon.it/tv/anticipazioni/le-5-soap-turche-che-hanno-conquistato-il-pubblico-italiano/n98105/.

Haarmann, U.W. (1988). Ideology and history, identity and alterity: the Arab image of the Turk from the Abbasids to modern Egypt. *International Journal of Middle East Studies*, 20(2), 175–96. https://doi.org/10.1017/S0020743800033924

Habermas, J. (1984). *The Theory of Communicative Action*, vol. 1: *Reason and the Rationalization of Society* (trans. Thomas McCarthy). Boston: Beacon Press.

Habibi, N. (2015). Turkey's TV drama (dizi) industry deserves more attention. Working Papers 84. Brandeis University, Department of Economics and International Business School. Retrieved from brandeis.edu/economics/RePEc/brd/doc/Brandeis_WP84.pdf.

Hafez, K. (2000). Zwischen Parallelgesellschaft, strategischer Ethnisierung und Transkultur in *Die türkische Medienkultur in Deutschland. Blätter für deutsche und internationale Politik*, 25(6), 728–36.

Halawa, T. (2013). المسلسلات التركية وفقاعة الاختراق والتأثير في الوطن العربي. Beta, 26 June. Retrieved from https://www.jadaliyya.com/Details/28842.

Hale, W. (2012). *Turkish Foreign Policy since 1774*. London & New York: Routledge.

Hamid, S. (2018). Turkey will not be a loyal ally to Arabs. Retrieved from https://alarab.co.uk/تركيا-لن-تكون-حليفا-مخلصا-للعرب

Hammond, A. (2007). *Popular Culture in the Arab World: Arts, Politics, and the Media*. Cairo: American University in Cairo Press.

Hathaway, J. (2019). *The Arab Lands under Ottoman Rule: 1516–1800* (2nd edn). London: Routledge. https://doi.org/10.4324/9781003015079

Heinrich, D. (2017). Turkey and Israel: Animosity ends when it comes to money. *Deutsche Welle*, 12 December. Retrieved from https://www.dw.com/en/turkey-and-israel-animosity-ends-when-it-comes-to-money/a-41766113.

Hobson, D. (2003). *Soap Opera*. Cambridge: Polity Press.

Horna, J.L. (1988). The mass media as leisure: a western-Canadian case. *Loisir et Société/Society and Leisure*, 11(2), 283–301.

Hoskins, C., & Mirus, R. (1988). Reasons for the US dominance of the international trade in television programmes. *Media, Culture & Society*, 10(4), 499–515.

Hürriyet (2010). 'Ayrılık' dizisinin mimarı da tutuklandı. 1 June. Retrieved from https://www.hurriyet.com.tr/dunya/ayrilik-dizisinin-mimari-da-tutuklandi-14900046.

REFERENCES

Hürriyet Daily News (2012). Arab tourist numbers up due to TV series. 10 July. Retrieved from https://www.hurriyetdailynews.com/arab-tourist-numbers-up-due-to-tv-series-25094.

Hürriyet Daily News (2014). Turkey world's second highest TV series exporter after US. 27 October. https://www.hurriyetdailynews.com/turkey-worlds-second-highest-tv-series-exporter-after-us-73478

Hürriyet Daily News (2016a). Netflix launches in 130 countries, including Turkey. 7 January. Retrieved from https://www.hurriyetdailynews.com/netflix-launches-in-130-countries-including-turkey-93526.

Hürriyet Daily News (2016b). Successful Turkish series awarded. 20 April. Retrieved from https://www.hurriyetdailynews.com/successful-turkish-series-awarded—98091.

Hürriyet Daily News (2018). Popularity of Turkish soap operas leads Latin American tourists to flock to Turkey: association. 22 October. Retrieved from https://www.hurriyetdailynews.com/popularity-of-turkish-soap-operas-leads-latin-american-tourists-to-flock-to-turkey-association-138141.

Hürriyet Daily News (2019a). Turkey reitreates [reiterates] support to end embargo on Cuba. 19 May. Retrieved from https://www.hurriyetdailynews.com/turkey-reitreates-support-to-end-embargo-on-cuba-143534.

Hürriyet Daily News. (2019b). Turkish TV series attract audience from 146 countries. 13 November. Retrieved from https://www.hurriyetdailynews.com/turkish-tv-series-attract-audience-from-146-countries-148651

Hurtas, S. (2015). Turkish media watchdog scrutinizes 'The Simpsons'. *Al-Monitor*, 13 February. Retrieved from https://www.al-monitor.com/originals/2015/02/turkey-tv-watchdog-conservative-pressure.html

IHA (2016). Cumhurbaşkanı Erdoğan Latin Amerika Turuna Çıkıyor. Ihlas Haber Ajansi. 27 January. Retrieved from https://www.iha.com.tr/ankara-haberleri/cumhurbaskani-erdogan-latin-amerika-turuna-cikiyor-1292225/.

Inbar, E. (2001). *The Israeli–Turkish Entente*. King's College London Mediterranean Studies. London: Tewkesbury Printing.

Inbar, E. (2011). Israeli–Turkish tensions and their international ramifications. *Orbis*, 55(1), 132–46.

Inglehart, R., & Baker, W.E. (2000). Modernization, cultural change, and the persistence of traditional values. *American Sociological Review*, 65(1), 19–51. Retrieved from http://www.jstor.org/stable/2657288

Iwabuchi, K. (2001). Becoming 'culturally proximate': the a/scent of Japanese idol dramas in Taiwan. In B. Moeran (ed.), *Asian Media Productions*, 54–74. London: Curzon Press.

Iwabuchi, K. (2002). *Recentering Globalization: Popular Culture and Japanese Transnationalism*. Durham, North Carolina: Duke University Press.

Jabbour, J. (2015). An illusionary power of seduction?: An assessment of Turkey's cultural power in the Arab world in light of its audio-visual presence in the region. *European Journal of Turkish Studies* 21, 1–23. https://doi.org/10.4000/ejts.5234

Jacobsen, U.C., & Jensen, P.M. (2020). Unfolding the global travel of Danish television drama series. In Jacobsen, U.C., & Jensen, P.M., *The Global Audiences of Danish Television Drama*. Gothenburg: Nordicom, University of Gothenburg. 9–19.

Jung, D. (2005). Turkey and the Arab world: historical narratives and new political realities. *Mediterranean Politics*, 10(1), 1–17. DOI: 10.1080/1362939042000338818

Kalin, I. (2011). Soft power and public diplomacy in Turkey. *Perceptions: Journal of International Affairs*, 16(3), 5–23.

Kaptan, Y., & Algan, E. (eds). (2020). *Television in Turkey: Local Production, Transnational Expansion, and Political Aspirations*. London: Palgrave Macmillan.

Karakartal, M. (2018). A new scale of censorship. *Hürriyet Daily News*. Retrieved from https://www.hurriyetdailynews.com/opinion/melike-karakartal/a-new-scale-of-censorship-127520.

Karaosmanoglu, A. (1985). Islam and foreign policy: a Turkish perspective. *Foreign Policy*, 12(1–2), 64–78.

Kardas, S. (2009). Erdogan searches for diplomatic response to Israeli invasion of Gaza. *Eurasia Daily Monitor*, 6(1). Retrieved from https://jamestown.org/program/erdogan-searches-for-diplomatic-response-to-israeli-invasion-of-gaza/.

Karpat, K.H. (1985). The Ottoman emigration to America, 1860–1914. *International Journal of Middle East Studies*, 17(2), 175–209.

Katz, E. (1993). *The Export of Meaning: Cross-Cultural Readings of Dallas*. Cambridge: Polity Press.

Katz, E., Blumler, J.G., & Gurevitch, M. (1973). Uses and gratifications research. *The Public Opinion Quarterly*, 37(4), 509–23.

Katz, M. (2020). לא רק הכלה מאיסטנבול: המלצה על חמש סדרות טורקיות Not just 'The Bride from Istanbul': a recommendation for five Turkish series. Retrieved from https://www.haaretz.co.il/gallery/television/.premium-MAGAZINE-1.8712996.

Katz, Y. (2010). Locked out of Turkey, IAF now searching for space to drill. *Jerusalem Post*. Retrieved from https://www.jpost.com/Israel/Locked-out-of-Turkey-IAF-now-searching-for-space-to-drill.

Kaya, I. (2004). *Social Theory and Later Modernities: the Turkish Experience*. Liverpool University Press.

Kaya, R. (1994). A fait accompli: transformation of media structures in Turkey. *METU Studies in Development*, 21(3), 383–404.

Kayali, H. (2014). Türklerin Araplara bakisi. *Al Jazeera Turk*. Retrieved from http://www.aljazeera.com.tr/gorus/turklerin-araplara-bakisi.

Kaynak, M.S. (2015). Noor and friends: Turkish culture in the world. In B.S. Çevik & P. Seib (eds), *Turkey's Public Diplomacy*, 233–53. Palgrave Macmillan Series in Global Public Diplomacy. New York: Palgrave Macmillan. https://doi.org/10.1057/9781137466983_12

Kerr, S. (2018). Top Saudi broadcaster caught up in Riyadh's corruption shakedown. *Financial Times*. Retrieved from https://www.ft.com/content/a50075d2-0069-11e8-9650-9c0ad2d7c5b5.

REFERENCES

Khalil, J.F. (2015). The future of television: an Arab perspective. In J.V. Pavlik (ed.), *Digital Technology and the Future of Broadcasting*, 109–23. New York & Abingdon: Routledge.

Khalil, J.F. (2019). Arab television industries: enduring players and emerging alternatives. In S. Shimpach (ed.), *The Routledge Companion to Global Television*, 401–10. New York & London: Routledge.

Khalil, J.F. (2020). Television in the Arab region: history, structure, and transformations, in J. Wasko & E.R. Meehan (eds), *A Companion to Television*, 439–58. Retrieved from wiley. https://doi.org/10.1002/9781119269465.ch22.

Khalil, J.F., & Kraidy, M.M. (2017). *Arab Television Industries*. London: Bloomsbury Publishing.

Khalil, J.F., & Zayani, M. (2021). De-territorialized digital capitalism and the predicament of the nation-state: Netflix in Arabia. *Media, Culture & Society*, 43(2), 201–18. https://doi.org/10.1177/0163443720932505

Khan, M., & Rohn, U. (2020). Transnationalization, exportation, and capitalization of Turkish television and its impact on the audience of the [sic] Egypt and Pakistan. *European Journal of Social Sciences*, 59(2), 123–37.

Khan, R.Q.G.A. (2006). King Abdullah to make historic visit to Turkey. *Arab News*, 25 February. Retrieved from https://www.arabnews.com/node/282954

Kharroub, T., & Weaver, A.J. (2014). Portrayals of women in transnational Arab television drama series. *Journal of Broadcasting & Electronic Media*, 58(2), 179–95.

Khashoggi, J. (2018). Saudi Arabia's crown prince already controlled the nation's media. Now he's squeezing it even further. *Washington Post*, 7 February. Retrieved from https://www.washingtonpost.com/news/global-opinions/wp/2018/02/07/saudi-arabias-crown-prince-already-controlled-the-nations-media-now-hes-squeezing-it-even-further/

Khorana, S. (2013). (ed.) *Crossover Cinema: Cross-Cultural Film from Production to Reception*. New York & Abingdon: Routledge.

Kimmelman, M. (2010). Turks put twist in racy soaps. *New York Times*, 17 June. Retrieved from https://www.nytimes.com/2010/06/18/arts/18abroad.html

Kirişci, K. (2011). Turkey's 'demonstrative effect' and the transformation of the Middle East. *Insight Turkey*, 13(2), 33–5.

Klich, I., & Lesser, J. (1996). Introduction: 'Turco' immigrants in Latin America. *The Americas*, 53(1), 1–14.

Kose, P. (2018). Türk dizilerinin yasaklanmasının ardındaki kirli oyun. *Yeni Safak*. Retrieved from https://www.yenisafak.com/hayat/turk-dizilerinin-yasaklanmasinin-ardindaki-kirli-oyun-3166022.

Kraidy, M.M. (2013). Mapping Arab television: structures, sites, genres, flows, and politics. In K. Wilkins, J. Straubhaar, & S. Kumar, eds, *Global Communication*, 35–49. New York & London: Routledge.

Kraidy, M.M. (2019). Boycotting neo-Ottoman cool: geopolitics and media industries in the Egypt–Turkey row over television drama. *Middle East Journal of Culture and Communication*, 12(2), 149–65.

Kraidy, M., & Khalil, J. (2007). The Middle East: transnational Arab television. In L. Artz & Y.R. Kamalipour (eds), *The Media Globe: Trends in International Mass Media*, 79–98. Lanham, Maryland: Rowman & Littlefield.

Kraidy, M.M., & Al-Ghazzi, O. (2013). Neo-Ottoman cool: Turkish popular culture in the Arab public sphere. *Popular Communication*, 11(1), 17–29. https://doi.org/10.1080/15405702.2013.747940

Ksiazek, T.B., & Webster, J.G. (2008). Cultural proximity and audience behavior: the role of language in patterns of polarization and multicultural fluency. *Journal of Broadcasting & Electronic Media*, 52(3), 485–503. https://doi.org/10.1080/08838150802205876

Kubala, P. (2005). The other face of the video clip: Sami Yusuf and the call for al-Fann al-Hadif. *Transnational Broadcasting Studies*, 14(2), 38–47.

Kunczik, M. (2016). *Images of Nations and International Public Relations*. New York: Routledge. https://doi.org/10.4324/9780203811917

Kürkçüoğlu, Ö. (1980). 'Dış Politika' Nedir? Türkiye'deki Dünü ve Bugünü. *Ankara Üniversitesi SBF Dergisi*, 35(1), 309–35.

La Pastina, A.C., & Straubhaar, J.D. (2005). Multiple proximities between television genres and audiences: the schism between telenovelas' global distribution and local consumption. *Gazette (Leiden, Netherlands)*, 67(3), 271–88. DOI: 10.1177/0016549205052231

Larkin, B. (2008). Itineraries of Indian cinema: African videos, Bollywood, and global media. In R. Dudrah, &. J. Desai (eds), *The Bollywood Reader*, 216–28. Maidenhead: Open University Press.

Lay, R.L. (2005). Interpretation of Islamic practices among non-Qatari students living in the University of Qatar's ladies hostels. *Dialectical Anthropology*, 29, 181–219. DOI 10.1007/s10624-005-0826-1

Lee, M., & Cho, C.H. (1990). Women watching together: an ethnographic study of Korean soap opera fans in the US. *Cultural Studies*, 4(1), 30–44. https://doi.org/10.1080/09502389000490031

Leonard, M., Stead, C., & Smewing, C. (2002). *Public Diplomacy*. London: Foreign Policy Centre.

Leung, L. (2001). College student motives for chatting on ICQ. *New Media & Society*, 3(4), 483–500. https://doi.org/10.1177/14614440122226209

Leung, L. (2008). Mediating nationalism and modernity: the transnationalization of Korean dramas on Chinese (satellite) TV. In I. Koichi, ed., *East Asian Pop Culture: Analyzing the Korean Wave*, 53–70. Hong Kong: Hong Kong University Press. DOI: 10.5790/hongkong/9789622098923.003.0004

Leung, L. (2013). Generational differences in content generation in social media: the roles of the gratifications sought and of narcissism. *Computers in Human Behavior*, 29(3), 997–1006. https://doi.org/10.1016/j.chb.2012.12.028

Leung, L., & Wei, R. (2000). More than just talk on the move: uses and gratifications of the cellular phone. *Journalism & Mass Communication Quarterly*, 77(2), 308–20. https://doi.org/10.1177/107769900007700206

REFERENCES

Levaggi, A.G. (2013). Turkey and Latin America: a new horizon for a strategic relationship. *Perceptions: Journal of International Affairs*, 18(4), 99–116.

Levaggi, A.G., & Donelli, F. (2021). Turkey's changing engagement with the global South. *International Affairs*, 97(4), 1105–1124. https://doi.org/10.1093/ia/iiab093

Lin, A., & Tong, A. (2008). Re-imagining a cosmopolitan 'Asian Us': Korean media lows and imaginaries of Asian modern femininities. In I. Koichi, ed., *East Asian Pop Culture. Analysing the Korean Wave*. Hong Kong: Hong Kong University Press.

Livingstone, S.M. (1988). Why people watch soap opera: an analysis of the explanations of British viewers. *European Journal of Communication*, 3(1), 55–80. https://doi.org/10.1177/0267323188003001004

Luxner, L. (2021). Diplomats see new era dawning as Turkey, Israel mend frosty relations. *Washington Diplomat*, 10 August. Retrieved from https://washdiplomat.com/diplomats-see-new-era-dawning-as-turkey-israel-mend-frosty-relations/.

Maluf, R. (2003). *Dubbing into Arabic: A Trojan Horse at the Gates*. Beirut: Lebanese American University.

Marcus, B., Weigelt, O., Hergert, J., Gurt, J., & Gelléri, P. (2017). The use of snowball sampling for multi source organizational research: some cause for concern. *Personnel Psychology*, 70(3), 635–73. https://doi.org/10.1111/peps.12169

Mardin, Ş. (2015). *Yeni Osmanlı Düşüncesinin Doğuşu*. Istanbul: İletişim Yayınları.

Martín-Barbero, J. (2002). Memory and form in the Latin American soap opera. In R.C. Allen (ed.), *To Be Continued...: Soap Operas around the World*, 286–94. London & New York: Routledge.

Martinez, I.H. (2021). Las 20 mejores series turcas de la historia. Retrieved from https://www.diezminutos.es/teleprograma/series-tv/g36458115/mejores-series-turcas/.

Masrawy (2018). Wall Street: Mohammed bin Salman is behind stopping the showing of Turkish series. 12 March. Retrieved from https://bit.ly/3C0YrbS

Matelski, M.J. (1999). *Soap Operas Worldwide: Cultural and Serial Realities*. Jefferson, North Carolina: McFarland Publishing.

McAnany, E.G., & Wilkinson, K.T. (1996). *Mass media and free trade: NAFTA and the cultural industries*. Austin: University of Texas Press. DOI 10.7560/751989

McCabe, J., & Akass, K. (eds). (2012). *TV's Betty Goes Global: from Telenovela To International Brand*. London: Bloomsbury Publishing.

McFadyen, S., Hoskins, C., & Finn, A. (2000). Cultural industries from an economic/business research perspective. 1999 Southam Lecture. In *Canadian Journal of Communication, 25(1)*. Toronto: University of Toronto Press. https://doi.org/10.22230/cjc.2000v25n1a1146

McPhail, T.L. (ed.) (2010). *Global Communication: Theories, Stakeholders, and Trends*. Hoboken, New Jersey: John Wiley & Sons.

McQuail, D. (1987). *Mass Communication Theory: An Introduction* (2nd edn). London: Sage Publications.

Meikle, G., & Young, S. (2012). *Media Convergence: Networked Digital Media In Everyday Life*. London & New York: Palgrave Macmillan. DOI: 10.1007/978-0-230-35670-2

Melamed, A. (2019). The Turks are back, and they've got all of Israel addicted: 'The Bride of Istanbul' is much more than a TV soap opera. *Haaretz*. Retrieved from https://www.haaretz.com/israel-news/.premium.MAGAZINE-the-bride-of-istanbul-turkey-back-in-israel-and-they-ve-got-everyone-addicted-1.6896105.

Melissen, J. (ed.) (2005). *The New Public Diplomacy*. Basingstoke: Palgrave Macmillan.

Mellor, N. (2013). Countering cultural hegemony: audience research in the Arab world. *Journal of Arab & Muslim Media Research*, 6(2–3), 201–16. DOI: 10.1386/jammr.6.2-3.201_1

Mellor, N., Rinnawi, K., Dajani, N., & Ayish, M.I. (2011). *Arab Media: Globalization and Emerging Media Industries*, vol. 1. Cambridge: Polity Press.

Metcalfe, B., Hutchings, K., & Cooper, B. (2009). Re-examining women's international management opportunities and experiences: a Middle Eastern perspective, In K. Ibeh & S. Davies (eds), *Contemporary Challenges to International Business*. Academy of International Business. UK Chapter. Conference. 232-47. London: Palgrave Macmillan. DOI: 10.1057/9780230237322_14

Milliyet (2008). İsrail'in operasyonu Türkiye'ye saygısızlık. Retrieved from https://www.milliyet.com.tr/siyaset/israilin-operasyonu-turkiyeye-saygisizlik-1033759.

Ministry of Foreign Affairs, Türkiye. (Undated.) Retrieved from http://www.mfa.gov.tr/i_turkeys-relations-with-the-latin-american-and-the-caribbean countries.

Modleski, T. (1979). The search for tomorrow in today's soap operas: notes on a feminine narrative form. *Film Quarterly*, 33(1), 12–21. https://doi.org/10.2307/1212060

Mosquera, P.M.R., Manstead, A.S., & Fischer, A.H. (2002). Honor in the Mediterranean and northern Europe. *Journal of Cross-Cultural Psychology*, 33(1), 16–36. DOI: 10.1177/0022022102033001002

Mourenza, A. (2020). Turquía: la inesperada fábrica global de telenovelas. *El Pais*. Retrieved from https://elpais.com/internacional/2020-06-06/turquia-la-inesperada-fabrica-global-de-telenovelas.html.

Moussley, M. (2008). Turkish soaps create drama in the Arab world. *Al Arabiya*. Retrieved from https://www.alarabiya.net/articles/2008%2F10%2F13%2F58148.

Munyar, V. (2016). Ekvador'da Yıldırım. *Hürriyet*. Retrieved from https://www.hurriyet.com.tr/yazarlar/vahap-munyar/ekvadorda-yildirim-40050717

Mutlu, E. (1999). *Televizyon ve Toplum (Television and Society)*. Ankara: Türkiye Radyo Televizyon Kurumu Yayınları (in Turkish).

Nachmani, A. (2003). *Turkey: Facing a New Millennium: Coping with Intertwined Conflicts*. (Europe in Change.) Manchester & New York: Manchester University Press.

Navani, P. (2022). What's behind the meteoric rise of Turkish dramas in the Middle East. *TRT World*. Retrieved from https://www.trtworld.com/magazine/what-s-behind-the-meteoric-rise-of-turkish-dramas-in-the-middle-east-54726.

REFERENCES

Neumann, K., & Charlton, M. (1988). Massenkommunikation als Dialog. Zumaktuellen Diskussionsstand der handlungstheoretisch orientierten Rezeptionsforschung. *Communications*, 14(3), 7–38. https://doi.org/10.1515/comm.1988.14.3.7

Northwestern University in Qatar (2016). Media industries in the Middle East 2016. Retrieved from http://www.mideastmedia.org/survey/2018/.

Northwestern University in Qatar (2018). Qatar's unique use of digital media. Retrieved from https://www.qatar.northwestern.edu/news/articles/2018/10-retrospective.html.

Northwestern University in Qatar (2019). Media use in the Middle East survey. Retrieved from https://www.qatar.northwestern.edu/news/articles/2019/12-media-use-survey-2019.html

NTV (2011). İsrail'de Menekşe ile Halil' çılgınlığı başladı. Retrieved from https://www.ntv.com.tr/yasam/israilde-menekse-ile-halil-cilginligi-basladi,9K7-jkW3y0SGA-kv6d0diw.

NTV (2017). Kara Sevda Uluslaraarasi Emmy Ödülü alan ilk Türk dizisi oldu. Retrieved from https://www.ntv.com.tr/galeri/yasam/kara-sevda-uluslararasi-emmy-odulu-alan-ilk-turk-dizisioldu.

Nydell, M. (2006). *Understanding Arabs: A Guide for Modern Times* (4th edn). Boston: Intercultural Press.

Nye, J.S. (1990). *Bound to Lead: The Changing Nature of American Power*. New York: Basic Books.

Nye Jr, J.S. (2004). *Soft Power: The Means to Success in World Politics*. New York: Public Affairs.

Nye Jr, J.S. (2008). Public diplomacy and soft power. *The Annals of the American Academy of Political and Social Science*, 616(1), 94–109.

Nye Jr, J.S. (2011). *The Future of Power*. New York: Public Affairs.

Nye Jr, J.S. (2016). *Bound to Lead: The Changing Nature of American Power*. New York: Basic Books.

Oğuzlu, T. (2007). Soft power in Turkish foreign policy. *Australian Journal of International Affairs*, 61(1), 81–97. DOI: 10.1080/10357710601142518

Oğuzlu, T. (2008). Middle Easternization of Turkey's Foreign Policy: Does Turkey Dissociate from the West? *Turkish Studies*, 9(1), 3–20. https://doi.org/10.1080/14683840701813960

Olson, S.R. (1999). *Hollywood Planet: Global Media and the Competitive Advantage of Narrative Transparency*. New York: Routledge. https://doi.org/10.4324/9781410604446

Onar, N.F. (2009). Neo-Ottomanism, historical legacies, and Turkish foreign policy. *Centre for Economic and Foreign Policy Studies, Discussion Paper Series*. Retrieved from https://www.scribd.com/document/38477119/Neo-Ottomanism-Historical-Legacies-and-Turkish-Foreign-Policy#

O'Neill, A. (2021). Total population in the Arab world 2019. Retrieved from https://www.statista.com/statistics/806106/total-population-arab-league.

Öniş, Z. (2011). Multiple faces of the 'new' Turkish foreign policy: underlying dynamics and a critique. *Insight Turkey*, 13(1), 47–65.

Ordóñez, M.D. (2012). Las 'narco telenovelas' colombianas y su papel en la construcción discursiva sobre el narcotráfico en América Latina. (Master's thesis, Universidad Andina Simón Bolívar, Sede Ecuador).

Otmazgin, N.K. (2008). Contesting soft power: Japanese popular culture in East and Southeast Asia. *International Relations of the Asia-Pacific*, 8(1), 73–101. DOI: 10.1093/irap/lcm009

Otmazgin, N., & Ben-Ari, E. (2012). *Popular Culture and the State in East and Southeast Asia*. Milton Park & London: Routledge.

Özalpman, D., & Sarikakis, K. (2018). The politics of pleasure in global drama: a case study of the TV series, *The Magnificent Century (Muhteşem Yüzyıl)*. *Global Media and Communication*, 14(3), 249–64. https://doi.org/10.1177/1742766518780168

Özdemir, Ö. (2022). Netflix ve televizyon kanallarının rekabeti dizi sektörünü nasıl değiştiriyor? *BBC News*. Retrieved from https://www.bbc.com/turkce/haberler-dunya-61750471.

Parris, M.R. (2009). Prospect for US–Turkish relations in the Obama era. *On the Record*, 11 February. Retrieved from https://www.brookings.edu/on-the-record/prospect-for-u-s-turkish-relations-in-the-obama-era/

Paul, K. (2018). Chairman of Saudi media group MBC allowed to travel to Dubai. *Reuters*. Retrieved from https://www.reuters.com/article/saudi-arrests-mbc/chairman-of-saudi-media-group-mbc-allowed-to-travel-to-dubai-idUSL5N1SZ25S.

Pavlik, J.V. (1996). *New Media Technology: Cultural and Commercial Perspectives*. Boston: Allyn & Bacon.

Pavlik, J.V., & McIntosh, S. (2004). *Converging Media. An Introduction to Mass Communication*. Boston: Allyn & Bacon.

Pintak, L. (2010). Arab media and the Al-Jazeera effect. In T.L. McPhail (ed.), *Global Communication: Theories, Stakeholders, and Trends*, 290–304. Hoboken, New Jersey: John Wiley & Sons.

Pontificia Universidad Católica De Chile (2015). Chile se ha convertido en la plataforma de exportación de las teleseries turcas con doblajes chilenos [Press release].

Prensario Internacional (2019). Perú: Latina celebró la segunda la segunda edición de los premios Latina Turkish Awards. Retrieved from https://prensario.tv/novedades/2826-peru-latina-celebro-la-segunda-la-segunda-edicion-de-los-premios-latina-turkish-awards.

Press-Barnathan, G. (2011). Does popular culture matter to International Relations scholars? Possible links and methodological challenges. In N. Otmazgin & E. Ben-Ari (eds), *Popular Culture and the State in East and Southeast Asia*, 29–45. London: Routledge. https://doi.org/10.4324/9780203801536

Press-Barnathan, G. (2017). Thinking about the role of popular culture in international conflicts. *International Studies Review*, 19(2), 166–84. https://doi.org/10.1093/isr/viw030

Quamar, M.M. (2018). AKP, the Arab Spring and the unravelling of the Turkey 'model'. *Strategic Analysis*, 42(4), 364–76. https://doi.org/10.1080/09700161.2018.1482622

Qureshi, K. (2007). Shifting proximities: news and 'belonging-security'. *European Journal of Cultural Studies*, 10(3), 294–310. https://doi.org/10.1177/1367549407079703

Rasmussen, T. (2014). *Personal Media and Everyday Life: A Networked Lifeworld*. Basingstoke: Palgrave Macmillan. DOI: 10.1057/9781137446466.0001

Raxhimi, A. (2011). Davutoglu: 'I'm not a neo-Ottoman'. *Balkan Insight*, 26 April. Retrieved from https://balkaninsight.com/2011/04/26/davutoglu-i-m-not-a-neo-ottoman/

REFERENCES

Reuters (2008). Saudi cleric slams Turkish soaps as 'wicked'. Retrieved from https://www.reuters.com/article/idINIndia-34699320080727.

Reuters (2009). Turkish TV series further strains ties with Israel. Retrieved from https://www.reuters.com/article/idUSLF714261.

Reuters (2014). New premier shares Erdogan's vision of Turkey's place in the world. Retrieved from https://www.reuters.com/article/turkey-government-davutoglu-idINL5N0QS1HM20140825.

Reuters (2018). Saudi-owned private broadcaster pulls the plug on Turkish dramas. Retrieved from https://www.reuters.com/article/us-saudi-turkey-tv/saudi-owned-private-broadcaster-pulls-the-plug-on-turkish-dramas-idUSKBN1GH18E.

Reuters (2019). Maduro isolated as Latin American nations back Venezuela opposition leader. Retrieved from https://www.reuters.com/article/us-venezuela-politics-latam-idUSKCN1PI01J.

Reuters (2021). Turkey and Israel want to improve ties after presidents' call—Turkish ruling party. Retrieved from https://www.reuters.com/world/middle-east/turkey-israel-want-improve-ties-after-presidents-call-turkish-ruling-party-2021-07-14/.

Robins, P. (2003). *Suits and Uniforms: Turkish Foreign Policy since the Cold War*. London: Hurst.

Rosengren, K.E., & Windahl, S. (1972). Mass media consumption as a functional alternative. In D. McQuail (ed.), *Sociology of Mass Communications: Selected Readings*, 166–94. Harmondsworth: Penguin.

Rousselin, M. (2013). Strategic depth through soft power: the domestic production and international projection of Turkish culture. *Euxeinos: Online Journal of the Center for Governance and Culture in Europe*, 10, 3–5.

Roy, S.K. (2009). Internet uses and gratifications: a survey in the Indian context. *Computers in Human Behavior*, 25(4), 878–86. DOI:10.1016/j.chb.2009.03.002

Rubin, A.M. (1985). Uses of daytime television soap operas by college students. *Journal of Broadcasting*, 29, 241–58. https://doi.org/10.1080/08838158509386583

Rubin, A.M. (2009). Uses-and-gratifications perspective on media effects. In R.L. Nabi & M.B. Oliver (eds), *The SAGE Handbook of Media Processes and Effects*, 147–59. Thousand Oaks, California: Sage Publications.

Rubin, A.M., & Rubin, R.B. (1985). Interface of personal and mediated communication: a research agenda. *Critical Studies in Media Communication*, 2(1), 36–53. https://doi.org/10.1080/15295038509360060

Rubin, B. (2015). *The Middle East: a Guide to Politics, Economics, Society and Culture*. New York: Routledge. https://doi.org/10.4324/9781315699417

Ruggiero, T.E. (2000). Uses and gratifications theory in the 21st century. *Mass Communication & Society*, 3(1), 3–37.

Rugh, W.A. (2004). *Arab Mass Media: Newspapers, Radio, and Television in Arab Politics*. Westport, Connecticut & London: Greenwood Publishing Group.

Sakr, N. (2002). *Satellite Realms: Transnational Television, Globalization, and the Middle East*. London: I.B.Tauris. Retrieved from https://westminsterresearch.westminster.ac.uk/item/93y39/satellite-realms-transnational-television-globalization-and-the-middle-east

Sakr, N. (2007). *Arab Television Today*. London & New York: I.B.Tauris.

Sakr, N., Skovgaard-Petersen, J., & Della Ratta, D. (2015). *Arab Media Moguls: An Introduction*. London: Bloomsbury Publishing.

Sakr, N., & Steemers, J. (eds). (2017). *Children's TV and Digital Media in the Arab World: Childhood, Screen Culture and Education*. London: Bloomsbury Publishing.

Salamandra, C. (2008). Creative compromise: Syrian television makers between secularism and Islamism. *Contemporary Islam*, 2(3), 177–89. DOI: 10.1007/s11562-008-0060-0

Salamandra, C. (2012). The Muhannad effect: media panic, melodrama, and the Arab female gaze. *Anthropological Quarterly*, 85(1), 45–77.

Saleh, H. (2021). Sexual violence in the Arab world: Egypt case shows the struggle for women's rights. *Financial Times*. Retrieved from https://www.ft.com/content/d8d0f901-4cb8-4b8e-b3ee-e8f88d2c2df5.

Salem, F. (2017). The Arab World Online 2017: digital transformations and societal trends in the age of the 4th industrial revolution. *Arab World Online*, 3, 1–63. Dubai: MBR School of Government.

Salem, P. (2011). Turkey's image in the Arab world. *TESEV Foreign Policy Programme Report*.

Saudi 24 News. (2020). 'Beirut Bride' stars stuck in Turkey! Retrieved from https://www.saudi24news.com/2020/04/beirut-bride-stars-stuck-in-turkey.html.

Sayin, E. (2021). Türk dizileri dünyanın dört bir yanına köprü oldu. *TRT Haber*. Retrieved from https://www.trthaber.com/haber/kultur-sanat/turk-dizileri-dunyanin-dort-bir-yanina-kopru-oldu-560791.html.

Schipani, A., & Pitel, L. (2021). Erdogan's great game: Turkey pushes into Africa with aid, trade and soaps. *Financial Times*. Retrieved from https://www.ft.com/content/0e3cec2a-bd80-499c-a6ab-e5d1a1e768cf.

Schönwälder, G. (2014). *Promoting Democracy: What Role for the Democratic Emerging Powers?* Discussion Paper *No. 2. Bonn: German Institute for Development*. Retrieved from http://hdl.handle.net/10419/199415

Schulte, P. (2010). Going off the reservation into the sanctuary: cross-border counterterrorist operations, fourth generation warfare and the ethical insufficiency of contemporary just war thinking. In D. Fisher & B. Wicker (eds), *Just War on Terror?: A Christian and Muslim Response*, 151-73. London: Routledge. https://doi.org/10.4324/9781315590820

Schutz, A., & Luckmann, T. (1973). *Structures of the Lifeworld*, vol. 1. Evanston, Illinois: Northwestern University Press.

Seib, P. (2013). Public diplomacy and the media in the Middle East. In *CPD Perspectives on Public Diplomacy*, Paper 6, 137-47. USC Center on Public Diplomacy. Los Angeles: Figueroa Press.

REFERENCES

Seńal News (2020). Calinos signs deal with Achla TV's 'Turkish Dramas + Channel' in Israel. Retrieved from https://senalnews.com/en/content/calinos-signs-deal-with-achla-tvs-turkish-dramas-channel-in-israel.

Seymour, R. (2013). Istanbul park protests sow the seeds of a Turkish spring. *The Guardian*, 31 May. Retrieved from https://www.theguardian.com/commentisfree/2013/may/31/istanbul-park-protests-turkish-spring

Shapira, E. (2020). יותר מחצי מיליון ישראלים רק השנה: כך חזרנו לטורקיה, ובגדול. More than half a million Israelis this year alone: this is how we returned to Turkey, and in a big way. *Walla News*. Retrieved from https://travel.walla.co.il/item/3336634.

Sharma, S. (2017). ANALYSIS: Erdogan, champion of Palestine and player to Arab street. *Middle East Eye*. Retrieved from https://www.middleeasteye.net/news/analysis-erdogan-champion-palestine-and-player-arab-street.

Shehab, A.J.A. (2008). Gender and racial representation in children's television programming in Kuwait: implications for education. *Social Behavior and Personality: An International Journal*, 36(1), 49–64. https://doi.org/10.2224/sbp.2008.36.1.49

Shin, D.H. (2009). A cross-national study of mobile internet services: a comparison of US and Korean mobile internet users. *Journal of Global Information Management (JGIM)*, 17(4), 29–54. DOI: 10.4018/jgim.2009070902

Shoult, A. (2006). *Doing Business with Saudi Arabia*. (3rd edn). London: GMB Publishing Ltd.

Simga, H. (2019). *A Question for Humanity: Sexism, Oppression and Women's Rights*. Münster: LIT Verlag.

Sinclair, J. (1998). *Latin American Television: A Global View*. Oxford: Oxford University Press.

Sinclair, J. (2009). Latin America's impact on world television markets. In G. Turner & J. Tay (eds), *Television Studies After TV: Understanding Television in the Post-Broadcast Era*, 141–58. New York: Routledge.

Singhal, A., & Udornpim, K. (1997). Cultural shareability, archetypes and television soaps: 'Oshindrome' in Thailand. *Gazette (Leiden, Netherlands)*, 59(3), 171–88 https://doi.org/10.1177/0016549297059003001

Skovgaard-Petersen, J. (2011). Islamic fundamentalism in Arab television: Islamism and Salafism in competition. *Fundamentalism in the Modern World*, 2, 264–91.

Slade, C. (2010). Telenovelas and soap operas: negotiating reality from the periphery in I. Stavans (ed.), *Telenovelas*, 51-60.

Smith, M. (2013). Young Saudis getting creative on YouTube. *Reuters*. Retrieved from https://in.reuters.com/article/saudi-youtube/young-saudis-getting-creative-on-youtube-idINDEE9AH0A520131118.

Snoj, J. (2019). Population of Qatar by nationality—2019 report. Priya Dsouza Communications. Retrieved from https://priyadsouza.com/population-of-qatar-by-nationality-in-2017/.

Sochaczewski, M. (2015). Brazil, Ottoman Empire and Modern Turkey: notes on ancient relations and recent proximity. Paper presented at the 2nd International Conference on Eurasian Politics & Society, Konya.

Sofuoglu, M. (2016). 13 key moments in Turkish–Israeli relations. *TRT World*. Retrieved from https://www.trtworld.com/in-depth/14-things-about-turkish-israeli-relations-you-didnt-know-93510.

Solomon, S. (2010). Israel struggles with upgrade from emerging to developed market. *Bloomberg*. Retrieved from https://www.bloomberg.com/news/articles/2013-08-22/israel-struggles-with-upgrade-from-emerging-to-developed-market.

Solomon, T. (2014). The affective underpinnings of soft power. *European Journal of International Relations*, 20(3), 720–41. https://doi.org/10.1177/1354066113503479

Soylu, R., & Inanc, Y.S. (2022). Turkey has not expelled any Hamas or Muslim Brotherhood members, sources say. *Middle East Eye*. Retrieved from https://www.middleeasteye.net/news/turkey-hamas-muslim-brotherhood-members-not-expelled-sources-say.

Spence, L. (2005). *Watching Daytime Soap Operas: The Power of Pleasure*. Middletown, Connecticut: Wesleyan University Press.

Strait Talk (2021). Turkish TV exports set to top $1 billion by 2023. *TRT World News*. Retrieved from https://www.youtube.com/watch?v=OIFb43O__9A.

Straubhaar, J.D., Castro, D., Duarte, L.G., & Spence, J. (2019). Class, pay TV access and Netflix in Latin America: transformation within a digital divide. *Critical Studies in Television*, 14(2), 233–54. DOI: 10.1177/1749602019837793

Strohecker, K. (2018). Graphic: Turkey's economic troubles in five charts. *Reuters*. Retrieved from https://www.reuters.com/article/us-turkey-markets-currency/graphic-turkeys-economic-troubles-in-five-charts-idUSKBN1GZ2MK.

Sundar, S.S. and Limperos, A.M. (2013). Uses and Grats 2.0: new gratifications for new media. *Journal of Broadcasting & Electronic Media*, 57(4), 504–25. https://doi.org/10.1080/08838151.2013.845827

Swanson, D.L. (1977). The uses and misuses of Uses and Gratifications 1. *Human Communication Research*, 3(3), 214–21. https://doi.org/10.1111/j.1468-2958.1977.tb00519.x

Sydney Morning Herald (2002). Miss Turkey triumphs. Retrieved from https://www.smh.com.au/entertainment/miss-turkey-triumphs-20021209-gdfxmm.html.

Tali, D. (2016). An unlikely story: Why do South Americans love Turkish TV? *BBC News*. Retrieved from https://www.bbc.com/news/business-37284938.

Tamimi, J.A. (2012). Challenge of the Turkish soap operas. *Gulf News*. Retrieved from https://gulfnews.com/business/challenge-of-the-turkish-soap-operas-1.1002249.

Taşpinar, Ö. (2011). The three strategic visions of Turkey. *US–Europe Analysis Series*, 50, 1–5.

Teller, M. (2014). Has wealth made Qatar happy? *BBC News*. Retrieved from https://www.bbc.com/news/magazine-27142647.

Terranova, T. (2021). Serie tv turche in Italia, le più amate del 2021: dove vederle. Retrieved from https://www.maridacaterini.it/soap-e-serie-tv-anticipazioni-puntate-trama/307552-serie-tv-turche-italia-2021-daydreamer-mr-wrong-love-is-in-the-air-brave-beautiful.html.

Times of Israel (2021). Turkey's ruling party says ties with Israel to improve after presidents' call. Retrieved from https://www.timesofisrael.com/turkeys-ruling-party-says-ties-with-israel-to-improve-after-presidents-call/.

REFERENCES

Tokyay, M. (2017). Arab world remains biggest market for Turkish TV series. *Arab News*. Retrieved from https://www.arabnews.com/node/1197036/media.

Tokyay, M. (2021). Turkey's latest donation of $30 million to Somalia stirs debate. *Arab News*. Retrieved from https://www.arabnews.com/node/1907106/middle-east.

Tol, G. (2012). The 'Turkish Model' in the Middle East. *Current History* 111(749), 350–55. https://doi.org/10.1525/curh.2012.111.749.350

Tol, G., & Başkan, B. (2018). From 'hard power' to 'soft power' and back again: Turkish foreign policy in the Middle East. Washington: Middle East Institute, 29 November. Retrieved from https://www.mei.edu/publications/hard-power-soft-power-and-back-again-turkish-foreign-policy-middle-east

TRT Español (2020). Los nombres turcos arrasan en los países latinoamericanos gracias a las series de televisión. Retrieved from https://www.trt.net.tr/espanol/cultura-y-arte/2019/11/14/los-nombres-turcos-arrasan-en-los-paises-latinoamericanos-gracias-a-las-series-de-television-1306660

TTV News (2020). Calinos announces volume deal with Israel's Achla TV. Retrieved from https://www.todotvnews.com/en/calinos-announces-volume-deal-with-israels-achla-tv/.

Tür, Ö. (2012). Turkey and Israel in the 2000s—from cooperation to conflict. *Israel Studies*, 17(3), 45–66. https://doi.org/10.2979/israelstudies.17.3.45

Türk, F. (2009). Adalet Ve Kalkinma Partisi Iktidarinda Türkiye Körfez Ülkeleri (Suudi Arabistan, Katar Ve Kuveyt) Ilişkileri. Sosyal ve Beşeri Bilimler Dergisi, 1(2), 21–32. Retrieved from https://dergipark.org.tr/en/download/article-file/117223

TVN (2018). Elif se instala como la teleserie turca más larga emitida en Chile. Retrieved from https://www.tvn.cl/teleseries/elif/destacados/elif-teleserie-turca-mas-larga-emitida-en-chile—2786185.

Tweissi, B. (2011). Turkey's new soft power. *Al Ghad*. Retrieved from https://bit.ly/3K5MuFT.

UPI (2002). Miss Turkey wins Miss World pageant. Retrieved from https://www.upi.com/Archives/2002/12/07/Miss-Turkey-wins-Miss-World-pageant/7241039237200/.

Uras, U. (2018). Saudi network ban on Turkey TV shows is 'political': minister. *Al Jazeera*. Retrieved from https://www.aljazeera.com/news/2018/3/6/saudi-network-ban-on-turkey-tv-shows-is-political-minister.

Uştuk, H. (2019). ABD'den sonra en fazla dizi ihraç eden ülke Türkiye. Retrieved from https://www.aa.com.tr/tr/kultur-sanat/abdden-sonra-en-fazla-dizi-ihrac-eden-ulke-turkiye/1641524.

Uzer, U. (2013). Turkish–Israeli relations: their rise and fall. *Middle East Policy*, 20(1), 97–110.

Van Ham, P. (2005). Power, public diplomacy, and the *Pax Americana*. In J. Melissen, ed., *The New Public Diplomacy. Studies in Diplomacy and International Relations*, 47-66. London: Palgrave Macmillan. https://doi.org/10.1057/9780230554931_3

Van Nieuwkerk, K. (2007). From repentance to pious performance. *ISIM Review* 20(1), 54–5.

Van Nieuwkerk, K. (2008). 'Repentant' artists in Egypt: debating gender, performing arts and religion. *Contemporary Islam*, 2(3), 191–210.

Varol, Z. (2016). The success story of Turkish TV series in Latin America. *Daily Sabah*. Retrieved from https://www.dailysabah.com/feature/2016/02/03/the-success-story-of-turkish-tv-series-in-latin-america

Vivarelli, N. (2017). Turkish TV Reaches More Viewers Abroad. *Variety*. Retrieved from https://variety.com/2017/tv/markets-festivals/turkish-tv-reaches-more-viewers-abroad-1202591287/

Walker, J.W. (2010). The United States and Turkey: can they agree to disagree? *Middle East Brief*, 46. Waltham, Massachusetts: Crown Center, Brandeis University. Retrieved from https://scholar.google.com/scholar?hl=en&as_sdt=0%2C5&q=The+United+States+and+Turkey%3A+can+they+agree+to+disagree&btnG=

Watson, I. & Comer, Y. (2009). Turkey denies government role in Gaza TV drama CNN. Retrieved from https://edition.cnn.com/2009/WORLD/europe/10/16/israel.turkey.tv.show/index.html?iref=nextin.

Williams, N. (2013). The rise of Turkish soap power. BBC News, 28 June. Retrieved from https://www.bbc.co.uk/news/magazine-22282563

Worldometer (2021). Latin America and the Caribbean population (LIVE). Retrieved from https://www.worldometers.info/world-population/latin-america-and-the-caribbean-population/.

Yaakoubi, A.E. (2021). Saudi state media companies to start moving from Dubai to Riyadh. *Reuters*. Retrieved from https://www.reuters.com/world/middle-east/saudi-state-media-companies-start-moving-dubai-riyadh-2021-09-03/.

Yalvaç, F. (2012). Strategic depth or hegemonic depth? A critical realist analysis of Turkey's position in the world system. *International Relations*, 26(2), 165–80. DOI: 10.1177/0047117811428331

Yanardağoğlu, E., & Karam, I.N. (2013). The fever that hit Arab satellite television: audience perceptions of Turkish TV series. *Identities*, 20(5), 561–79. https://doi.org/10.1080/1070 289X.2013.823089

Yanatma, S. (2016). Media capture and advertising in Turkey: the impact of the state on news. Oxford: Reuters Institute Fellowship Paper, University of Oxford.

Yanatma, S. (2021). Advertising and media capture in Turkey: how does the state emerge as the largest advertiser with the rise of competitive authoritarianism? *International Journal of Press/Politics*, 26(4), 797–821. DOI: 10.1177/19401612211018610

Yavuz, S. (2017). More Elif than Veronica as Chileans embrace Turkish soaps. Retrieved from https://www.aa.com.tr/en/americas/more-elif-than-veronica-as-chileans-embrace-turkish-soaps/768375.

Yeni Safak (2021). Turkish dramas captivate Hispanic audiences. Retrieved from https://www.yenisafak.com/en/life/turkish-dramas-captivate-hispanic-audiences-3573825.

Yilmaz, Ş. (2004). Impact of lobbies on Turkish–American relations. In M. Aydin & C. Erhan (eds), *Turkish–American Relations: Past, Present and Future*, 181–212. London & New York: Routledge.

Yilmaz, T. (2010). Türkiye–İsrail İlişkileri: Tarihten Günümüze. *Akademik Orta Doğu*, 5(1), 9–24.

REFERENCES

Yörük, Z., & Vatikiotis, P. (2013). Turkey, the Middle East & the media | Soft power or illusion of hegemony: the case of the Turkish soap opera 'colonialism'. *International Journal of Communication*, 7, 2361–85 .

Yörükoğlu, M., & Atasoy, H. (2010). The effects of the global financial crisis on the Turkish financial sector. *BIS Paper*, 54, 387–405.

Zaharopoulos, T. (1990). Cultural proximity in international news coverage: 1988 US presidential campaign in the Greek press. *Journalism Quarterly*, 67(1), 190–94. https://doi.org/10.1177/107769909006700128

Zaman, A. (2011). Turkey's growing ties with Arab world. BBC News. Retrieved from https://www.bbc.com/news/business-12290479.

Zimet, D. (2014). חרם על טורקיה? הסחר עם ישראל בשיא (Boycott of Turkey? Trade with Israel is at its peak). *Ynet*. Retrieved from https://www.ynet.co.il/articles/0,7340,L-4557677,00.html.

Index

Albayrak, Hakan 151
Al-Ghazzi, O. 35
Altunişik, M.B. 44, 148
Amor Eterno 123
Ang, I. 104, 109–10, 115, 130, 141–2, 166
Arab television market, Turkish serials entering 25–7
Arab women, Turkish dramas resonate with 7
Arab world, Turkish drama serials in 5–6, 25–7
   Arab adaptation of Turkish serials 39–40
   banned on network TV but on digital media 35–9
   early to mid-1990s 31
   meeting Arab audiences 34–5
   past and present 29–32
   Ramadan TV 34–5
   socio-cultural factors in 6–7
   television audiences and markets 32–3
Arbell, D. 149
Arici, Abdurrahman 56
Asi 28
A-Team, The 14
Ayish, M.I. 31
Ay Yapim 39, 176

Ben-Ari, E. 58, 156
Bitter Lands 19–20
Black Money Love 128
BluTV platform 23, 39
Bourdieu, P. 77, 158
Bride of Beirut, The 39, 176

Bride of Istanbul 39, 146, 153, 157–8, 175–6, 192
Brunsdon, C. 103
Bryant, R. 52

Cara Sucia 14
Cetin, K.B.E. 17
Cevik, B.S. 44, 52
Charlie's Angels 13
Charlton, M. 138
Chile, Turkish drama serials in 7–8, 114–45
   Chilean audiences 3
   introduction to Türkiye 124–8
   emotional realism 140–2
   entertainment as main motive 129–31
   entry to 121–4
   genre and production values 142–3
   LAC relations with Türkiye 116–19
   lifeworld concept 138
   perceived ethnic similarities 131–2
   romance, importance 139–40
   Türkiye's multidimensional policy enabling 120–1
   value, thematic proximity, and similar lifeworlds, interplay between 132–9
   younger Chilean audiences 128–9
Cho, C.H. 100
Çiller, Tansu 148
Cosby Show, The 14
Cull, Nicholas 180
cultural blend offered by Turkish serials 86–8
cultural proximity 73–4, 76–80, 183, 193

INDEX

Dal, E.P. 46
Dallas 14, 110, 141
Davutoğlu, Ahmet 48–9, 117
Demirel, Süleyman 148
Demirören Media 24, 173
digital media and streaming platforms 22–5
Donelli, Federico 119
drama serials, soft power of 6
Dramax 24, 173
dubbing 76–80, 167
Dynasty 110

Elif 123, 136–7
emotional realism 107–10, 140–2, 163–7
Empire of Lies (*Imperio de Mentiras*) 128
Erdoğan, Tayyip 42, 50, 53, 55, 66–7, 150, 152, 180
Ergenç, Halit 82, 122
Ertugrul 64
Exxen platform 24

family values' significance in serials 85–6
Fatmagül 137
Forbidden Love 13

GAİN platform 24
genre proximity 91–2, 163–7, 183
Geraghty, C. 106, 110
Gezi Park protests 52, 59
Great Arab Revolt of 1916 46
Gül, Abdullah 27
Gulf Cooperation Council (GCC) 44

Haaretz 153
Hale, William 47
Hatay, M. 52
Hernández, Patricio 121
Herzog, Chaim 148
Herzog, Isaac 152
Hussain bin Ali 46
Hussein, Saddam 57

iftars 34
Ignatius, David 50
Islamic religion importance in serials 83–5

Ismail, Fadi 26, 79
Israel, Turkish drama serials in 18–22, 146–69
   creating positive perception of Türkiye 153–7
   cultural proximity importance in 157–61
   face-to-face interviews 9
   focus-group discussions 9
   genre proximity and emotional realism 163–7
   Israeli audiences 3
   on Israeli television, arrival 152–3
   production values importance 167–8
   semi-structured interviews 9
   subtitling instead of dubbing 167
   value and thematic proximity 161–3
   young Israeli audiences 157
   see also Turkish–Israeli relations, past and present
I've Known You All My Life (*Te Acuerdas de Mí*) 128
Iwabuchi, K. 80

Jong-il, Kim 57
Jung, Dietrich 46

Kaptan, Y. 14
Katz, Mika 153
Kaya, I. 14–15
Khair, Adib 79
Khalil, J.F. 30–2, 37
Kingdom of Fire 54
Kingdom of Saudi Arabia (KSA) 28
Kirişci, K. 61
Knight Rider 14
Kraidy, M. 32, 35
Kunczik, M. 57
Kutlay, Mustafa 26

La Pastina, A.C. 74, 140, 161, 164
Las Mil y Una Noches (*Binbir Gece/One Thousand and One Nights*) 121–2, 129–30, 153
Latin American and Caribbean (LAC) relations with Türkiye 2, 116–19

241

Lee, M. 100
Levaggi, Ariel 119
Lionsgate 38
Little House on the Prairie, The 13

Magnificent Century 19, 64, 81–2
Maria La Del Barrio 14
Marimar 14
Martin-Barbero, J. 140
Mavi Marmara incident 151
Medyapim 39, 176
Melamed, Ariana 158
Menekşe and Halil 146, 152
Middle East and North Africa (MENA) region 2, 28–33, 37–8, 41, 72, 120, 147
Middle East Broadcasting Center (MBC) 2, 28
Mirna and Khalil 28
Modleski, Tania 108
Mother 157
Mothers-in-Law (*Kaynanalar*) 13
Muslims 179

Nachmani, A. 47
'Neo-Ottoman cool' 78
Neumann, K. 138
Noor (*Gümüs*) serial 2, 25–6, 28, 34, 45, 78, 153, 171, 174
'Noormania and Muhannad effect' 72
Nye, J.S. 50–1, 62, 178, 195

Oğuzlu, T. 49
Olmert, Ehud 149
Organization of Islamic Cooperation (OIC) 44
Otmazgin, Nissim 57–8, 156
Over-the-top (OTT) services 22, 28
Özal, Ahmet 14
Özal, Turgut 14, 48

Peres, Shimon 50, 150
Pintak, L. 31
Pitel, Laura 119
Press-Barnathan, G. 57, 155, 195

production values importance 167–8
proximity 73–4, 76–80, 161–3
  genre proximity 163–7
  thematic proximity 77, 161–3
  value proximity 77, 161–3
Puhu platform 23

Qatar, situation of women in 96–7
  socio-cultural structure 96–7
  women viewers responses 95–113
Queen of the Night 128
Qureshi, K. 84

Radio and Television Supreme Council (RTÜK) 15, 90, 198n30
Ramadan TV 34–5
religion importance in serials 83–5
Resurrection: Ertugrul 19, 64, 81
romance importance, between reality and fantasy 102–6
Roots 13
Rubin, A.M. 31

Savci, Timur 19, 82
Schipani, Andres 119
Seddülbahir 19
Separation: Palestine at Love and War 150
set-top box media services 22
Şinasi, Ibrahim 13
Sinclair, J. 77
soft power of drama serials 48–52, 55–8
Solomon, Ty 155, 195
StarzPlay Arabia 38–9
Strategic Depth 48
Straubhaar, J.D. 74, 77, 140, 161, 164
subscription video-on-demand (SVOD) services 30, 174
subtitling 73, 76, 78, 167
successful subscription video-on-demand (SVOD) platform 23

Tanzimat era 48
Tatlıtuğ, Kıvanç 152
thematic proximity 132–9, 161–3

INDEX

Turkish–Arab relations 6, 41–71
   catalysts for increased awareness 58–62
   de facto neo-Ottomanist foreign policy 49
   ever-changing nature of 52–5
   hard power in generating soft power 66–8
   historical overview 46–8
   Ottoman history, changing perception of 62–4
   Saudi–Turkish opposition 54
   soft power of drama serials 48–52
   2000 to 2013, golden period 42–5
   as window onto model society 64–6
Turkish dramas resonating with Arab women 95–113
   as vehicle for engaging with Turkish modernity 110–12
   see also women viewers responses in Qatar
Turkish International Cooperation and Development Agency (TIKA) 119
Turkish–Israeli relations, past and present 147–52
   1956 Suez Crisis 147
   1990s Turkish–Israeli relations 148–50
   Arab–Israeli conflict 147
   Jerusalem Act 147
   Operation Cast Lead 150
Turkish Radio and Television Corporation (TRT) 12
Turkish serials among Arab viewers 72–94
   audience preferences 74
   cultural and ethnic similarity role 80–3
   cultural blend 86–8
   cultural proximity in 73–4, 76–80
   dubbing, success of 76–80
   family values, significance 85–6
   genre proximity 91–2
   Islamic religion importance in 83–5
   as 'just' a women's genre 74–6
   overlapping histories 80–3
   period dramas 82
   portrayal of women 88–91
   socio-cultural factors in 72–94
   Syrian colloquial dialect 78
Turkish television industry 5, 11–27
   current conditions in 18–22
   digital media and streaming platforms 22–5
   entering Arab television market 25–7
   from national to transnational 5
   historic overview 12–15
   Türkiye's success in scripted serials 15–18
Türkiye's success in scripted serials 15–18
Tür, Özlem 147

United Arab Emirates (UAE) 28
Uşaklıgil, Halid Ziya 13
uses and gratifications (U&G) theory 97–8

Valley of the Wolves 81
value proximity 132–9, 161–3

Wedding of a Poet, The 13
Weizman, Ezer 148
What Is Fatmagül's Crime?/Fatma 89–90, 102
women portrayal in Turkish serials 88–91
women viewers responses in Qatar 7, 95–113
   emotional involvement and realism 107–10
   entertainment 98–9
   findings 98–112
   'honour' concept 97
   personal agency intersection 99–101
   romance importance, between reality and fantasy 102–6
   shifting viewing patterns 99–102
   socio-cultural structure 96–7
   viewing motivations 97–8
World Television: From Global to Local 139

Yalvac, Faruk 49
Yilmaz, Ş. 45, 149
Yo Soy Betty, La Fea 123
Yönder, Tunca 13

Zayani, M. 37

CPSIA information can be obtained
at www.ICGtesting.com
Printed in the USA
JSHW020006100723
44337JS00001B/4

9 781804 130421